# Azure Synapse Analytics Cookbook

Implement a limitless analytical platform using effective recipes for Azure Synapse

**Gaurav Agarwal**

**Meenakshi Muralidharan**

BIRMINGHAM—MUMBAI

# Azure Synapse Analytics Cookbook



**Publishing Product Manager**: Dhruv Jagdish Kataria
**Senior Editor**: David Sugarman
**Content Development Editor**: Priyanka Soam
**Technical Editor**: Rahul Limbachiya
**Copy Editor**: Safis Editing
**Project Coordinator**: Aparna Ravikumar Nair
**Proofreader**: Safis Editing
**Indexer**: Rekha Nair
**Production Designer**: Shankar Kalbhor
**Marketing Coordinators**: Abeer Dawe, Shifa Ansari

First published: April 2022

Production reference: 1130422

Published by Packt Publishing Ltd.
Livery Place
35 Livery Street
Birmingham
B3 2PB, UK.

ISBN 978-1-80323-150-1

www.packt.com

# Foreword

Digitalization of economies, across all sectors such as health, mobility, energy, and finance, has seen a significant generation of data. We are living in an age where data is becoming central to how organizations, and indeed our economies and society, function. The increasing value of data is driving organizations to retain more of it so that they can explore new opportunities to increase customer loyalty, bring new services to market, and compete more effectively.

However, the exponential growth in the volume, variety, and velocity of data poses challenges in unlocking the value from that data – at the scale, scope, and speed of business. Today, for organizations that are innovating and transforming with data, the hyperscale cloud is the technology of choice for collecting, transforming, processing, and analyzing data at scale.

Azure Synapse Analytics is a limitless analytics service on Microsoft Azure that brings together data integration, enterprise data warehousing, and big data analytics. It gives you the freedom to query data on your terms, using either serverless or dedicated options—at scale. Azure Synapse brings these worlds together with a unified experience to ingest, explore, prepare, transform, manage, and serve data for immediate Business Intelligence (BI) and Machine Learning (ML) needs.

I am delighted to present to you this book on Azure Synapse Analytics. The audience for this book is data architects, data engineers, and developers who want to learn and understand the main concepts of Azure Synapse analytics and implement them in real-world scenarios.

This is a practical, hands-on book to help the reader learn how to load data into Synapse, create robust data pipelines using the Synapse notebook, learn how to visualize data, and manage other big data scenarios. Synapse SQL architecture components and how to leverage scale out capabilities in Azure for distributed processing of data across nodes are described. Data transformation and analytics in real-time using Azure Synapse Link and Cosmos DB will enable the reader to learn how to perform real-time analytics for many applications, including IoT. Big data processing and transformation with Synapse notebooks will enable the reader to work with Azure Data Lake Storage Gen2. Data enrichment using Azure ML helps the reader harness the power of Azure Machine Learning along with Spark MLlib with Synapse Studio. Visualization and reporting with petabytes of data using Power BI, data cataloging, and governance within Synapse truly enable exploration of data using the power of serverless pool. Finally, the book helps the reader migrate legacy data warehouses using Azure Synapse Pathway.

I invite you to leverage this book to unlock the value of data at scale, using the best of SQL technologies used in enterprise data warehousing, spark technologies used for big data, data explorer for log and time series analytics, pipelines for data integration, and ETL/ELT and take advantage of the deep integration of Azure Synapse Analytics with other Azure services such as Power BI, CosmosDB, and AzureML.

*Rohini Srivathsa*

*National Technology Officer - Microsoft India*

# Contributors

## About the authors

**Gaurav Agarwal** is a cloud solution architect at Microsoft India Corp. Ltd, working closely with Microsoft clients on Azure data and AI, Azure ML, big data, IoT, and Power BI. He has extensive experience in architecting and transforming data solutions for the modern cloud, and expertise in building large-scale enterprise data warehouse solutions.

**Meenakshi Muralidharan** leads modern data platforms and is a renowned chief architect for an Indian multinational information technology services and consulting company. She has extensive experience in building large-scale data platforms and applications in Microsoft Azure.

# About the reviewers

**Shaleen Thapa** is a partner technology strategist for ISVs at Microsoft India and has over 20 years of experience. With more than 15 years of Microsoft experience, his primary job responsibilities are to help ISVs and start-ups adopt the latest technologies on Azure, build solutions on Azure, and strategize ISVs'/start-ups' roadmaps for their product development and GTM. He primarily focuses on Azure apps and infra, Azure services, Azure Synapse Analytics, blockchain, Azure DevOps, and GitHub. He has authored several articles published in MSDN Magazine on various Azure and on-premises technologies. He has delivered technical talks on various internal as well as external forums, such as Microsoft Ready, Open Source India, Barracuda Networks, and others.

**Ajay Agarwal** was born and brought up in India. He completed his master's of technology at BITS. He has significant experience in product management in the analytics domain. For years, he has managed and evolved multiple cloud capabilities and analytics products in the data science and machine learning domains. He is known for his passion for technology and leadership.

# Table of Contents

# 3
# Processing Data Optimally across Multiple Nodes



# 4
# Engineering Real-Time Analytics with Azure Synapse Link Using Cosmos DB

# 5
# Data Transformation and Processing with Synapse Notebooks



# 6
# Enriching Data Using the Azure ML AutoML Regression Model

# 7

## Visualizing and Reporting Petabytes of Data



# 8

## Data Cataloging and Governance



# 9

## MPP Platform Migration to Synapse

# Preface

As data warehouse management becomes increasingly integral to successful organizations, choosing and running the right solution is more important than ever. Microsoft Azure Synapse is an enterprise-grade, cloud-based data warehousing platform, and this book holds the key to using Synapse to its full potential. If you want the skills and confidence to create a robust enterprise analytical platform, this cookbook is a great place to start.

You'll learn about and execute enterprise-level deployment on medium-to-large data platforms. Using the step-by-step recipes and accompanying theory covered in the book, you'll understand how to integrate various services with Synapse to make it a robust solution for all your data needs. Whether you're new to Azure Synapse or just getting started, you'll find the instructions you need to solve any problem you may face, including using Azure services for data visualization as well as **Artificial Intelligence** (**AI**) and **Machine Learning** (**ML**) solutions.

By the end of this Azure book, you'll have the skills you need to implement an enterprise-grade analytical platform, enabling your organization to explore and manage heterogeneous data workloads and employ various data integration services to solve real-time industry problems.

## Who this book is for

This book is for data architects, data engineers, and developers who want to learn and understand the main concepts of Azure Synapse Analytics and implement them in real-world scenarios.

# What this book covers

*Chapter 1, Choosing the Optimal Method for Loading Data to Synapse*, will help you learn how to choose between different options when loading data into Synapse and the optimal way to perform different data loadings.

*Chapter 2, Creating Robust Data Pipelines and Data Transformation*, will help you understand Synapse notebooks and its interfaces to create a file that will contain the real code – the logic. You will also learn how to visualize data within a notebook and other big data scenarios.

*Chapter 3, Processing Data Optimally across Multiple Nodes*, explores the Synapse SQL architecture components and how to leverage the scale-out capabilities to distribute the computational processing of data across multiple nodes.

*Chapter 4, Engineering Real-time Analytics with Azure Synapse Link Using Cosmos DB*, describes how you can architect and perform real-time analytics with Synapse, integrate Synapse Link for Cosmos DB, and enable the **Internet of Things** (**IoT**).

*Chapter 5, Data Transformation and Processing with Synapse Notebooks*, teaches you how to use Python to read data from Azure Data Lake Storage Gen2 into a Spark DataFrame using Azure Synapse Analytics.

*Chapter 6, Enriching Data Using the Azure ML AutoML Regression Model*, helps you uncover the power of Azure Machine Learning along with Spark MLlib and Synapse Studio.

*Chapter 7, Visualizing and Reporting Petabytes of Data*, teaches you how to present data using visualizations with Power BI, integrate Power BI with Synapse, and use the power of the serverless SQL pool for data exploration.

*Chapter 8, Data Cataloging and Governance*, teaches you how to provide comprehensive data governance for an analytical workload and embed data discovery and classification with Synapse using Azure Purview integration.

*Chapter 9, MPP Platform Migration to Synapse*, teaches you how to get started with the migration of a legacy data warehouse using Azure Synapse Pathway.

# To get the most out of this book

| Software/hardware covered in the book | Operating system requirements |
|---|---|
| An Azure subscription, SQL Server Management Studio, Power BI Desktop, and Azure Synapse Pathway | Windows 8.1/Windows Server 2012 R2 or later and Internet Explorer 11 or later<br>Memory (RAM) – at least 2 GB available; 4 GB or more recommended |

**If you are using the digital version of this book, we advise you to type the code yourself or access the code from the book's GitHub repository (a link is available in the next section). Doing so will help you avoid any potential errors related to the copying and pasting of code.**

# Download the example code files

You can download the example code files for this book from GitHub at `https://github.com/PacktPublishing/Azure-Synapse-Analytics-cookbook`. If there's an update to the code, it will be updated in the GitHub repository.

We also have other code bundles from our rich catalog of books and videos available at `https://github.com/PacktPublishing/`. Check them out!

# Download the color images

We also provide a PDF file that has color images of the screenshots and diagrams used in this book. You can download it here: `https://static.packt-cdn.com/downloads/9781803231501_ColorImages.pdf`.

# Conventions used

There are a number of text conventions used throughout this book.

`Code in text`: This indicates code words in text, database table names, folder names, filenames, file extensions, pathnames, dummy URLs, user input, and Twitter handles. Here is an example: "Define and load the entire DataFrame to pandas using the toPandas() function and define the chart type that you want to plot.

A block of code is set as follows:

```
mydataframeplot = mydataframe1.toPandas()
ax = mydataframeplot['passenger_count'].plot(kind='hist', bins=
20, facecolor='orange')
ax.set_title('Total Passenger distribution')
ax.set_xlabel('No. of Passengers')
ax.set_ylabel('Counts')
chartplt.suptitle('Trend')
chartplt.show()
```

When we wish to draw your attention to a particular part of a code block, the relevant lines or items are set in bold:

```
[default]
exten => s,1,Dial(Zap/1|30)
exten => s,2,Voicemail(u100)
exten => s,102,Voicemail(b100)
exten => i,1,Voicemail(s0)
```

Any command-line input or output is written as follows:

```
SELECT name, is_auto_create_stats_on
FROM sys.databases
```

**Bold**: This indicates a new term, an important word, or words that you see onscreen. For instance, words in menus or dialog boxes appear in **bold**. Here is an example: "Go to the existing Synapse Analytics workspace and navigate to Synapse Studio."

> **Tips or Important Notes**
> Appear like this.

# Get in touch

Feedback from our readers is always welcome.

**General feedback**: If you have questions about any aspect of this book, email us at `customercare@packtpub.com` and mention the book title in the subject of your message.

**Errata**: Although we have taken every care to ensure the accuracy of our content, mistakes do happen. If you have found a mistake in this book, we would be grateful if you would report this to us. Please visit `www.packtpub.com/support/errata` and fill in the form.

**Piracy**: If you come across any illegal copies of our works in any form on the internet, we would be grateful if you would provide us with the location address or website name. Please contact us at `copyright@packt.com` with a link to the material.

**If you are interested in becoming an author**: If there is a topic that you have expertise in and you are interested in either writing or contributing to a book, please visit `authors.packtpub.com`.

# Share Your Thoughts

Once you've read *Azure Synapse Analytics Cookbook*, we'd love to hear your thoughts! Scan the QR code below to go straight to the Amazon review page for this book and share your feedback.

`https://packt.link/r/1-803-23150-5`

Your review is important to us and the tech community and will help us make sure we're delivering excellent quality content.

# 1
# Choosing the Optimal Method for Loading Data to Synapse

In this chapter, we will cover how to enrich and load data to **Azure Synapse** using the most optimal method. We will be covering, in detail, different techniques to load data, considering the variety of data source options. We will learn the best practices to be followed for different data loading options, along with unsupported scenarios.

We will cover the following recipes:

- Choosing a data loading option
- Achieving parallelism in data loading using PolyBase
- Moving and transforming using a data flow
- Adding a trigger to a data flow pipeline
- Unsupported data loading scenarios
- Data loading best practices

# Choosing a data loading option

**Data loading** is one of the most important aspects of data orchestration in Azure Synapse Analytics. Loading data into Synapse requires handling a variety of data sources of different formats, sizes, and frequencies.

There are multiple options available to load data to Synapse. To enrich and load the data in the most appropriate manner, it is very important to understand which option is the best when it comes to actual data loading.

Here are some of the most well-known data loading techniques:

- Loading data using the `COPY` command
- Loading data using PolyBase
- Loading data into Azure Synapse using **Azure Data Factory** (**ADF**)

We'll look at each of them in this recipe.

## Getting ready

We will be using a public dataset for our scenario. This dataset will consist of New York yellow taxi trip data; this includes attributes such as trip distances, itemized fares, rate types, payment types, pick-up and drop-off dates and times, driver-reported passenger counts, and pick-up and drop-off locations. We will be using this dataset throughout this recipe to demonstrate various use cases:

- To get the dataset, you can go to the following URL: `https://www.kaggle.com/microize/newyork-yellow-taxi-trip-data-2020-2019`.
- The code for this recipe can be downloaded from the GitHub repository: `https://github.com/PacktPublishing/Analytics-in-Azure-Synapse-Simplified`.
- For a quick-start guide of how to create a Synapse workspace, you can refer to `https://docs.microsoft.com/en-us/azure/synapse-analytics/quickstart-create-workspace`.
- For a quick-start guide of how to create SQL dedicated pool, check out `https://docs.microsoft.com/en-us/azure/synapse-analytics/quickstart-create-sql-pool-studio`.

Let's get started.

# How to do it...

Let's look at each of the three methods in turn and see which is most optimal and when to use each of them.

## Loading data using the COPY command

We will be using the new `COPY` command to load the dataset from external storage:

1. Before we get started, let's upload the data from the Kaggle New York yellow taxi trip data dataset to the **Azure Data Lake Storage Gen2** (**ADLS2**) storage container named `taxistagingdata`. You can download the dataset to your local machine and upload it to the Azure storage container, as shown in *Figure 1.1*:

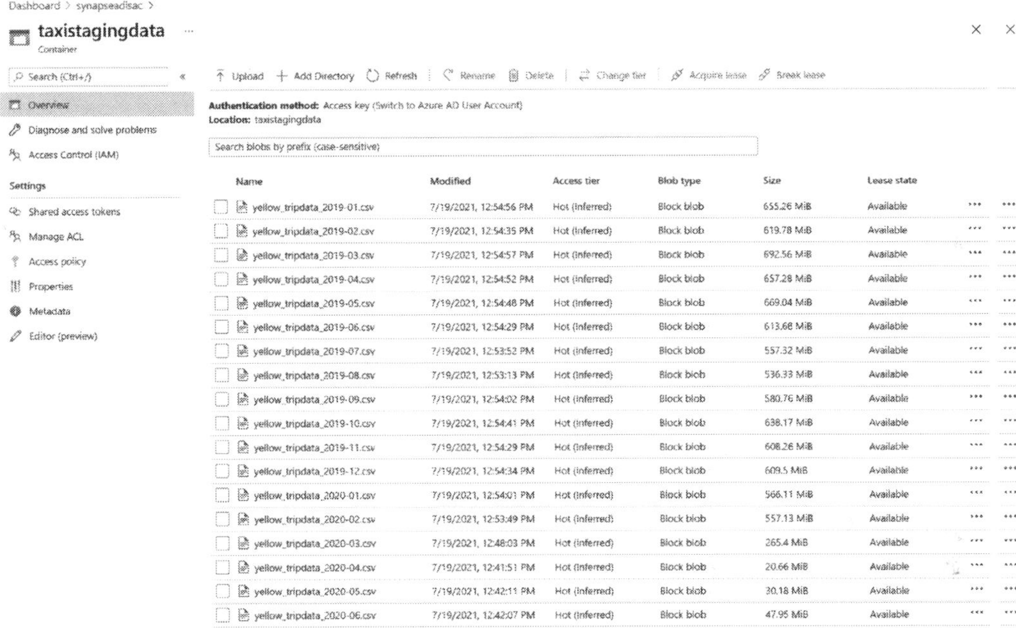


Figure 1.1 – The New York taxi dataset

2. Let's create a table to load the data from the data lake storage. You can use **SQL Server Management Studio** (**SSMS**) to run the following queries against the SQL pool that you have created:

```
CREATE SCHEMA [NYCTaxi];
IF NOT EXISTS (SELECT * FROM sys.objects WHERE NAME =
'TripsStg' AND TYPE = 'U')
CREATE TABLE [NYCTaxi].[TripsStg]
  (
```

```
VendorID nvarchar(30),
tpep_pickup_datetime nvarchar(30),
tpep_dropoff_datetime nvarchar(30),
passenger_count nvarchar(30),
trip_distance nvarchar(30),
RatecodeID nvarchar(30),
store_and_fwd_flag nvarchar(30),
PULocationID nvarchar(30),
DOLocationID nvarchar(30),
payment_type nvarchar(30),
fare_amount nvarchar(10),
extra nvarchar(10),
mta_tax nvarchar(10),
tip_amount nvarchar(10),
tolls_amount nvarchar(10),
improvement_surcharge nvarchar(10),
total_amount nvarchar(10)
)
WITH
 (
DISTRIBUTION = ROUND_ROBIN,
HEAP
)
```

3. Use the `COPY INTO` command to load the data from ADLS2. This helps by reducing multiple steps in the data loading process and its complexity:

```
COPY INTO [NYCTaxi].[TripsStg]
FROM 'https://mystorageaccount.blob.core.windows.net/
myblobcontainer/*.csv'
WITH
(
    FILE_TYPE = 'CSV',
CREDENTIAL=(IDENTITY= 'Shared Access Signature', SECRET=
'<Your_Account_Key>'),
IDENTITY_INSERT = 'OFF'
)
GO
```

Next, let's look at using PolyBase.

## Loading data using PolyBase

In this section, we will use **PolyBase** technology to load data to Synapse SQL pool. PolyBase will help in connecting external data sources, such as ADLS2 or Azure Blob storage. The PolyBase command syntax is like T-SQL, so it's easy to understand and learn this new technology without much effort:

1. Create the master key and credentials, as shown in the following code block:

```
CREATE MASTER KEY;
--Credential used to authenticate to External Data Source
CREATE DATABASE SCOPED CREDENTIAL AzureStorageCredential
WITH
    IDENTITY = 'polybaseuser',
    SECRET = '<Access Key>'
;
```

2. Create the external data source, pointing to ADLS/Azure Blob storage:

```
CREATE EXTERNAL DATA SOURCE NYTBlob
WITH
(
    TYPE = Hadoop,
    LOCATION = 'wasbs://myblobcontainer @myaccount.blob.
core.windows.net/',
CREDENTIAL = AzureStorageCredential
);
Create the external file format using below query
CREATE EXTERNAL FILE FORMAT csvstaging
WITH (
    FORMAT_TYPE = DELIMITEDTEXT,
    FORMAT_OPTIONS (
FIELD_TERMINATOR = ',',
        STRING_DELIMITER = '',
        USE_TYPE_DEFAULT = False,
FIRST_ROW = 2
    )
);
```

3. Create the schema and external table. Make sure to specify the location, data source, and file format, which were previously created:

```
CREATE SCHEMA [NYTaxiSTG];
CREATE EXTERNAL TABLE [NYTaxiSTG].[Trip]
(
    [VendorID] varchar(10) NULL,
    [tpep_pickup_datetime] datetime NOT NULL,
    [tpep_dropoff_datetime] datetime NOT NULL,
    [passenger_count] int  NULL,
    [trip_distance] float  NULL,
    [RateCodeID] int NULL,
    [store_and_fwd_flag] varchar(3) NULL,
    [PULocationID] int NULL,
    [DOLocationID] int NULL,
    [payment_type] int NULL,
    [fare_amount] money NULL,
    [extra] money NULL,
    [mta_tax] money NULL,
    [tip_amount] money NULL,
    [tolls_amount] money NULL,
    [improvement_surcharge] money NULL,
    [total_amount] money NULL,
    [congestion_surcharge] money NULL
)
WITH
(
    LOCATION = '/',
    DATA_SOURCE = NYTBlob,
    FILE_FORMAT = csvstaging,
FORMAT_OPTIONS (FIELD_TERMINATOR = ','),
    REJECT_TYPE = value,
    REJECT_VALUE = 0
);
```

4. Check the data and table structure in SSMS connecting with the SQL pool, as shown here:

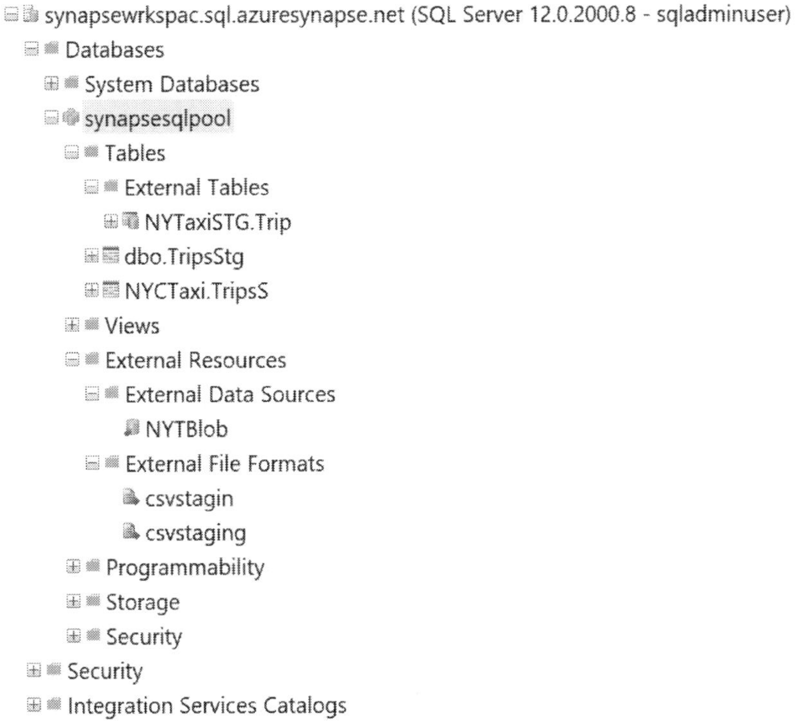

- synapsewrkspac.sql.azuresynapse.net (SQL Server 12.0.2000.8 - sqladminuser)
  - Databases
    - System Databases
    - synapsesqlpool
      - Tables
        - External Tables
          - NYTaxiSTG.Trip
        - dbo.TripsStg
        - NYCTaxi.TripsS
      - Views
      - External Resources
        - External Data Sources
          - NYTBlob
        - External File Formats
          - csvstagin
          - csvstaging
      - Programmability
      - Storage
      - Security
  - Security
  - Integration Services Catalogs

Figure 1.2 – SSMS screen

Finally, let's see the ADF method.

## Loading data using ADF

ADF gives you the option to perform a data sink using three different options: PolyBase, the `Copy` command, and bulk insert using a dynamic pipeline. For a quick-start guide to creating a data factory using the Azure portal, you can refer to `https://docs.microsoft.com/en-us/azure/data-factory/quickstart-create-data-factory-portal`.

OK, let's start:

1. Create and define the pipeline and use the **Copy data** activity.
2. Define the source as the ADLS2 container where the data files were uploaded.
3. Define the sink as the Synapse Analytics SQL pool.

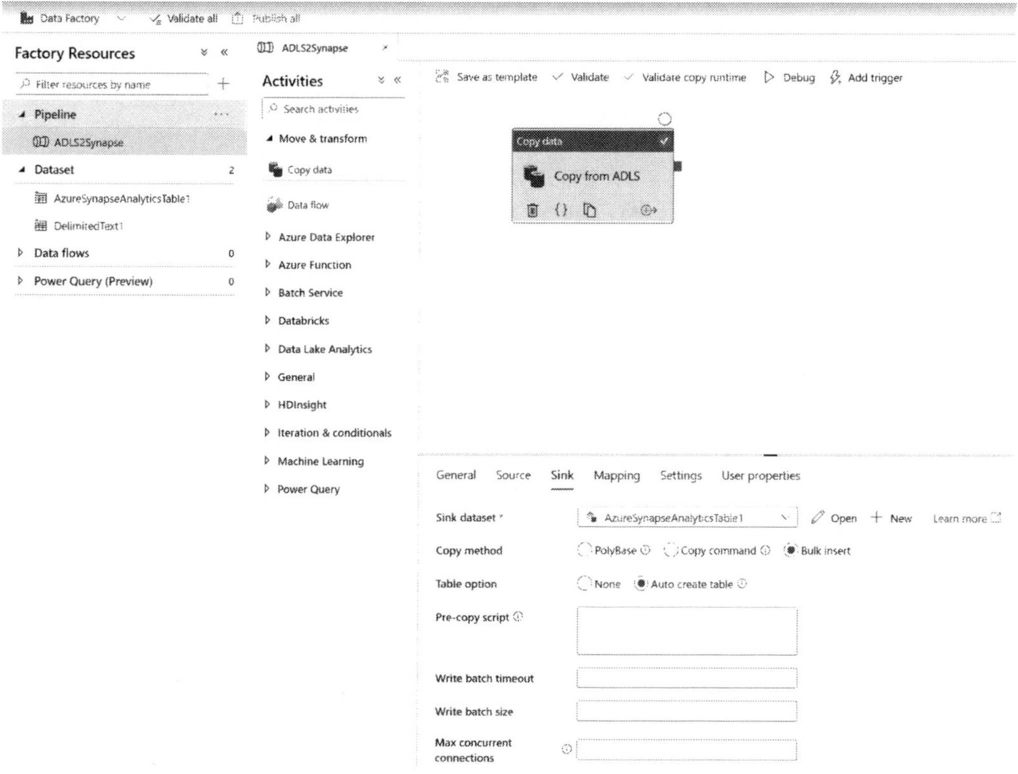


Figure 1.3 – ADF pipeline for Copy data

We have seen the three different ways of loading data to Azure Synapse. Each of them has its own relevance. We will see how to choose which one is appropriate for your task in the *How it works...* section.

## How it works...

To choose the best method of data loading, it is very important to understand *what* we are loading. Some of the key aspects we need to consider include the following:

- What does our data source look like?
- What is the format of our data source?
- How big is our dataset?
- How big is the data file size?
- How much transformation do we need to perform?
- How frequently do we want to load the data?
- Does it require incremental load or is it a full load?

We have seen the three different methods of data loading and have a fair idea of how to use each method. We will go through each method one by one and learn the benefits and considerations for data loading.

> DWUs
>
> We are assuming that you already know a bit about **Data Warehouse Units** (**DWUs**). If not, you can refer to this page to learn more: `https://docs.microsoft.com/en-us/azure/synapse-analytics/sql-data-warehouse/what-is-a-data-warehouse-unit-dwu-cdwu`.

The use of the `COPY` command gives the developer the most flexible way of loading data with numerous advantages and benefits, such as the ability to do the following:

- Execute a single T-SQL statement without having to create any additional database objects.
- Flexibly define a custom row terminator for CSV files.
- Easily use SQL Server date formats for CSV files.
- Specify a custom row terminator for CSV files.
- Specify wildcards and multiple files in the storage location path.
- Parse and load CSV files where delimiters (string, field, and row) are escaped within string-delimited columns.

- Use a different storage account for the ERRORFILE location (REJECTED_ROW_LOCATION).
- CSV supports GZIP and Parquet supports GZIP and Snappy.
- ORC supports DefaultCodec and Snappy.

When loading multiple files, it is recommended to use the file-splitting guidelines shown in the following figure. Also, there is no need to split Parquet and ORC files because the COPY command will automatically split files.

For optimal performance, Parquet and ORC files in an Azure Storage account should be 256 MB or larger.

| DWU | 100 | 200 | 300 | 400 | 500 | 1,000 | 1,500 | 2,000 | 2,500 | 3,000 | 5,000 | 6,000 | 7,500 | 10,000 | 15,000 | 30,000 |
|---|---|---|---|---|---|---|---|---|---|---|---|---|---|---|---|---|
| No. of Files | 60 | 60 | 60 | 60 | 60 | 120 | 180 | 240 | 300 | 360 | 600 | 720 | 900 | 1,200 | 1,800 | 3,600 |

Figure 1.4 – File splitting based on DWU

> **Tip**
>
> Make sure you create new statistics once you have completed the data load to your production warehouse. Bad statistics can be a common source of poor query performance in Azure Synapse Analytics. They can lead to suboptimal **Massively Parallel Processing** (**MPP**) plans, which result in unproductive data movement.

When loading data using PolyBase technology, you can retrieve data from external data stores, which could be in ADLS, Azure Blob storage, or Hadoop. The best part of PolyBase is that it uses T-SQL-like syntax so it is very convenient for database developers to write the data loading and transformation query.

Another benefit is that PolyBase can combine both relational and non-relational data and load it into a single dataset. Since PolyBase uses the MapReduce principle, it's also one of the fastest data loading techniques on scale.

PolyBase supports data loading from UTF-8 and UTF-16 text files. The Hadoop data file formats supported are the famous Parquet, OCR, and RC File. Currently, extended ASCII, nested, and fixed-width formats are not supported. So, you can't load formats such as JSON, WinZip, or XML.

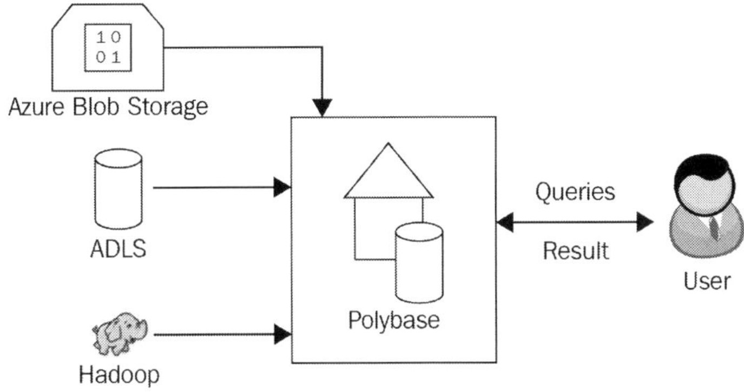


Figure 1.5 – PolyBase data loading

## There's more...

Here are a few more things to consider when using PolyBase for Synapse workloads:

- The load performance of PolyBase is directly proportional to the compute DWUs.
- PolyBase automatically achieves parallelism during the data load process, so you don't have to explicitly break the input data into multiple files and issue concurrent loads, unlike some traditional loading practices.
- A single PolyBase load operation provides the best performance.
- PolyBase moves data directly from Hadoop data nodes to Synapse compute nodes using MPP architecture.

Finally, let's understand the ADF data loading mechanism. As ADF provides the most seamless way to integrate with PolyBase or create your own pipeline connecting to multiple data sources, it is very convenient for ETL developers to work on the development of an ADF data pipeline.

ADF provides an interface where developers can drag and drop to create a complex data loading end-to-end pipeline. For data sources that are PolyBase compatible, you can directly invoke the Copy activity to use the PolyBase mechanism and avoid writing complex T-SQL queries.

If your source data is not originally supported by PolyBase, the copy activity additionally provides a built-in staged copy to automatically convert data into a compatible format before using PolyBase to load the data.

ADF further enriches the PolyBase integration to support the following:

- Loading data from ADLS2 with an account key or managed identity authentication.
- To connect the data source securely, you can use and create the **Azure Integration Runtime**, which will eventually create an ADF **Virtual Network** (**VNET**), and the Integration Runtime will be provisioned with the managed VNET.
- With the help of a **managed VNET**, you don't have to worry about managing the VNET to ADF yourself. You don't need to create a subnet for the Azure Integration Runtime, which could eventually use many private IPs from your VNET and would require prior network infrastructure planning – it will be done for you.
- Managed VNETs, along with managed private endpoints, protect against data breakout.
- ADF supports private links. A private link enables you to access Azure data services, such as Azure Blob storage, Azure Cosmos DB, and Azure Synapse Analytics.
- It's recommended that you create managed private endpoints to connect to all your Azure data sources.

# Achieving parallelism in data loading using PolyBase

PolyBase is the one of best data loading methods when it comes to performance after the `COPY Into` command. So, it's recommended to use PolyBase where it's supported or possible when it comes to parallelism.

How it achieves parallelism is similar to what a parallel data warehouse system does. There will be a control node, followed by multiple compute nodes, which are then linked to multiple data nodes. The data nodes will consist of the actual data, which will get the process by the compute nodes in parallel, and all these operations and instructions are governed by the control node.

In the following architecture diagrams, each **Hadoop Distributed File System** (**HDFS**) bridge of the service from every compute node can connect to an external resource, such as Azure Blob storage, and then bidirectionally transfer data between a SQL data warehouse and the external resource. This is fully scalable and highly robust: as you scale out your DWU, your data transfer throughput also increases.

If you look at the following architecture, all the incoming connections go through the control node to the compute nodes. However, you can increase and decrease the number of compute resources as required.

Data loading parallelization is achieved as there will be multiple compute nodes that perform multithreading to process the file and load the data as quickly as possible.

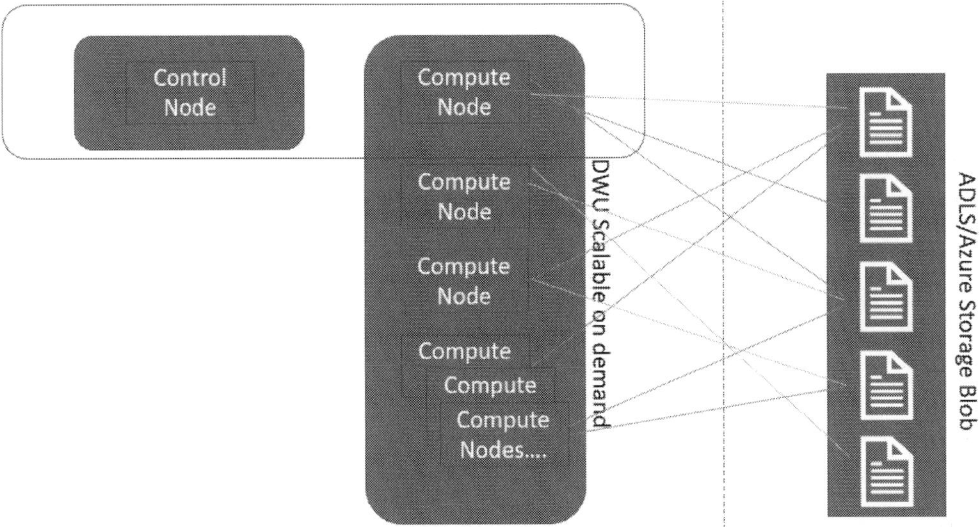


Figure 1.6 – PolyBase data loading architecture

# Moving and transforming using a data flow

Azure data flows are a low-code/no-code visual transformation tool that provides data engineers with a simple interface to develop the transformation logic without writing code. Azure data flows provide flexibility to ETL developers so that they can use the drag-and-drop user experience to build the data flow from one source to another, applying various transformations.

In this recipe, we will discuss and create a data flow considering the following data flow components:

- Select
- Optimize partition type
- Derived column
- Sink to Azure Synapse

## Getting ready

We will be using the same dataset that we used in a previous recipe, *Choosing a data loading option*. Access the New York yellow taxi trip data dataset from the ADLS2 storage container named `taxistagingdata`. The code can be downloaded from the GitHub repository here: `https://github.com/PacktPublishing/Analytics-in-Azure-Synapse-Simplified`.

Also, we will be using the same pipeline that we created in the earlier recipe here and will create a data flow.

## How to do it...

Let's start:

1. Go to Synapse Studio and open the **Develop** tab.
2. Create and define a new data flow under **Develop** within Synapse Studio.

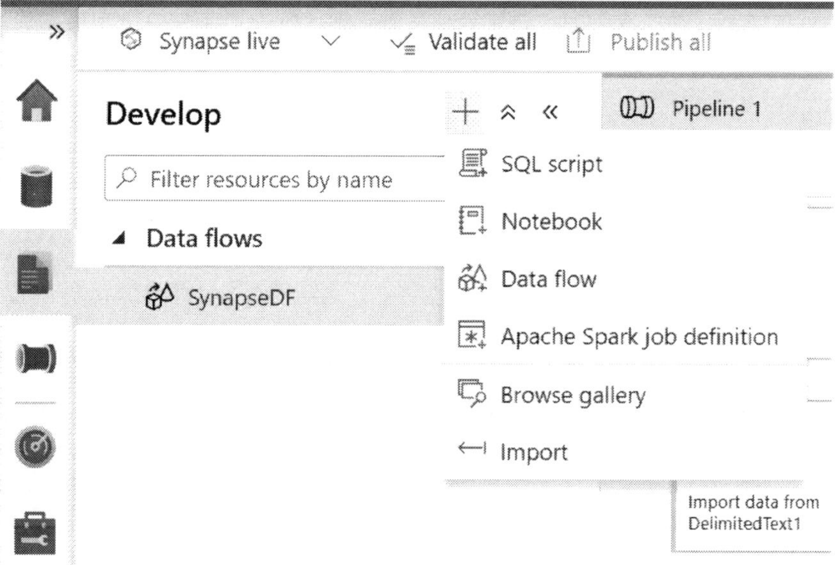


Figure 1.7 – Defining a data flow

3. Define the source. In our case, it will be ADLS2, where we uploaded the files in our previous recipe.

Source settings Source options Projection Optimize Inspect Data preview

Output stream name * Source Learn more

Source type * Integration dataset Inline

Dataset * DelimitedText1 Test connection Open New

Options Allow schema drift

Infer drifted column types

Validate schema

Skip line count

Sampling * Enable Disable

Figure 1.8 – Source setting

4. Under **Optimize**, please select the partition type, from a list of **Round Robin**, **Hash**, **Dynamic Range**, **Fixed Range**, or **Key**.

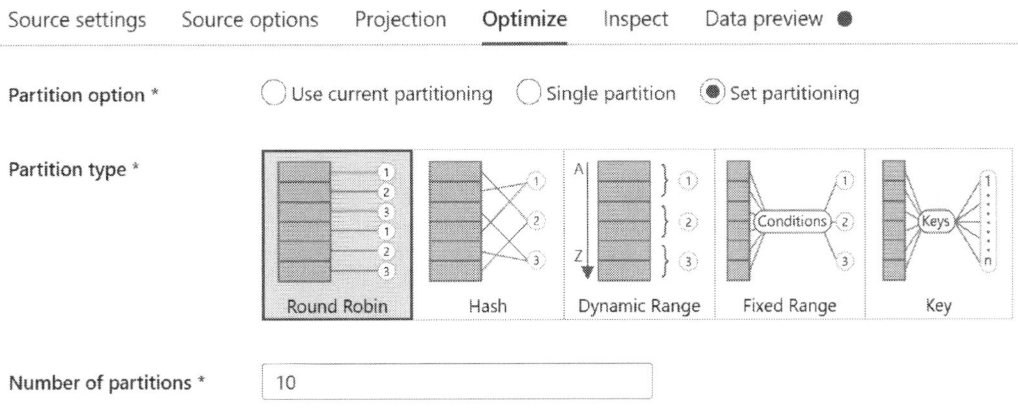


Figure 1.9 – Setting the partition type

5. To get the data preview, make sure you have enabled the **Data flow debug** mode.

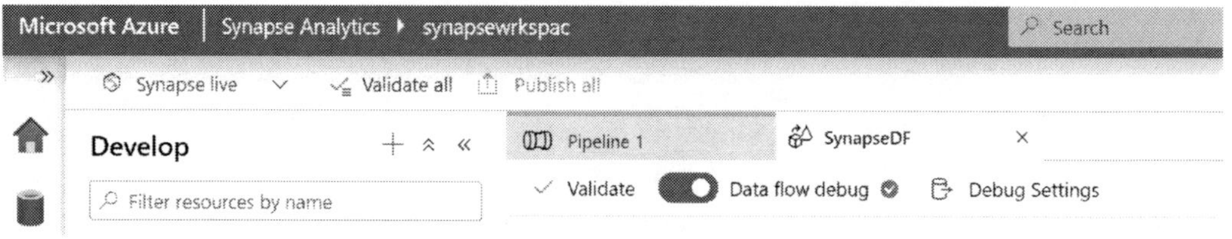


Figure 1.10 – Data flow debug mode on

6. You can use the different transformations, schema modifiers, and so on. I have used derived column in our example to get the `totalfare = tip_amount + tolls_amount` result.

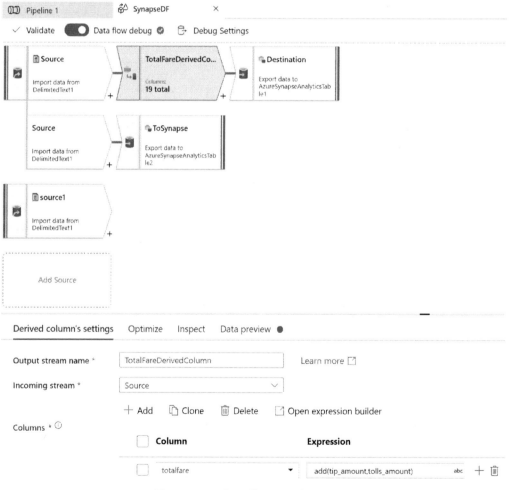

Figure 1.11 – Data flow transformation

7. Define the sink/destination to load the data. In our case, it will be the Azure Synapse pool database.

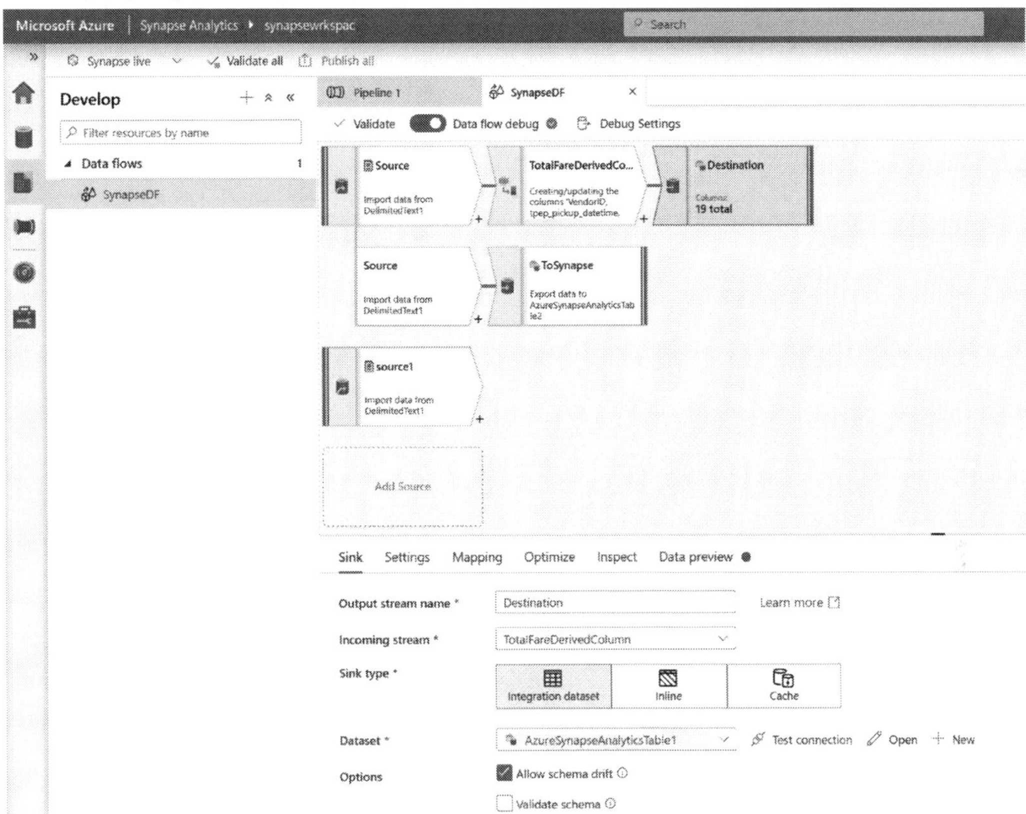


Figure 1.12 – Sink data flow

8. Finally, publish the flow by clicking **Publish all**.

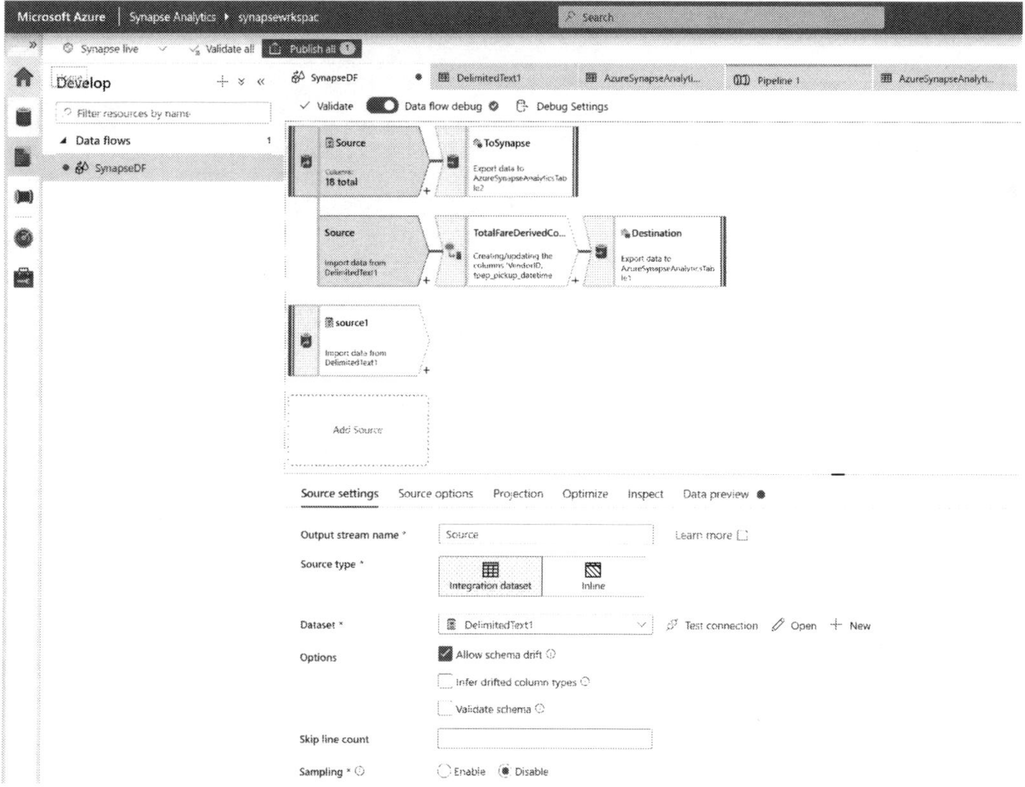


Figure 1.13 – Publish data flow

9. Create a pipeline to call the existing flow that we have just created. Click on the integrate icon on the left and add a new pipeline.

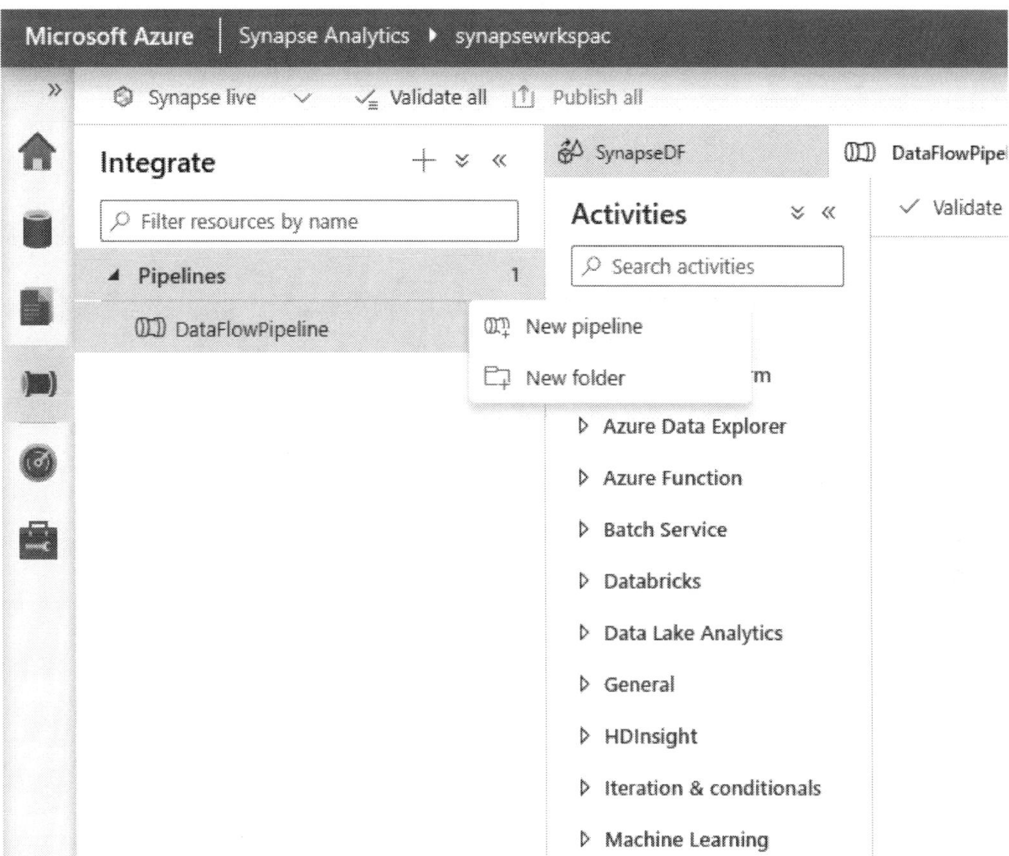


Figure 1.14 – Create pipeline

10. Select the **SynapseDF** data flow under the **Settings** tab, which we created in *Step 6*.

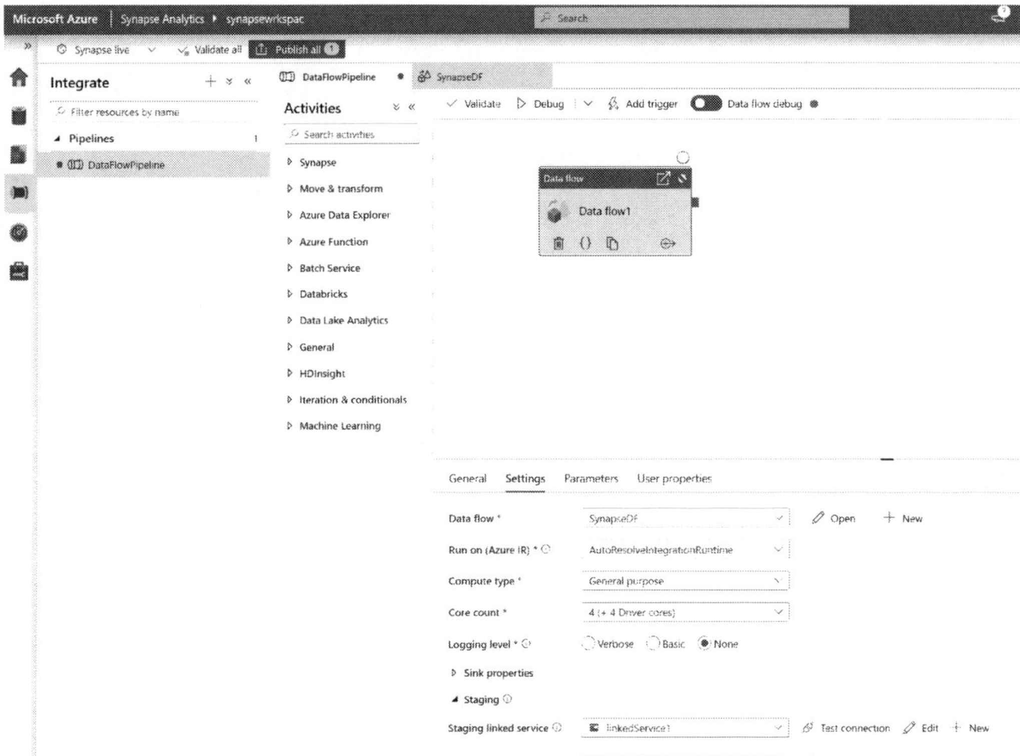

Figure 1.15 – Creating and calling a data flow pipeline

Now we have a customized pipeline that we can reuse any time.

## How it works...

This is one way you can use Azure data flows to create data pipelines and consume data. The main purpose of having a flow pipeline is that you can call, schedule, or trigger this at any time so that it can be part of the data load schedule.

You can also take advantage of the end-to-end monitoring of a pipeline so that it is easier for you or another developer to debug it if there are any data loading issues or failures.

# Adding a trigger to a data flow pipeline

In the *Moving and transforming data using a data flow* recipe, we created a data flow and manually performed the execution of pipelines, also known as on-demand execution, to test the functionality and the results of the pipelines that we created. However, in a production scenario, we need the pipeline to be triggered at a specific time as per our data loading strategy. We need an automated method to schedule and trigger these pipelines, which is done using **triggers**.

The schedule trigger is used to execute ADF pipelines or data flows on a wall-clock schedule.

## Getting ready

Make sure you have the pipeline demonstrated in the previous recipes created and published.

The data flow is created by calling the existing pipeline, as we did in the previous recipe.

## How to do it...

Let's begin:

1. An ADF trigger can be created under the **Manager** page, by clicking on the **Add trigger | New/Edit | Create Trigger** option from the triggers window, as shown in the following screenshot:

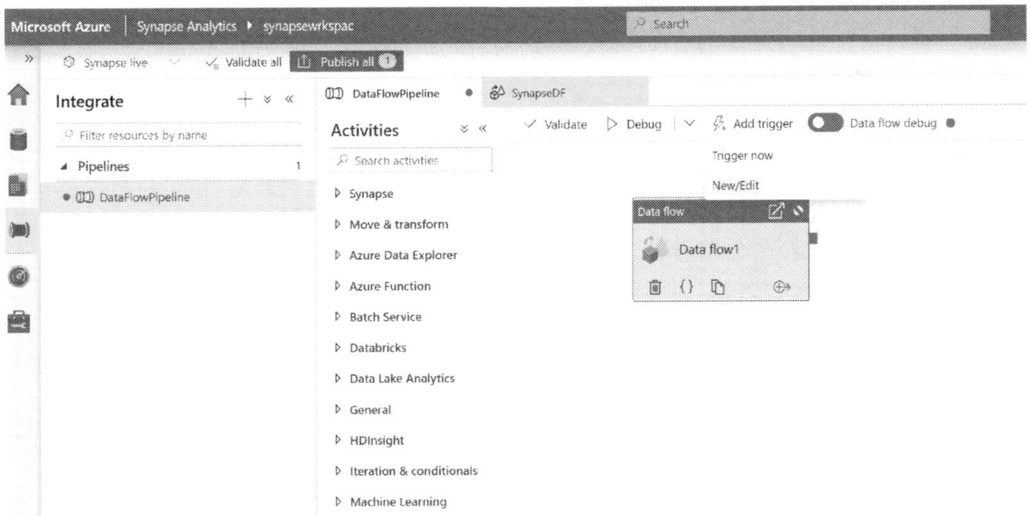


Figure 1.16 – Adding a trigger

The schedule trigger executes the pipeline on a wall-clock schedule, the tumbling window trigger executes the pipeline at a periodic interval and retains the pipeline state, and the event-based trigger responds to a blob-related event.

2. A scheduled trigger will have a start date, the time zone that will be used in the schedule, the end date of the trigger, and the frequency of the trigger (this is optional), with the ability to configure the trigger frequency to be called every specific number of minutes or hours, as shown in the following screenshot:

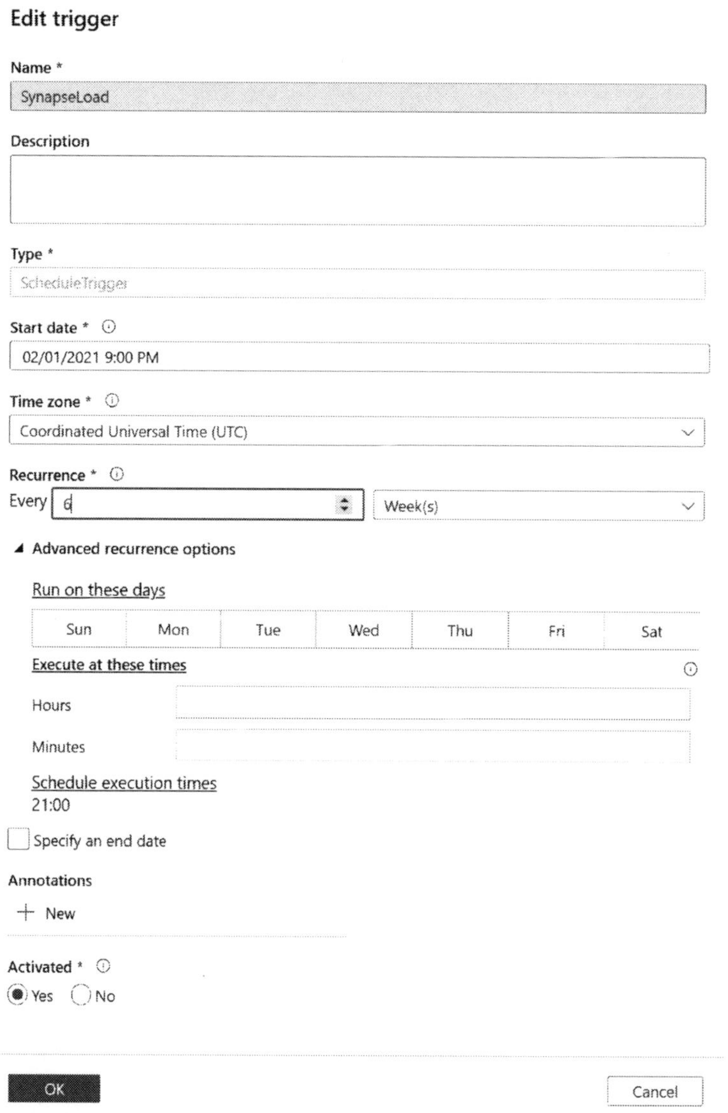

Edit trigger

Name *
SynapseLoad
Description
Type *
ScheduleTrigger
Start date *
02/01/2021 9:00 PM
Time zone *
Coordinated Universal Time (UTC)
Recurrence *
Every 6 Week(s)
Advanced recurrence options
Run on these days
Sun Mon Tue Wed Thu Fri Sat
Execute at these times
Hours
Minutes
Schedule execution times
21:00
Specify an end date
Annotations
+ New
Activated *
Yes No
OK Cancel

Figure 1.17 – Schedule-based trigger

3. An event-based trigger executes pipelines in response to a blob-related event, such as creating or deleting a blob file, in Azure Blob storage, as shown in *Figure 1.18*:



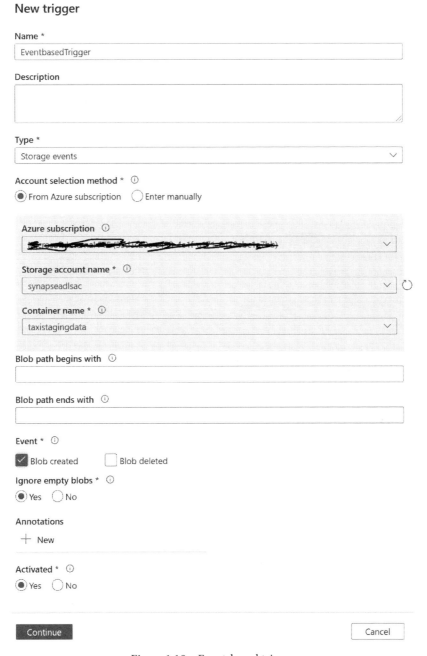

Figure 1.18 – Event-based trigger

## How it works...

A trigger execution is typically initiated by passing the arguments to the parameters that you have created and defined in the pipeline. Every pipeline is associated with a unique pipeline run ID, which is a unique GUID that is responsible for that particular run.

# Unsupported data loading scenarios

In the case of migration scenarios when migrating your database from another SQL database, there is a possibility that some of the data types are not supported on Synapse SQL.

## How to do it...

In order to identify the unsupported data types in your current SQL scheme, you can use the following T-SQL query:

```
SELECT  t.[name], c.[name], c.[system_type_id], c.[user_type_
id], y.[is_user_defined], y.[name]
FROM sys.tables  t
JOIN sys.columns c on t.[object_id]     = c.[object_id]
JOIN sys.types    y on c.[user_type_id] = y.[user_type_id]
WHERE y.[name] IN ('geography','geometry','hierarchyid','
image','text','ntext','sql_variant','xml')
 AND  y.[is_user_defined] = 1;
```

## There's more...

A list of the data types that are unsupported and an alternative workaround that you can use is shown in the following table. This list is from the official Microsoft documentation:

| Unsupported data type | Workaround |
|---|---|
| geometry | varbinary |
| geography | varbinary |
| hierarchyid | nvarchar(4000) |
| image | varbinary |
| text | varchar |
| ntext | nvarchar |
| sql_variant | Split column into several strongly typed columns. |
| table | Convert to temporary tables or consider storing data to storage using CETAS. |
| timestamp | Rework code to use datetime2 and the CURRENT_ TIMESTAMP function. Only constants are supported as defaults, therefore current_timestamp cannot be defined as a default constraint. If you need to migrate row version values from a timestamp typed column, then use BINARY(8) or VARBINARY(8) for NOT NULL or NULL row version values. |
| xml | varchar |
| user-defined type | Convert back to the native data type when possible. |
| default values | Default values support literals and constants only. |

Figure 1.19 – A table showing unsupported data types

# Data loading best practices

Azure Synapse Analytics has a rich set of tools and methods available to load data into SQL pool. You can load data from relational or non-relational data stores; structured or semi-structured data; on-premises systems or other clouds; in batches or streams. The loading can be done using various methods, such as with PolyBase, using the COPY into command, using ADF, or creating a data flow.

## How to do it...

In this section, we'll look at some basic best practices to keep in mind as you work.

## Retaining a well-engineered data lake structure

Retaining a well-engineered data lake structure allows you to know that the data you're loading regularly is consistent with the data requirements for your system.

When loading large datasets, it's recommended to use the compression capabilities of the file format. This ensures that less time is spent on the process of transferring data, using instead the power of Azure Synapse's MPP compute capabilities for decompression.

## Setting a dedicated data loading account

A common error that many of us make while performing data exploration is to use the service administrator account. This account is limited to using the `smallrc` dynamic resource class, which can use between 3% and 25% of the resources depending on the performance level of the provisioned SQL pool.

Hence, it is best to create a dedicated account assigned to different resources classes dependent on the projected task:

1. Create a login within the master database so you can connect SQL pool using SSMS:

```
-- Connect to master
CREATE LOGIN loader WITH PASSWORD = '<strong password>';
```

2. Connect to the dedicated SQL pool and create a user:

```
-- Connect to the SQL pool
CREATE USER loader FOR LOGIN loader;
GRANT ADMINISTER DATABASE BULK OPERATIONS TO loader;
GRANT INSERT ON <yourtablename> TO loader;
GRANT SELECT ON <yourtablename> TO loader;
GRANT CREATE TABLE TO loader;
GRANT ALTER ON SCHEMA::dbo TO loader;
CREATE WORKLOAD GROUP LoadData
WITH (
    MIN_PERCENTAGE_RESOURCE = 100
    ,CAP_PERCENTAGE_RESOURCE = 100
    ,REQUEST_MIN_RESOURCE_GRANT_PERCENT = 100
    );
```

```
CREATE WORKLOAD CLASSIFIER [wgcELTLogin]
WITH (
        WORKLOAD_GROUP = 'LoadData'
    ,MEMBERNAME = 'loader'
);
```

## Handling data loading failure

The frequent **Query aborted-- the maximum reject threshold was reached while reading from an external source** failure error message indicates that your external data contains dirty records.

This error occurs when you meet any of the following criteria:

- If there is a mismatch between the number of columns or the data type of the column definition of the external table
- If the dataset doesn't fit the specified external file format

To handle dirty records, please make sure you have the correct definition for the external table and the external file format so that your external data fits under these definitions.

## Using statistics after the data is loaded

In order to improve the query performance, one of the key things you can do is to generate statistics for your data once the data is loaded to the dedicated SQL pool.

Turn the `AUTO_CREATE_STATISTICS` option on for the database. This will enable SQL dedicated pool to analyze the incoming user query for any missing statistics and optimize them.

The query optimizer creates statistics for individual columns if there are any missing statistics.

To enable dedicated SQL pool on `AUTO_CREATE_STATISTICS`, you can execute the following command:

```
ALTER DATABASE <yourdwname>
SET AUTO_CREATE_STATISTICS ON
```

These tips should prove useful throughout the book and your Synapse experience.

# 2
# Creating Robust Data Pipelines and Data Transformation

In this chapter, we will cover how to load and enrich data using the power of Apache Spark in Azure Synapse Analytics. We will learn about and understand various concepts and recipes for writing Spark data frames to read data from **Azure Data Lake Storage** (**ADLS**) and writing to a SQL pool using PySpark.

This chapter comprises the following recipes:

- Reading and writing data from ADLS Gen2 using PySpark
- Visualizing data in a Synapse notebook

# Reading and writing data from ADLS Gen2 using PySpark

Azure Synapse can take advantage of reading and writing data from the files that are placed in the ADLS2 using Apache Spark. You can read different file formats from Azure Storage with Synapse Spark using Python.

Apache Spark provides a framework that can perform in-memory parallel processing. On top of that, Spark pools help developers to debug and work more effectively as regards their production workloads.

## Getting ready

We will be using the same public dataset that we used in *Chapter 1*, *Choosing the Optimal Method for Loading Data to Synapse*. To retrieve the dataset, you can go to the following URL: `https://www.kaggle.com/microize/newyork-yellow-taxi-trip-data-2020-2019`.

The prerequisites for this recipe are as follows:

- The public dataset must be uploaded to ADLS2.
- You must have an Apache Spark pool created within Synapse Studio. You can refer to the following document for more information on how to create a Spark pool in Synapse: `https://docs.microsoft.com/en-us/azure/synapse-analytics/quickstart-create-apache-spark-pool-portal`.

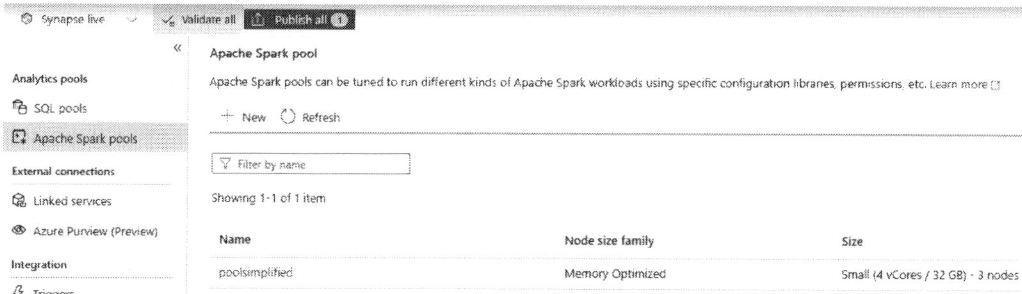


Figure 2.1 – Apache Spark pool

## How to do it...

Let's begin this recipe and see how you can read the data from ADLS2 using the Spark notebook within Synapse Studio. We will leverage the notebook capability of Azure Synapse to get connected to ADLS2 and read the data from it using PySpark:

1. Let's create a new notebook under the **Develop** tab with the name `PySparkNotebook`, as shown in *Figure 2.2*, and select **PySpark (Python)** for **Language**:

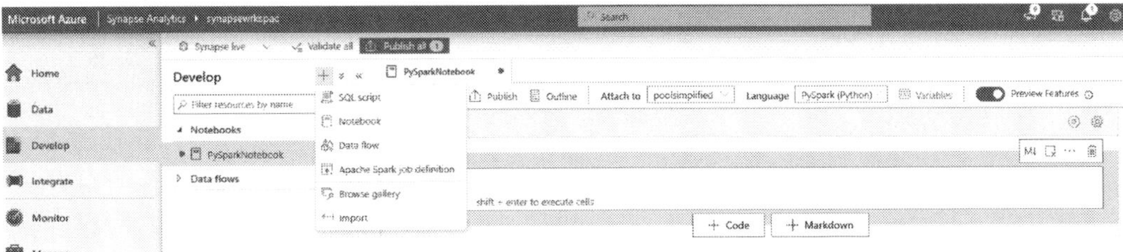


Figure 2.2 – Creating a new notebook

2. You can now start writing your own Python code to get started. The following code is how you can read a CSV file from ADLS using Python:

```
from pyspark.sql import SparkSession
from pyspark.sql.types import *
adls_path ='abfss://%s@%s.dfs.core.windows.
net/%s' % ("taxistagingdata", "synapseadlsac","")
mydataframe = spark.read.option('header','true') \
.option('delimiter', ',') \
.csv(adls_path + '/yellow_tripdata_2020-06.csv')
mydataframe.show()
```

Please refer to *Figure 2.3* for a better understanding of the execution and the results:

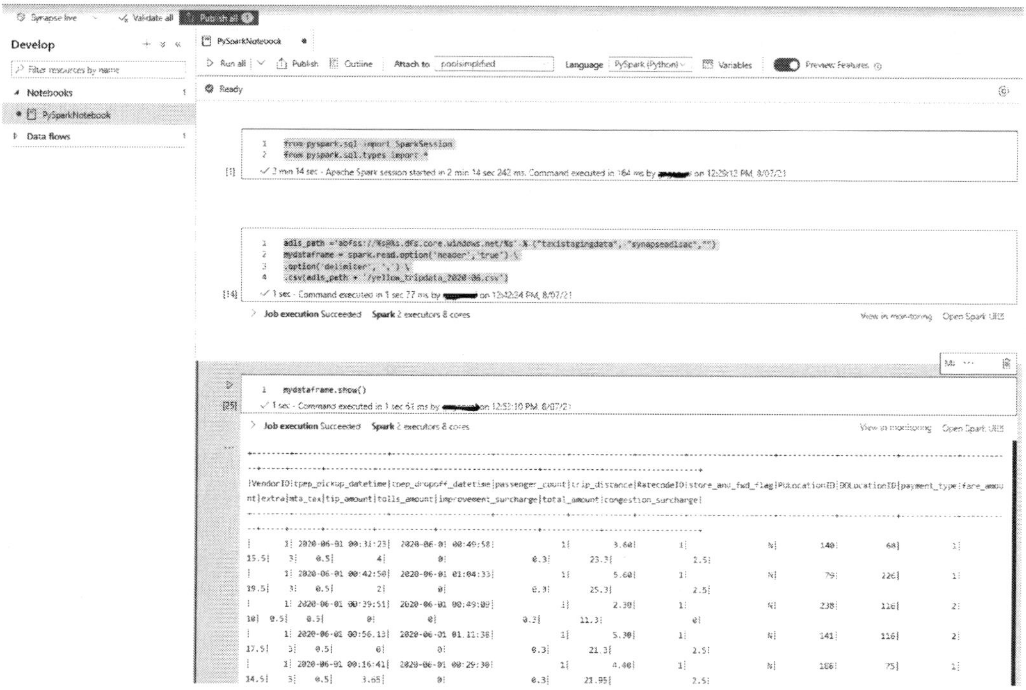

Figure 2.3 – Reading data from a CSV file

3. You can use different transformations or datatype conversions, aggregations, and so on, within the data frame, and explore the data within the notebook. In the following query, you can check how you are converting `passenger_count` to an `Integer` datatype and using `sum` along with a `groupBy` clause:

```
mydataframe1 = mydataframe.withColumn("passenger_
count" ,mydataframe["passenger_count"].
cast(IntegerType()))
```

```
mydataframe1.groupBy("VendorID","payment_type").
sum("passenger_count").show()
```

You can refer to *Figure 2.4* to see how it looks:

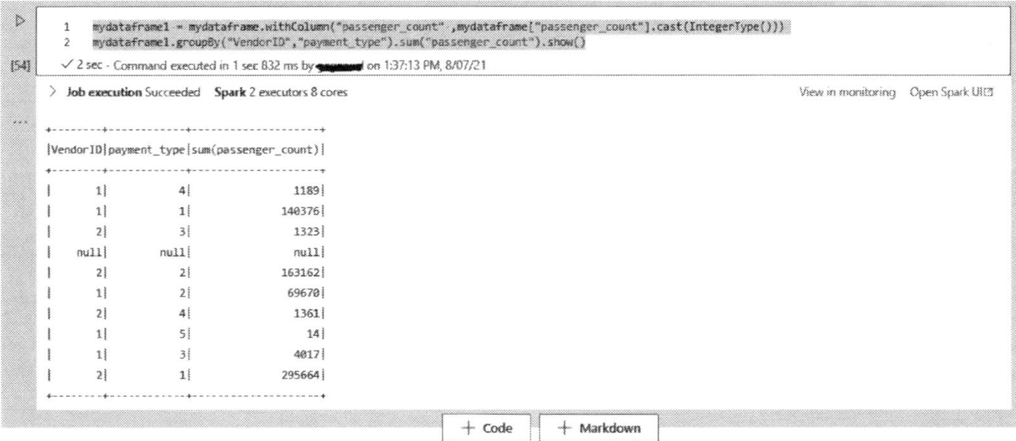


Figure 2.4 – Column datatype conversation

4. Another aspect is the fact that you can write the external table data to the Spark pool from your data frame with the simple command shown here:

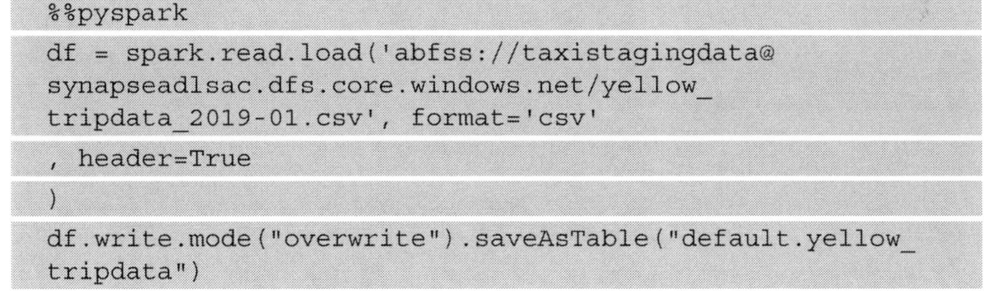

```
%%pyspark
df = spark.read.load('abfss://taxistagingdata@
synapseadlsac.dfs.core.windows.net/yellow_
tripdata_2019-01.csv', format='csv'
, header=True
)
df.write.mode("overwrite").saveAsTable("default.yellow_
tripdata")
```

The following screenshot shows the result:

Figure 2.5 – Writing data to a Spark table

5. Finally, you can query and read the data from the Spark table that you have created and play around with the data, as shown in *Figure 2.6*:

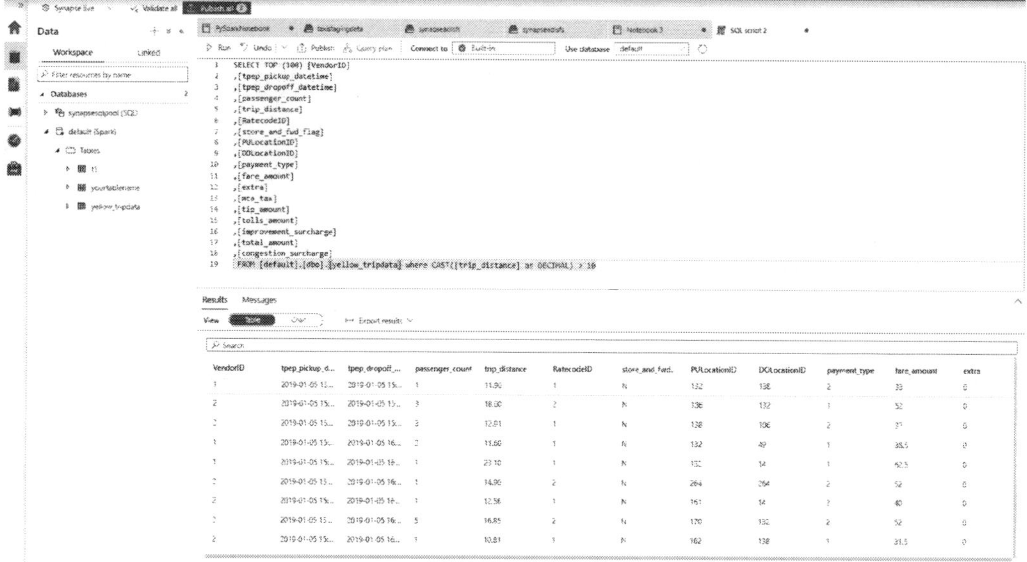

Figure 2.6 – Querying the Spark table

You can also create charts to analyze it on the fly, as shown in *Figure 2.7*:

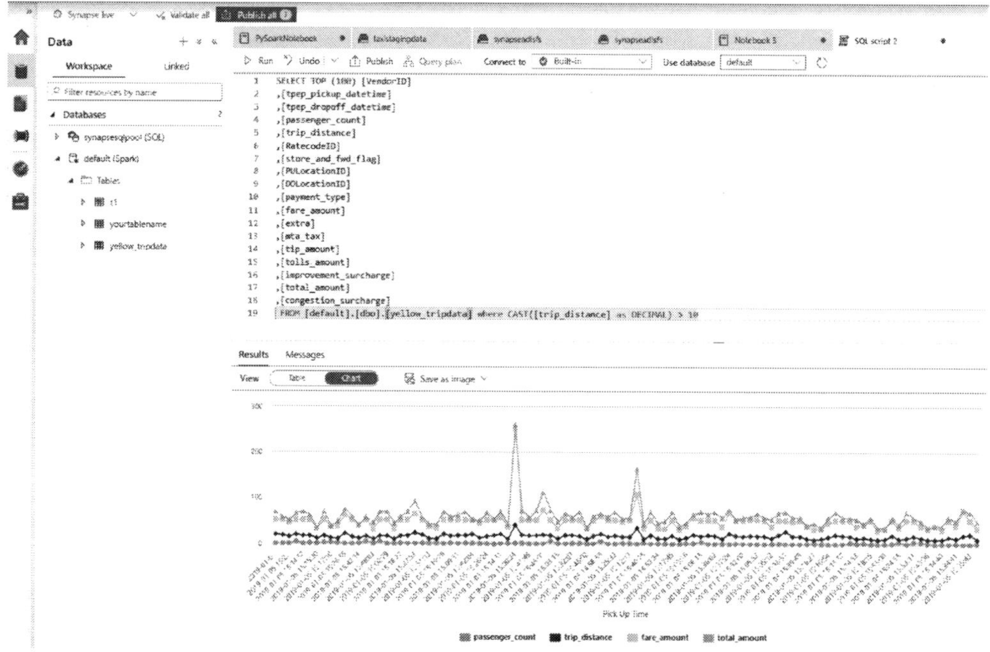

Figure 2.7 – Charting data

## How it works...

The Spark pool gives you the flexibility to define the compute as per your needs. You can define the node size as Small, Large, xLarge, xxLarge, or xxxLarge, with up to 80 vCores/505 GB. The autoscale features provide you with the ability to automatically scale up and down based on the level of load and activity.

You can monitor the compute allocation using the Spark pool monitor to understand the vCore allocation, active applications, and concluded applications by date and time. This allows the developer to plan resource allocation more optimally, as you can see in *Figure 2.8*:

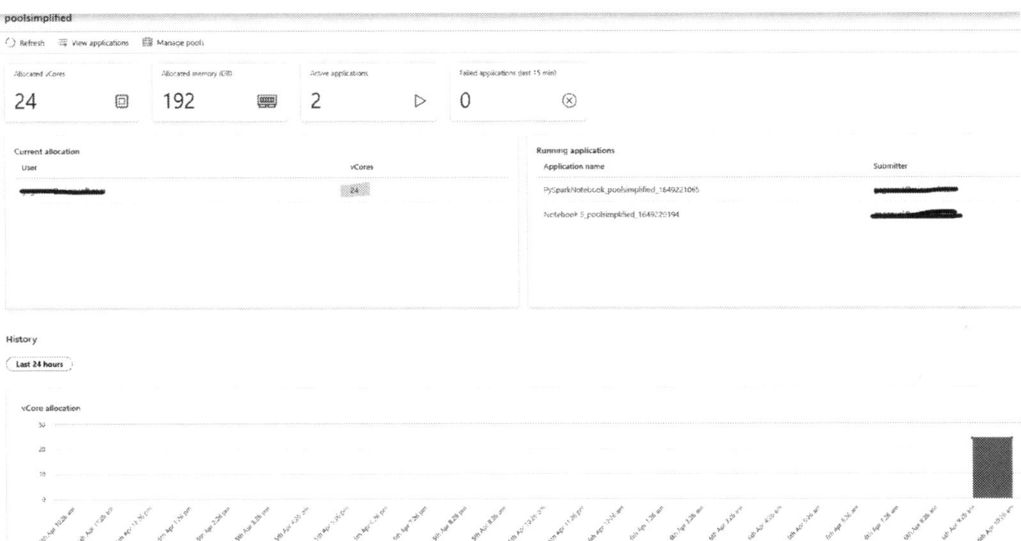


Figure 2.8 – Apache Spark pool monitor

# Visualizing data in a Synapse notebook

Let's now look at an interesting aspect of data exploration that will involve plotting some interesting visuals within the Synapse notebook. We all know that it is always easier to understand pictures or graphs compared to a typical dataset in rows and columns, for example, when you are dealing with a very large dataset, which may contain a lot of key insights. To obtain data-driven insights, we try to work on data pointers that will lead us to those insights; to do that, we plot the data in the form of a visual.

This is exactly what we will be doing in this recipe, and you will learn how to do this within the notebook experience.

## Getting ready

We will be leveraging the same data frame that we created in the *Reading and writing data from ADLS Gen2 using PySpark* recipe.

Basic knowledge of `matplotlib` is required, which will help you to create static and interactive Python visuals.

## How to do it...

Let's get back to the same notebook, **PySparkNotebook**, that we published in the *Reading and writing data from ADLS Gen2 using PySpark* recipe:

1. Import `matplotlib.pyplot`:

   ```
   import matplotlib.pyplot as plt
   ```

   This is the visualization plotting library in Python, as shown in *Figure 2.6*:

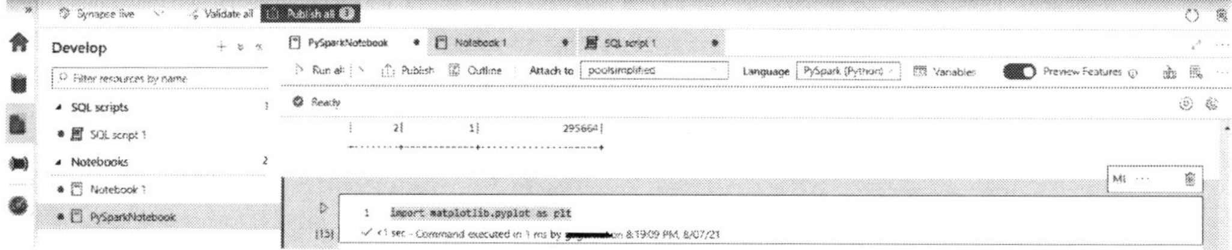

Figure 2.9 – matplotlib import

2. Define and load the entire data frame to pandas using the `toPandas()` function, and define the chart type that we want to plot. In our case, it will be a histogram, which will give us the distribution for the total passenger count:

   ```
   mydataframeplot = mydataframe1.toPandas()
   ax = mydataframeplot['passenger_count'].
   plot(kind='hist', bins= 20, facecolor='orange')
   ax.set_title('Total Passenger distribution')
   ax.set_xlabel('No. of Passengers')
   ax.set_ylabel('Counts')
   chartplt.suptitle('Trend')
   chartplt.show()
   ```

*Figure 2.10* shows the output:

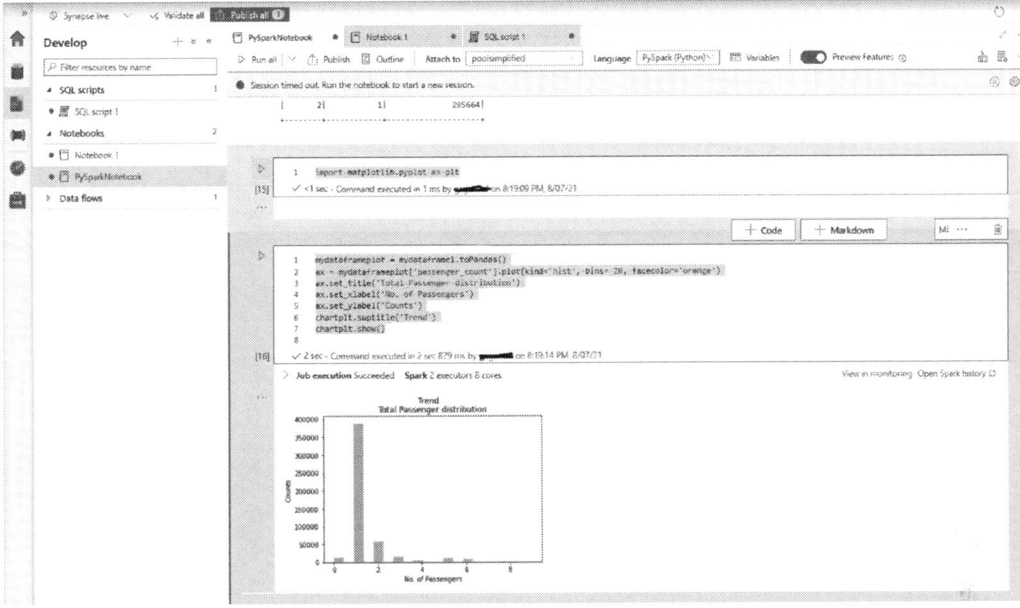


Figure 2.10 – Plotting a histogram

## How it works...

This leverages the power of the Spark pool that you have created to perform data exploration. It makes the process of extracting useful insights from the data extremely fast. The notebook experience within Synapse makes it a one-stop-shop for the developer and the data analyst to collaborate and perform their respective activities.

# 3
# Processing Data Optimally across Multiple Nodes

In this chapter, we will cover the **Synapse SQL** architecture components that are required for running data transformation pipelines and leverage the scale-out capabilities to distribute computational data processing and transformation across multiple nodes. Synapse SQL architecture is designed in such a way that the compute is totally separated from storage and, as needed, the compute can be scaled independently of the data. Since compute and data are separated, the queries handled by compute enable massively parallel processing, performance, and greater speed in retrieving the data.

We will cover the following recipes:

- Working with the resource consumption model of Synapse SQL
- Optimizing analytics with dedicated SQL pool and working on data distribution
- Working with serverless SQL pool
- Processing and querying very large datasets
- Script for statistics in Synapse SQL

# Working with the resource consumption model of Synapse SQL

In this section, we will understand the architecture components of Synapse SQL, the definition of analytical storage, and how storage and compute work together to distribute computational processing of data across multiple nodes. Then we will cover the resource consumption model of Synapse SQL, which enables you to choose the right model for your analytical storage and queries.

## Architecture components of Synapse SQL

Synapse SQL has two main types of SQL pools for analytical storage:

- **Dedicated SQL**
- **Serverless SQL**

### Dedicated SQL

The Synapse dedicated SQL underlying architecture is node-based. Applications issue T-SQL to a control node, which is considered a single-entry point for Synapse SQL.

The Synapse SQL control node utilizes a massively parallel processing distributed query engine to optimize queries for parallel processing and then splits them into different sets of queries for each compute node for parallel execution.

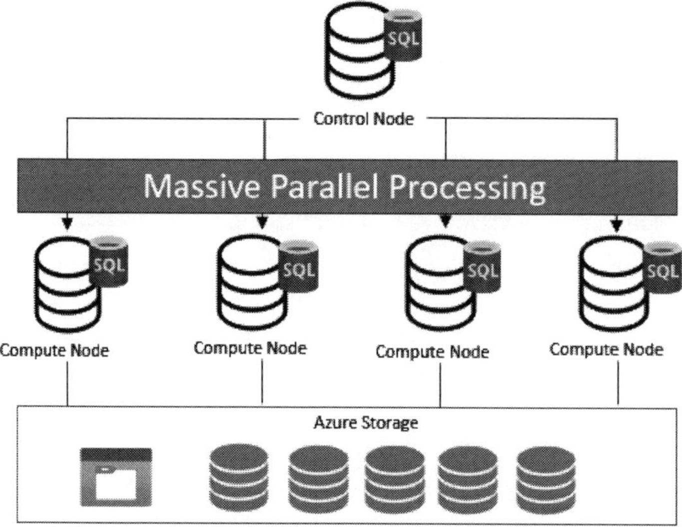


Figure 3.1 – Dedicated SQL pool under the hood

The data that is required for compute nodes is stored in Azure Storage. The **Data movement service** (**DMS**) is an internal system-level service that helps you move data across nodes and compute nodes run queries in parallel, returning results to the application that issued the T-SQL commands.

## Serverless SQL

The scaling of compute resources for serverless SQL is done automatically according to query and resourcing requirements.

Serverless SQL pool has a **control node** that utilizes the **distributed query processing engine**, which orchestrates the distributed parallel execution of queries issued by the user. It splits larger queries into smaller queries, which are executed by compute nodes and orchestrated by the control node. Data is stored in **Azure Storage** and the compute node processes the data in storage with queries, which provides the necessary results.

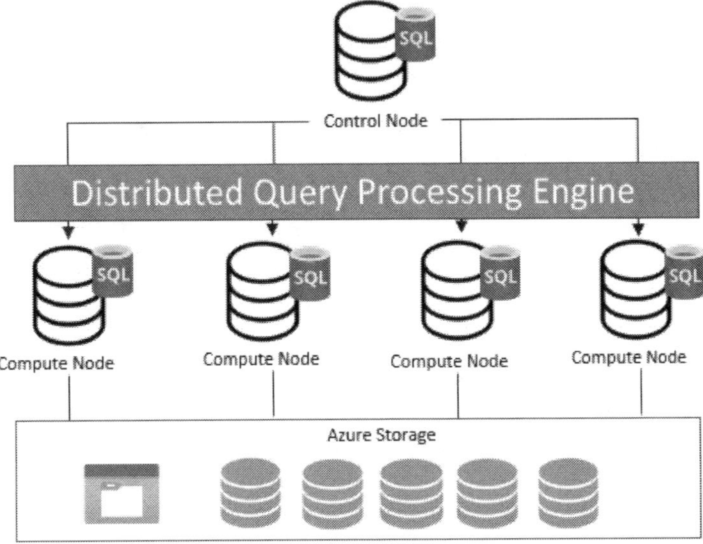


Figure 3.2 – Serverless SQL pool under the hood

There are differences between serverless SQL pool and dedicated SQL pool in how and where the data resides. Serverless SQL pool queries data lake files directly from Azure Storage, whereas dedicated SQL pool queries ingest data from data lake files in Azure Storage to SQL in the compute node. Data that is ingested into dedicated SQL pool will be sharded into distributions for optimal performance. The sharding patterns are as listed:

- **Hash**
- **Round robin**
- **Replicate**

## Sharding pattern or distribution

Dedicated SQL pool in a compute node will split into 60 smaller queries that run in parallel. Each of the 60 smaller queries runs on one of the distribution or sharding patterns. Dedicated SQL pool has one distribution per compute node. If we choose Dedicated SQL pool with minimum compute resources, then all the data distribution will run on one compute node.

- **Hash distribution**: This delivers the highest performance for joins and aggregations on larger tables. Dedicated SQL pool uses the hash function to assign each row to a distribution. One of the columns will be defined as the distribution column. The hash functions use values in the distribution column and assign each row to a distribution.
- **Round-robin distribution**: This delivers fast performance when used as a staging table, particularly for loads. A round-robin distributed table distributes data evenly across the table. This distribution is random and round robin requires shuffling of data, which increases the latency on query retrieval.
- **Replicated tables**: This delivers the fastest query performance for smaller tables. The table is replicated on each compute node and a full copy of the table is cached. Since the table is replicated, transferring data between the compute nodes is not required when we do a join or aggregation. The performance is outstanding for smaller tables but it adds more overhead when writing data and hence is not suitable for larger tables.

## Resource consumption

The following are the resource consumption models for Synapse SQL:

- **Serverless SQL pool**: A pay-per-query service where resources are increased or decreased automatically based on consumption.
- **Dedicated SQL pool**: The unit of scale is an abstraction of compute power and is called a data warehouse unit. The analytical storage is a combination of compute, memory, and IO, bundled as data warehouse units.

Increasing the data warehouse units would do the following:

- Increase the performance of scans, aggregations, and **CREATE TABLE AS SELECT (CTAS)** statements.
- Increase the number of readers and writers for PolyBase load operations.
- Increase the capacity in running concurrent queries and increase concurrency slots.

| Category | Description | Maximum limits |
|---|---|---|
| Data warehouse units (DWUs) | Maximum DWUs for dedicated SQL pool | Gen1: DW6000<br>Gen2: DW30000c |
| Default Database Transaction Unit (DTU) per server | A DTU allows a specific number of DWUs based on generation as described above | 54,000<br>This is the default quota and it is for safety limits. We can increase the quota with a support ticket. To calculate DTUs, we need to use the below formulae:<br>DW6000 x 7.5 = 45,000 DTUs DW7500c x 9 = 67,500 DTUs. |

Figure 3.3 – Table showing data warehouse units

# Optimizing analytics with dedicated SQL pool and working on data distribution

In this section, we will understand the in-depth details of dedicated SQL pool for optimizing analytics on a larger dataset. We need to understand the basics of column storage; know when to use round robin, hash distribution, and replicated data distributions; know when to partition a table and check for data skew and space usage; know the best practices and how to effectively use workload management for dedicated SQL pool.

## Understanding columnstore storage details

A columnar store is logically organized as a table with rows and columns. It is physically stored in a column-wise data format. Generally, a **rowgroup** (group of rows) is compressed in columnar store format. A rowgroup consists of the maximum number of rows per rowgroup. The columnstore index slices the table into rowgroups and then compresses the rowgroups column-wise.

A clustered **columnstore** index is the primary storage for the entire table and it is useful for data warehousing and analytics workloads. It is used to store fact tables and large dimension tables. It improves query performance and data compression by 10 times compared to a nonclustered index.

A nonclustered index is a secondary index that is created on a **rowstore** table and is useful for real-time operational analytics in an **Online transaction processing** (**OLTP**) workload.

A columnstore index provides a high level of data compression and significantly reduces data warehouse storage costs. Columnstore indexes are the preferred data storage format for data warehousing and analytics workloads.

## Knowing when to use round-robin, hash-distributed, and replicated distributions

A distributed table is actually a single table outwardly but rows are stored in 60 distributions. The distribution of rows either uses hash or the round-robin algorithm. Hash is used for large fact tables. Round robin is useful for improving loading speed. Replicated tables are used for smaller datasets.

To choose between three distribution options, for all design scenarios, consider asking yourself the following set of questions:

- What is the size of the table?
- What is the frequency at which we access the table and refresh the table?
- Are we going to use fact and dimension tables in dedicated SQL pool?

If the answers to the preceding questions are as follows, then consider using hash distribution:

- Larger fact tables and the table size is more than 2 GB on disk.
- Data will be refreshed frequently and accessed by concurrent users for reporting. It has frequent **Create, Read, Update, Delete**, and **List** (**CRUDL**) operations.
- Both fact and dimension tables are needed in dedicated SQL pool.

### Hash distribution

Hash distribution distributes table rows across the compute nodes by using a deterministic hash function, which assigns each row one distribution in each compute node. All identical values will be stored in the same distribution. SQL Analytics will store the location of the row, and this will help to minimize data movement, which improves query performance. It works out well if we have a very large numbers of rows.

### Round-robin distribution

Round robin distributes table rows evenly across all distributions. Rows with equal values will not be assigned to the same distribution and assignment is completely random. Hence there are more data movement operations to organize the data and shuffling frequently hits the performance. Consider using round robin for the following scenarios:

- None of the columns are suitable candidates for hash distribution.
- The table does not share a common join key and there is no join key.
- When we need to use this for temporary staging.

### Replicated tables

Replicated tables hold a full copy of the table on the compute node. Replicating a table removes the need to transfer data between compute nodes. Since the table has multiple copies, a replicated table works out if the table size is less than 2 GB compressed.

Consider using a replicated table when the following applies:

- The table size is less than 2 GB irrespective of the number of rows.
- The table used in joins requires data movement. If one of the tables is small, consider a replicated table.

Replicated tables will not provide the best query performance in the following scenarios:

- The table has frequent CRUDL operations. This slows down the performance.
- The SQL pool is scaled frequently. Scaling requires us to copy the replicated tables frequently to the compute node, which slows the performance.
- The table has many columns but read operations are targeted only to a small number of columns. It would be effective to distribute the table and create an index on frequently queried columns instead of using replicated tables.

## Knowing when to partition a table

Table partitions help to segregate data into smaller groups of data. Mostly, they are created on the date column. Table partitioning is supported on all table types with different sets of indexes and also on different distribution types.

The benefit is that it improves query performance because it limits the scan only to qualified partitions. This avoids a full table scan and scans only a limited set of data.

A design with too many partitions can affect the performance. At least 1 million rows per distribution and partition are required for optimal compression and performance of columnstore index tables. If there are 1 million rows per distribution and a full table scan can be avoided, we recommend using partitions.

## Checking for skewed data and space usage

We learned in previous sections that data should be evenly distributed across a distribution. When data is not distributed evenly, it results in data skew. If there is data skew, some processing in a compute node will take a longer time and others will finish more quickly. This is not an ideal scenario and you must therefore choose your distribution column in such a way that it has many unique values, no date column, and does not contain `NULL` values or has only a few NULL values.

Check data skew with `DBCC PDW_SHOWSPACEUSED` as shown in the following line of code:

```
DBCC PDW_SHOWSPACEUSED('dbo.FactSales');
```

Data skew identification is necessary so that we can finish the processing quickly and, as in the preceding line, we need to check the tables frequently.

## Best practices

We will learn a few best practices and tips that help in the design of optimized analytics for dedicated SQL pool.

Batching the `insert` statements together will reduce the number of round trips and improve efficiency. If there are larger volumes of data that have to be loaded into dedicated SQL pool, choose PolyBase and select hash distribution. While partitioning helps in query performance, too many partitions can be detrimental to performance.

`INSERT`, `UPDATE`, and `DELETE` statements always run in a transaction. The transaction is rolled back if there is a failure. Minimize the transaction size to reduce long rollbacks, which is achieved by dividing these statements into parts. For instance, if an `UPDATE` statement is expected to get completed in 1 hour, we can break this into four equal parts so that each part takes 15 minutes to complete. Any error in the middle of a transaction will have a quicker rollback.

Reduce the number of query results and use the `top` statement to return only a specific set of rows. Designing the smallest possible column size is helpful because the overall table will be smaller and the query results will also be smaller. Temporary tables should be used for loading transient data.

Designing a columnstore index for tables of more than 60 million rows is a good solution. When we partition data, each partition is expected to have 1 million rows to benefit from a columnstore index. Hence a table with 100 partitions should have 100 million rows to benefit from columnstore indexing (since by default there will be 60 distributions and 100 partitions, which actually need 1 million rows).

# Workload management for dedicated SQL pool

Dedicated SQL pool offers workload management with the following three concepts:

- **Workload classification**
- **Workload importance**
- **Workload isolation**

This enables us to maintain query performance at an optimized level throughout. We can choose an appropriate capacity for DWU and it offers memory, distribution, and concurrency limits based on DWU.

**Workload classification** involves classifying the workload group based on loading the data with `INSERT`, `UPDATE`, and `DELETE` and then querying the data with `Select`. A data warehousing solution will have one kind of workload policy for loads that are classified as a high-resource class, which requires more resources, and a different workload policy for `Select` queries where loading might take precedence compared to querying. The first step is to classify the workload into a workload group.

**Workload importance** involves the order or priority in which a request gets access.

**Workload isolation** involves reserving resources for a workload group. We can define the quantity of resources that are assigned based on resource classes.

All these workload groups have a configuration for query timeout and requests. The workload groups require constant monitoring and management to maintain optimal query performance.

# Working with serverless SQL pool

Azure Synapse Analytics has serverless SQL pool endpoints that are primarily used to query data in Azure Data Lake (Parquet, Delta Lake, delimited text formats), Azure Cosmos DB, and Dataverse.

We can access the data using T-SQL queries without the need to copy and load data in a SQL store through serverless SQL pool. Serverless SQL pool is ideally a wrapper service for interactive querying and distributed data processing for large-scale analysis of big data systems. It is a completely serverless and managed service offering from Microsoft Azure, built with fault tolerance, high reliability, and high performance for larger datasets.

Serverless SQL pool is suitable for the following scenarios:

- Basic exploration and discovery where data in **Azure Data Lake Storage** (**ADLS**) with different formats such as Parquet, CSV, Delta, and JSON can be used to derive insights.
- A relational abstraction layer on top of raw data without transformation, allowing you to get an up-to-date view of data. This will be created on top of Azure Storage and Azure Cosmos DB.
- Simple, scalable, and performance-efficient data transformation with T-SQL.

In this recipe, we will learn how to explore data from Parquet stored in ADLS Gen 2 with serverless SQL pool.

## Getting ready

We will be using a public dataset for our scenario. This dataset will consist of New York yellow taxi trip data: this includes attributes such as trip distances, itemized fares, rate types, payment types, pick-up and drop-off dates and times, driver-reported passenger counts, and pick-up and drop-off locations. We will be using this dataset throughout this recipe to demonstrate various use cases.

- To get the dataset, you can go to the following URL: `https://www.kaggle.com/microize/newyork-yellow-taxi-trip-data-2020-2019`.

- The code for this recipe can be downloaded from the GitHub repository: `https://github.com/PacktPublishing/Analytics-in-Azure-Synapse-Simplified`.

Let's get started.

## How to do it...

Let's first create our Synapse Analytics workspace and then create serverless SQL pool on top of it. We will upload a Parquet file and explore it with serverless SQL.

Synapse Analytics workspace creation requires us to create a resource group or access to an existing resource group with owner permissions. Let's use an existing resource group where you will find owner permissions for the user:

1. Log in to the Azure portal: `https://portal.azure.com/#home`.
2. Search for `synapse` on the **Microsoft Azure** page and then navigate to **Azure Synapse Analytics**.
3. Select **Azure Synapse Analytics**.

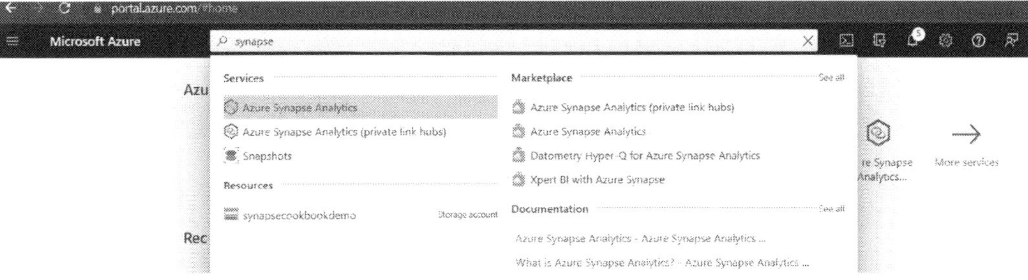


Figure 3.4 – Search for Synapse Analytics

4. Create an Azure Synapse Analytics workspace using the **Create** button or the **Create Synapse workspace** button.

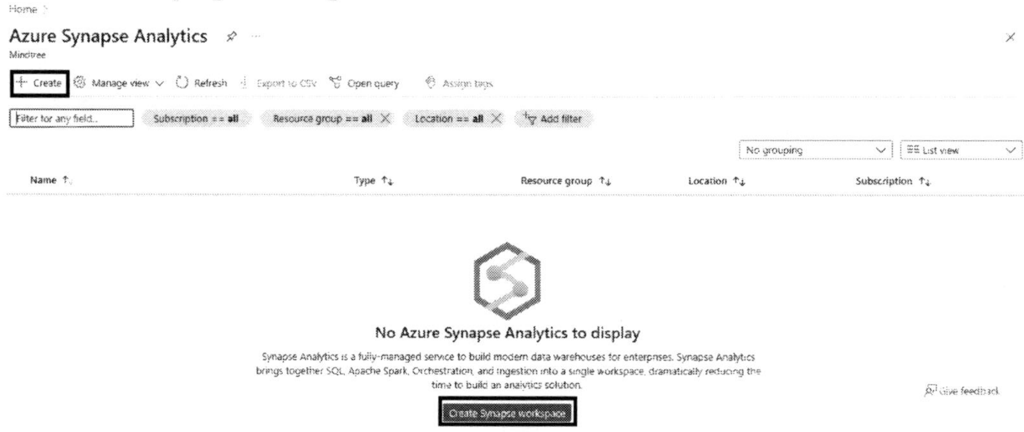


Figure 3.5 – Create Synapse Analytics workspace

5. On the **Basics** tab, enter the resource group workspace name as `synapsecookbook`.
6. Associate it with already created ADLS Gen 2 account name and the container.

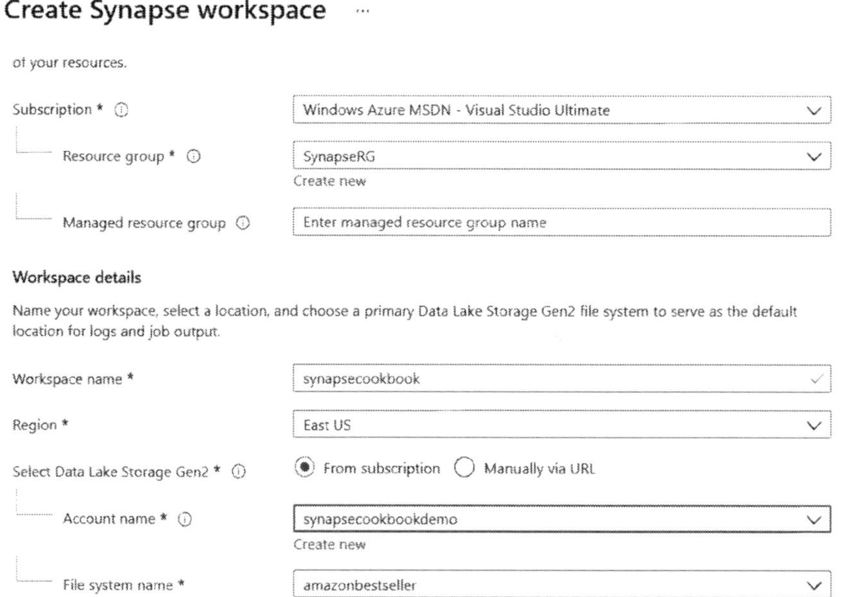


Figure 3.6 – Create Synapse workspace Basics tab

7. Enter the SQL administrator password to access the Synapse workspace upon login.

*Basics ***Security** Networking Tags Review + create

Configure security options for your workspace.

**SQL administrator credentials**

Provide credentials that can be used for administrator access to the workspace's SQL pools. If you don't provide a password, one will be automatically generated. You can change the password later.

SQL Server admin login * ⓘ sqladminuser

SQL Password ⓘ ••••••••••

Confirm password ••••••••••

**System assigned managed identity permission**

Choose the permissions that you would like to assign to the workspace's system-assigned identity. Learn more

☑ Allow pipelines (running as workspace's system assigned identity) to access SQL pools. ⓘ

☐ Allow network access to Data Lake Storage Gen2 account. ⓘ

ⓘ The selected Data Lake Storage Gen2 account does not restrict network access using any network access rules, or you selected a storage account manually via URL under Basics tab. Learn more

Figure 3.7 – Create Synapse workspace Security tab

8. Review and create the workspace.
9. Go to the existing **Synapse Analytics workspace** and navigate to **Synapse Studio**.

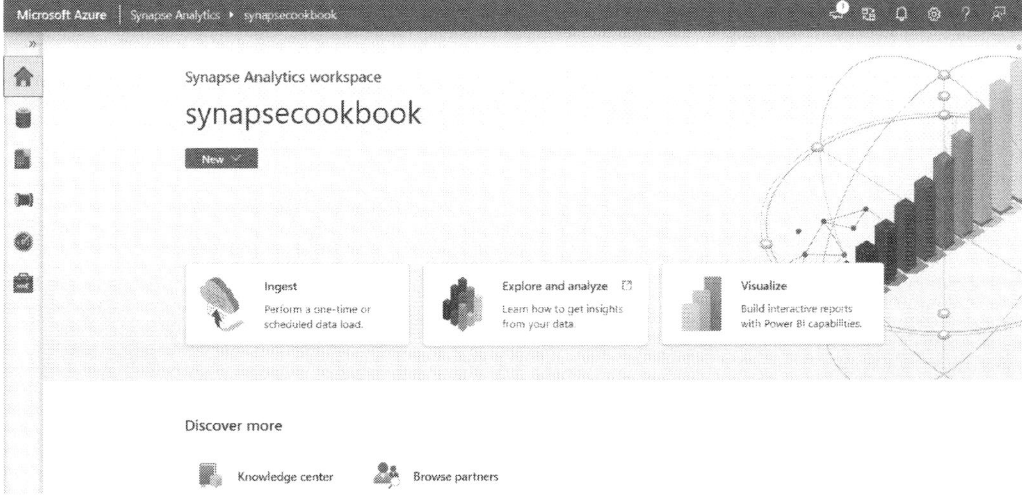


Figure 3.8 – Synapse Studio

10. Create a **Serverless** SQL database in Synapse Studio.

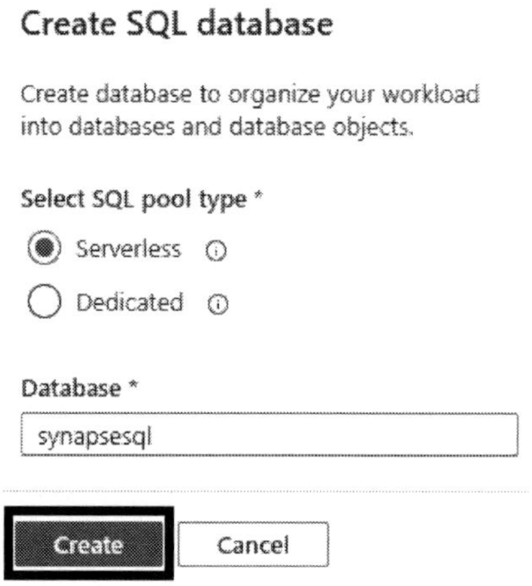

Figure 3.9 – Create serverless SQL pool

11. Upload the `NYCTripSmall.parquet` file in any existing storage account.
12. Query the Parquet file as external storage with T-SQL as follows:

```
select top 10 *
from openrowset(
    bulk 'abfss://amazonbestseller@synapsecookbookdemo.
dfs.core.windows.net/NYCTripSmall.parquet',
    format = 'parquet') as rows
```

That completes the recipe!

## There's more...

Serverless SQL pool allows us to query files in ADLS. It does not have storage like dedicated SQL pool or ingestion capabilities. The following list suggests some best practices for serverless SQL pool:

- Always co-locate client applications such as Power BI in the same region as serverless SQL pool for good performance.
- Co-locate ADLS, Cosmos DB, and serverless SQL pool in the same region.
- Optimize storage using partitioning and files in Azure Storage between 100 MB and 1 GB.

- Cache results on the client side (Power BI or **Azure Analysis Services** (**AAS**)) and refresh it frequently. Serverless SQL pool is not suitable for complex queries or processing a large amount of data in Power BI DirectQuery mode.

# Processing and querying very large datasets

Synapse SQL uses distributed query processing, the data movement service, and scale-out architecture, leveraging the advantages of the scalability and flexibility of compute and storage. Data transformation is not required prior to loading it to Synapse SQL. We need to use the built-in massively parallel processing capabilities of Synapse, load data in parallel, and then perform the transformation.

Loading data using `PolyBase` external tables and `COPY SQL` statements is considered one of the fastest, most reliable, and scalable ways of loading data. We can use external data stored in **ADLS** and Azure Blob storage, and load data using the `COPY` statement. This data is then loaded to production tables and exposed as views, which creates a query view for the client applications to derive meaningful business insights.

## Getting ready

We will be performing a series of steps in order to extract, load, and create a materialized view of data for larger datasets. The Azure documentation has the syntax for all the steps, which should be referred to for actual implementation:

- `https://docs.microsoft.com/en-us/azure/synapse-analytics/sql/develop-tables-external-tables?tabs=hadoop#create-external-data-source`
- `https://docs.microsoft.com/en-us/azure/synapse-analytics/sql/develop-tables-external-tables?tabs=hadoop#create-external-file-format`
- `https://docs.microsoft.com/en-us/azure/synapse-analytics/sql/develop-tables-external-tables?tabs=hadoop#create-external-table`
- `https://docs.microsoft.com/en-us/sql/t-sql/statements/copy-into-transact-sql?view=azure-sqldw-latest`

## How to do it...

Let's now dive deep into the step-by-step process of extracting, loading, and creating the materialized view of data:

1. *Extract* the source data into text, Parquet, or CSV files. Let's take an example where the source data is in Oracle. Use Oracle's built-in wizards or third-party tools to move the data from Oracle to delimited text or CSV files. Converting to Parquet will be useful and is supported in Synapse SQL. Load the data from UTF-8 and UTF-16 as delimited text or CSV files.
2. *Load* the data into Azure Blob storage or ADLS. Synapse data integration or Azure Data Factory can be used to load the text files created earlier or CSV files into Azure Blob storage or ADLS. If we are loading this larger dataset on-premises, it is highly recommended to have Azure ExpressRoute or Site-to-Site VPN established between on-premises and Azure.
3. *Prepare* the data for loading. We need to prepare the data before we load it to Synapse SQL tables.
4. *Define* the tables. First, define the tables before loading them to dedicated SQL pool. We can define external tables in dedicated SQL pool before loading. External tables are similar to database views. These external tables will have the table schema and data that is stored outside dedicated SQL pool.

   There are several different ways of defining tables, which are listed as follows:

   - `CREATE EXTERNAL DATA SOURCE`
   - `CREATE EXTERNAL FILE FORMAT`
   - `CREATE EXTERNAL TABLE`

5. *Load the data into Synapse SQL* using PolyBase or the `COPY` statement. Data is loaded to staging tables. The options for loading are as follows:

   - `COPY` statement: The following code is the sample for loading Parquet files into Synapse SQL:

```
COPY INTO test_parquet
FROM 'https://myaccount.blob.core.windows.net/
myblobcontainer/folder1/*.parquet'
WITH (
    FILE_FORMAT = myFileFormat,
    CREDENTIAL=(IDENTITY= 'Shared Access Signature',
SECRET='<Your_SAS_Token>')
)
```

6. *Configure* PolyBase in Azure Data Factory or Synapse data integration.
7. *Transform* the data and move it to production tables. The data is in staging tables now and you can perform transformations with a T-SQL statement and move data into the production table. The `INSERT INTO ... SELECT` statement moves the data from the staging table to the production table.
8. *Create* materialized views for consumption. Materialized views are views where data gets automatically updated as data changes in underlying production tables. Views significantly improve the performance of complex queries (typically queries with lot of joins, aggregations, and complex joins) and offer simple maintenance.

Processing and querying large datasets requires us to load them in parallel, process them with massively parallel processing clusters, and create materialized views that refresh the data automatically. These materialized views will be used by the reporting tool for dashboards and deriving insights.

# Script for statistics in Synapse SQL

Once the data is loaded into a dedicated SQL pool, statistics collection from data is very important for continuous query optimization. The dedicated SQL pool query optimizer is a cost-based optimizer that compares query plans and chooses the plan with the lowest cost. The dedicated SQL pool engine will analyze incoming user queries where the statistics are constantly analyzed and the database `AUTO_CREATE_STATISTICS` option is set to `ON`. If the statistics are not available, then the query optimizer will create statistics on individual columns.

## How to do it...

By default, statistics creation is turned on. Check the data warehouse configuration for `AUTO_CREATE_STATISTICS` using the following command:

```
SELECT name, is_auto_create_stats_on
FROM sys.databases
```

Enable statistics with the following command:

```
ALTER DATABASE <datawarehousename>
SET AUTO_CREATE_STATISTICS ON
```

Once the statistics command is received, it will trigger the automatic creation of statistics for the following statements:

- `SELECT`
- `INSERT-SELECT`
- `CTAS`
- `UPDATE`
- `DELETE`
- `EXPLAIN`

## Creating and updating statistics

The following command is used to create and update statistics for a table with a set of columns or all columns:

```
CREATE STATISTICS [statistics_name]   ON [schema_name].[table_name]([column_name]);
UPDATE STATISTICS [schema_name].[table_name]([stat_name]);
UPDATE STATISTICS [schema_name].[table_name];
```

Serverless SQL pool supports the automatic creation of statistics only for Parquet files. For CSV files, statistics have to be created manually.

We can create stored procedures and views with all statistics enabled. These stored procedures can be used to automatically execute on the creation and updating of statistics of selected columns in tables.

## There's more...

System views and functions are used to get information on statistics. `STATS_DATE()` allows you to view the statistics created or updated. The following table lists the system views that we can use to get relevant information on statistics:

| Views | Description |
|---|---|
| sys.columns | One row for each column |
| sys.objects | One row for each object in the database |
| sys.schemas | One row for each schema in the database |
| sys.stats | One row for each statistics object |
| sys.stats_columns | One row for each column in the statistics object. Links back to sys.columns |
| sys.tables | One row for each table (includes external tables) |
| STATS_DATE | Date the statistics object was last updated |
| sys.table_types | One row for each data type |

Figure 3.10 – Table providing information on system views

# 4
# Engineering Real-Time Analytics with Azure Synapse Link Using Cosmos DB

In this chapter, we will cover how to perform real-time analytics with Cosmos DB by integrating Azure Synapse Link. Designing and implementing **Internet of Things** (**IoT**) end-to-end solutions from data ingestion, data processing, and deriving insights will be explored in depth. This will help us to learn about real-world use cases involving Synapse Link and Cosmos DB, where we will use it effectively for real-time analytics and reporting.

We will cover the following recipes:

- Integrating an Azure Synapse ETL pipeline with Cosmos DB
- Setting up Azure Cosmos DB analytical store
- Enabling Azure Synapse Link and connecting Azure Cosmos DB to Azure Synapse
- IoT end-to-end solutions and getting real-time insights
- Use cases with Synapse Link

# Integrating an Azure Synapse ETL pipeline with Cosmos DB

In this section, we will understand Azure Synapse Link for Cosmos DB and its usage for real-time analytics. We will learn about the following topics:

- The basics of Cosmos DB
- Azure Synapse Link integration with Cosmos DB
- Feature support of Cosmos DB with Synapse
- Synapse runtime support
- Structured streaming support
- Security features of Cosmos DB

## Introducing Cosmos DB

**Azure Cosmos DB** is a fully isolated columnar store for large-scale analytics with operational data and a transactional store that is schema-agnostic, which allows us to use it with transactional applications without the overhead of managing schema or indexes.

Azure Cosmos DB analytical store is optimized for use for analytical workloads, which offers good analytical query performance.

When operational data is stored in a transaction store in row store format, analytical queries would be expensive, since we need provisioned throughput on the data scan stored in row format. This will impact the performance of transactional workloads that are used by real-time applications. Hence, larger operational data will be stored in a data warehouse as a separate data storage layer. This data will then be analyzed by Spark-based clusters for efficient analytics. Separation of analytical storage and compute for this operation data incurs more costs since it involves both Spark clusters and data warehouse storage. It also results in additional latency because the ETL pipelines are run less frequently than the transaction workloads. The `upsert` and `merge` statements on this operation data in analytical storage will become complex and it is not fast like newly ingested data.

Cosmos DB analytical store addresses the complexity and latency challenges of designing ETL pipelines. It can sync the operational data into a separate columnstore automatically instead of having a data warehouse. As you know, columnstore is the preferred storage format for all large-scale analytical queries, which results in faster query performance.

## Azure Synapse Link integration

**Azure Synapse Link for Azure Cosmos DB** is a cloud-native managed offering from Microsoft that enables **hybrid transactional and analytical processing** (**HTAP**) to run near real-time analytical queries with operation data stored in Azure Cosmos DB.

**Synapse Link** enables no-**ETL** (**Extract-Transform-Load**) analytics in Azure Synapse Analytics for all operational data at a larger scale. Synapse Spark or Synapse SQL is used along with Synapse Link and Cosmos DB by enabling near real-time business intelligence, analytics, and machine learning analytical pipelines. The existing transactional workload on Cosmos DB is not impacted because of enabling analytical store and Synapse Link.

No separate connectors are required and we can now directly connect Azure Cosmos DB containers with Azure Synapse Analytics using Synapse Link. There is no additional data transformation required to analyze the operation data. The analytical store in Cosmos DB can be analyzed with the following:

- **An Apache Spark pool of Synapse**, where existing data transformations are written for the operational data
- **Serverless SQL pool** and integration support with BI tools such as **Power BI**

# Supported features of Azure Synapse Link

Azure Cosmos DB supports two types of containers:

- **HTAP container** – This container supports both transactional and analytical storage. It has Synapse Link integration enabled.
- **Online Transactional Processing (OLTP) container** – This container supports only transactional stores and it does not have Synapse Link enabled with it.

You can use an Apache Spark pool and serverless SQL pool. The following table shows the supported features of Synapse Link:

| | Apache Spark pool | Serverless SQL pool |
|---|---|---|
| Azure Synapse runtime support to access Cosmos DB | Yes | Yes |
| Azure Cosmos DB API support | SQL/Mongo DB APIs are supported | SQL/Mongo DB APIs are supported |
| Object support | Dataframes, views, and tables are supported | Only views are supported |
| Azure Cosmos DB container support for read operations | OLTP/HTAP | HTAP |
| Azure Synapse runtime support for write operations to Cosmos DB containers | Yes | No |

Figure 4.1 – Table showing the supported features of Synapse Link

Hybrid transactional and analytical processing containers support the following code-generated actions for serverless SQL pool:

- Use T-SQL syntax and infer schema automatically from a Cosmos DB container.
- Create a SQL view that directly accesses the Cosmos DB container for BI.
- Combine queries from Cosmos DB containers with queries from Azure Blob storage or ADLS using `CETAS (CREATE EXTERNAL TABLE AS SELECT)`.

Here are the important points with respect to Synapse Link:

- Synapse Link is now supported by the Azure Cosmos DB SQL Core API and MongoDB API.
- It is not supported by Gremlin, Cassandra, and the Table API.
- Likewise, there is no support for Azure Cosmos DB serverless.
- Once you have enabled the Synapse Link capability, it cannot be disabled.

## Azure Synapse runtime support

The following table details the actions supported by Azure Synapse runtime.

| Azure Synapse runtime | Current support |
|---|---|
| Azure Synapse Spark pools | Read, write (through a transactional store), tables, and temporary vews |
| Azure Synapse serverless SQL pool | Read, view |
| Azure Synapse SQL provisioned | Not available |

Figure 4.2 – Table showing Synapse runtime support

## Structured streaming support

Currently, Spark structured streaming support for Azure Cosmos DB is implemented using the change feed functionality of the transactional store. Streaming is not supported by analytical store.

## Network and data security support for Azure Synapse Link with Cosmos DB

Managed private endpoints (**Private Link**) can be established between both a transactional store and analytical store with the same Azure Cosmos DB account in an Azure Synapse Analytics workspace.

Data is encrypted at rest using customer-managed keys stored in **Azure Key Vault**. Data is encrypted at transit using HTTPS/SSL.

# Setting up Azure Cosmos DB analytical store

In this recipe, we will learn how to set up Azure Cosmos DB analytical store, which helps us to run near real-time analytical queries with operation data. CosmosDB is used as storage for real-time data and data that's near real-time, such as from IoT sensory devices.

## Getting ready

Before we begin the recipe, create the resource group **SynapseRG** in the Azure portal.

## How to do it...

We will create an Azure Cosmos DB account and learn how to set up the container in it. Let's get started:

1. Log in to Azure portal: `https://portal.azure.com/#home`.
2. Search for `cosmos` by using the top search bar on the **Microsoft Azure** page and navigate to **Azure Cosmos DB**.

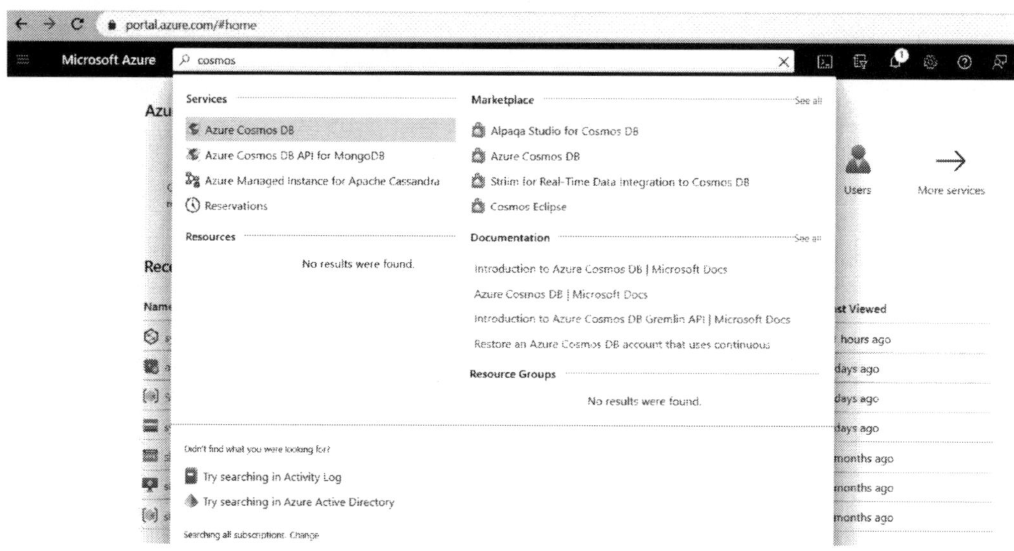


Figure 4.3 – Search for Azure Cosmos DB

3. Click on **Azure Cosmos DB**.

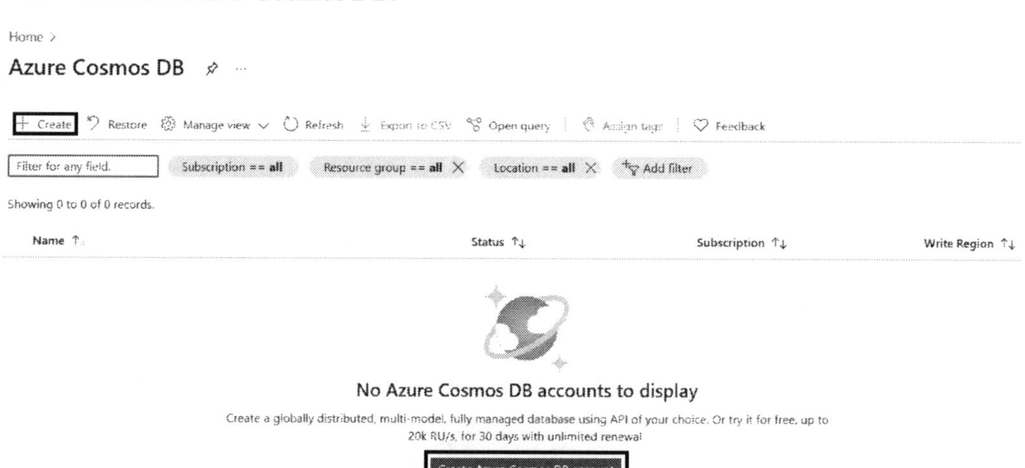


Figure 4.4 – Create an Azure Cosmos DB account

4. Select **Core (SQL)** by clicking **Create.**

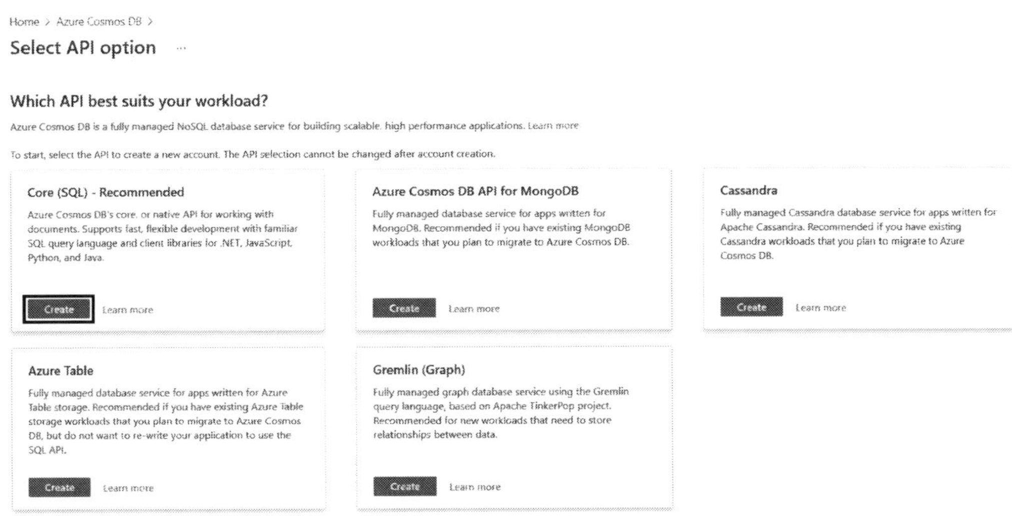


Figure 4.5 – Select Core (SQL)

5. On the **Basics** tab, select the existing resource group and fill in **Account Name**. Select **Location** so that it's the same as the Synapse workspace, which in our case is **(US) East US**. **Capacity mode** has two options, **Provisioned throughput** and **Serverless**. Choose **Provisioned throughput**.

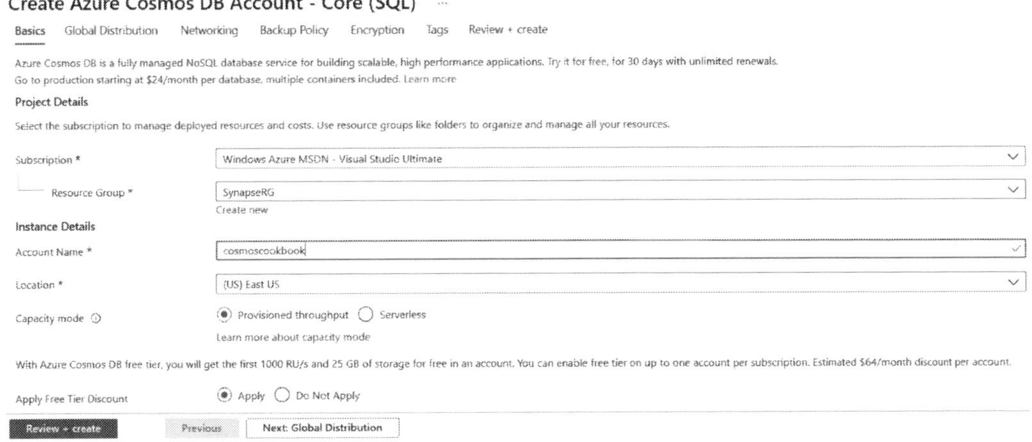


Figure 4.6 – Basics tab of Cosmos DB account

6. Select **Global distribution**. Cosmos DB supports geo-redundancy and multi-region writes in selected availability zones. We are disabling these settings for this Azure Cosmos DB account.

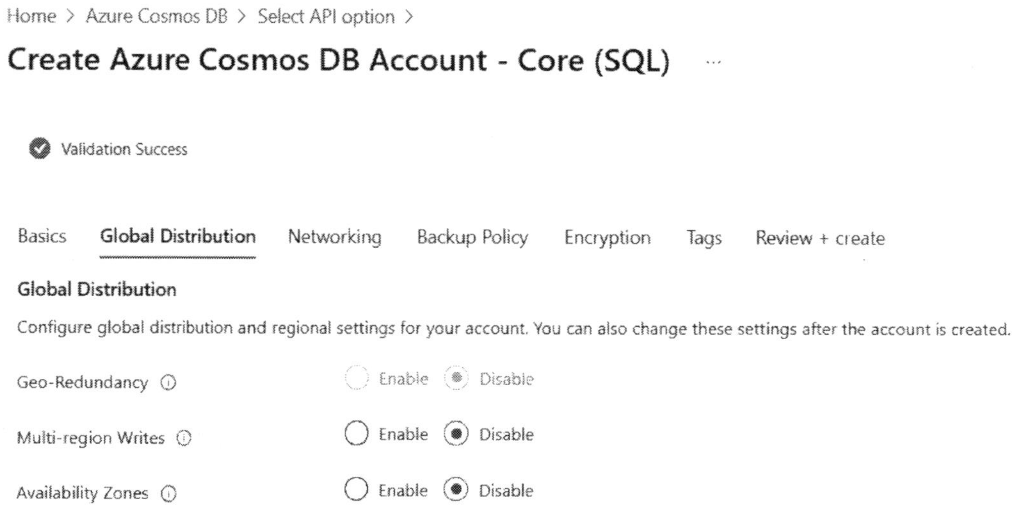

Figure 4.7 – Global Distribution of Cosmos DB account

7. Select **Networking** and select the connectivity choices listed in the following screenshot. We are allowing connectivity for **All networks**.

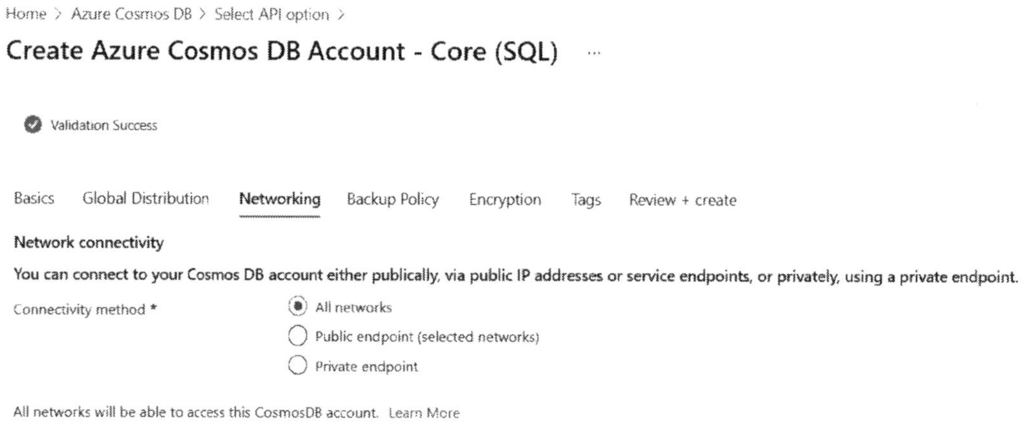

Figure 4.8 – Networking for Cosmos DB account

8. In the **Backup Policy** tab, specify **Backup policy** as **Periodic**, **Backup interval** in minutes, and **Backup retention** in hours. In case of disaster, we are enabling two copies to be retained and enabling **Backup storage redundancy** as **Geo-redundant backup storage**.

Create Azure Cosmos DB Account - Core (SQL) ...

Validation Success

Basics Global Distribution Networking **Backup Policy** Encryption Tags Review + create

Azure Cosmos DB provides two different backup policies. You will not be able to switch between backup policies after the account has been created. Learn more about the differences of the two backup policies and pricing details. Learn more

Backup policy ⓘ ◉ Periodic ◯ Continuous

Backup interval ⓘ 240 Minute(s) 60-1440

Backup retention ⓘ 8 Hours(s) 8-720

Copies of data retained 2

Backup storage redundancy * ⓘ ◉ Geo-redundant backup storage ◯ Zone-redundant backup storage ◯ Locally-redundant backup storage

Figure 4.9 – Backup Policy of Cosmos DB account

9. Create data encryption keys by selecting **Service-managed key**.

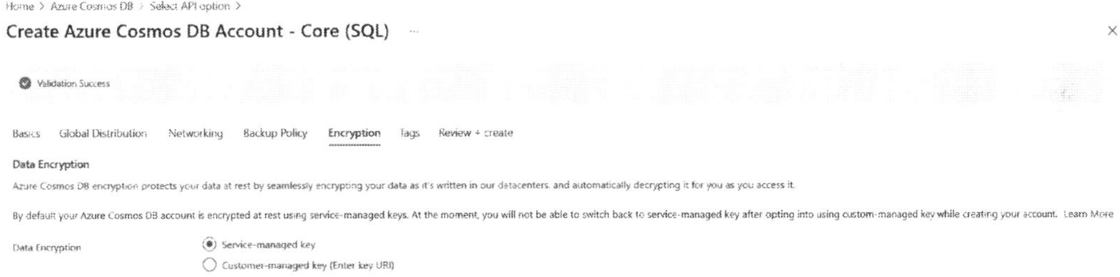


Figure 4.10 – Encryption of Cosmos DB account

10. Review and create the Azure Cosmos DB account.

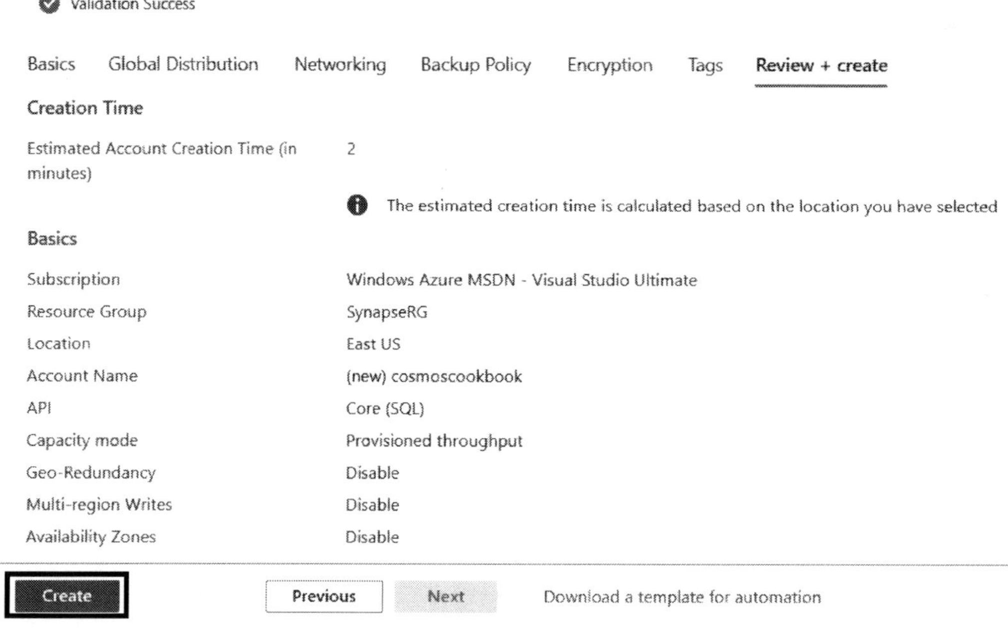


Figure 4.11 – Review + create of Cosmos DB account

11. Click **Add Container** and create a new Azure Cosmos DB container.

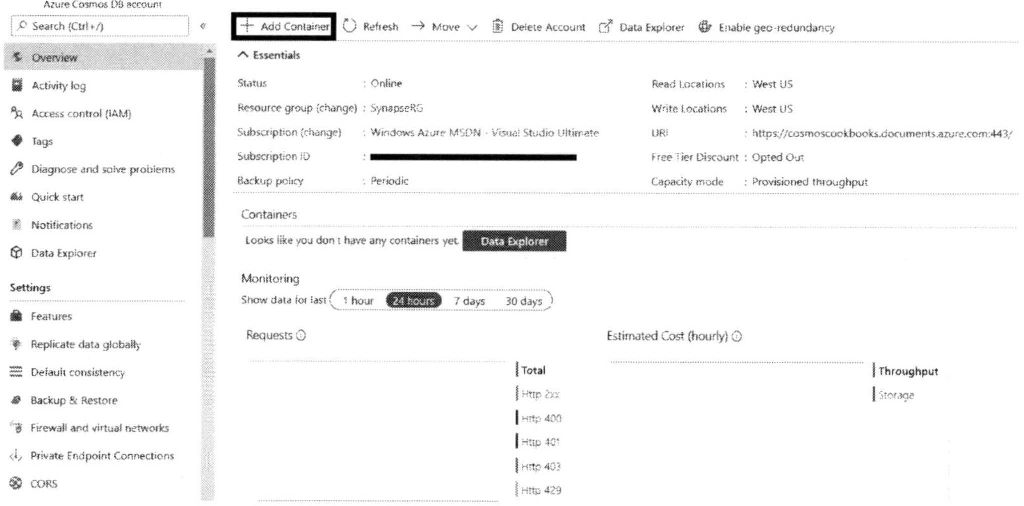


Figure 4.12 – Add Container for Azure Cosmos DB

12. Create a database ID, select a database throughput, and enter a container ID and a partition key. Click **OK**.

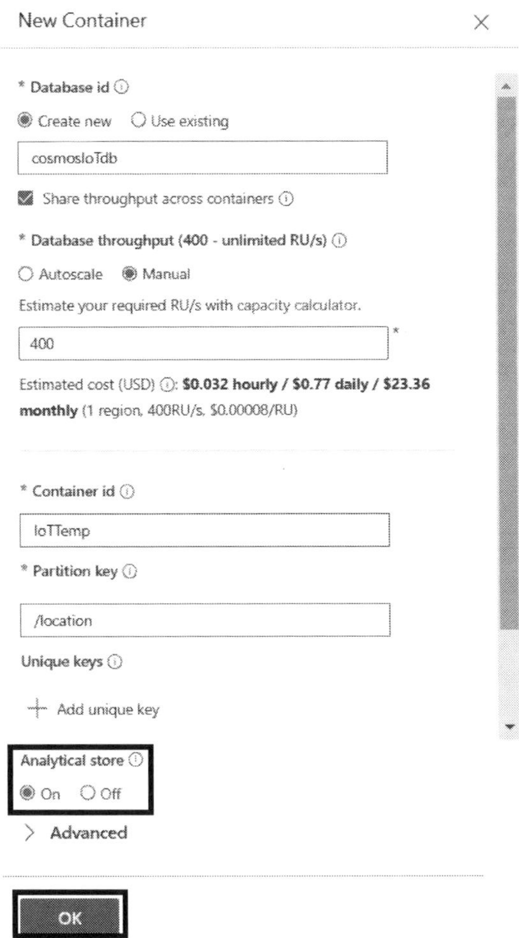


Figure 4.13 – Add a new container for the Cosmos DB account

We have successfully created an Azure Cosmos DB account and Cosmos DB container.

# Enabling Azure Synapse Link and connecting Azure Cosmos DB to Azure Synapse

In this recipe, we will learn how to enable Synapse Link and connect Azure Cosmos DB to Azure Synapse. For large-scale analytics that provide high-scale performance without impacting on operational load, we recommend enabling Synapse Link. This helps to achieve HTAP capability for the Cosmos DB container.

## Getting ready

Create a resource group called **SynapseRG** in the Azure portal.

## How to do it...

We need to enable the features of Azure Synapse Link in the Azure Cosmos DB account and a linked service is required to connect to the Azure Cosmos DB database. Let's explore step by step how to enable Synapse Link in the Cosmos DB account by adding linked servers in Synapse Studio:

1. Go to the previously created Azure Cosmos DB account from the *Setting up Azure Cosmos DB analytical store* recipe and select the **Features** settings. Select **Azure Synapse Link**.

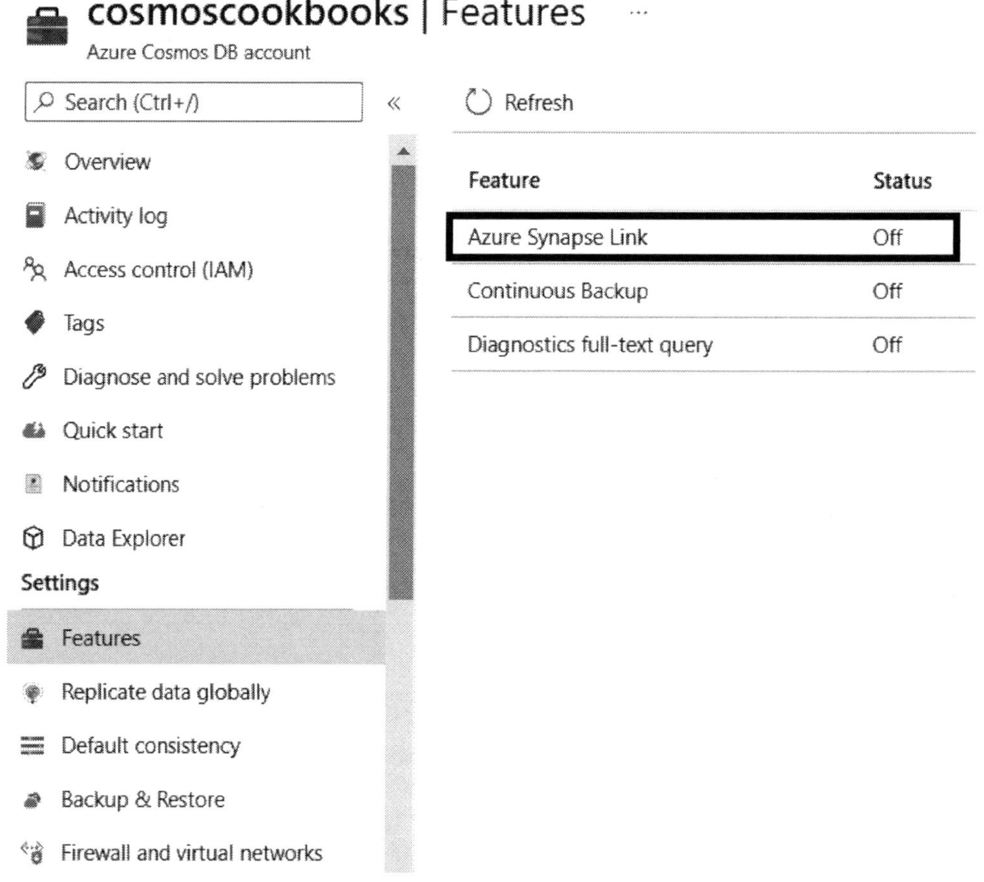


Figure 4.14 – Select Azure Synapse Link

2. **Enable** Azure Synapse Link.

Azure Synapse Link ×

Azure Synapse Link for Cosmos DB creates a tight integration between Azure Cosmos DB and Azure Synapse Analytics enabling customers to run near real-time analytics over their operational data with no-ETL and full performance isolation from their transactional workloads

By combining the distributed scale of Cosmos DB's transactional processing with build-in analytical store and the computing power of Azure Synapse Analytics, Azure Synapse Link enables Hybrid Transactional/Analytical Processing (HTAP) architectures for optimizing your business processes. This integration eliminates ETL processes, enabling business analysts, data engineers & data scientists to self-serve and run near real-time BI, analytics and ML pipelines over operational data.

Learn More

Figure 4.15 – Enable Azure Synapse Link

3. Go to the existing **Synapse Analytics workspace** and navigate to **Synapse Studio**.

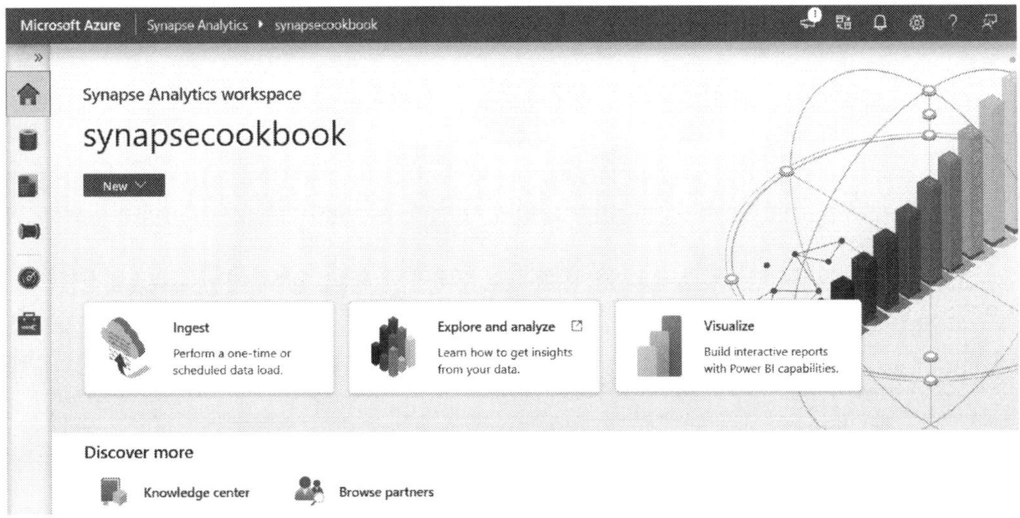


Figure 4.16 – Synapse workspace

4. Navigate to the **Data** tab and **Add new resource**.

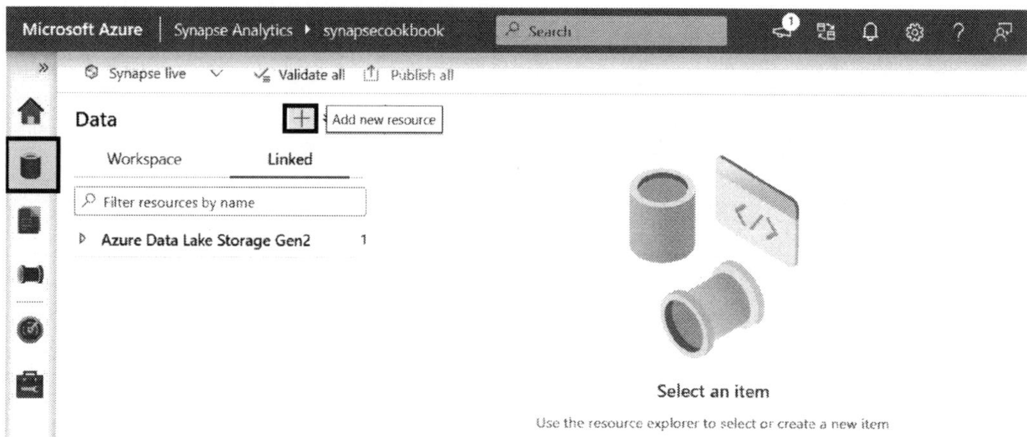


Figure 4.17 – Add new resource

5. Select **Azure Cosmos DB (SQL API)** and click **Create**.

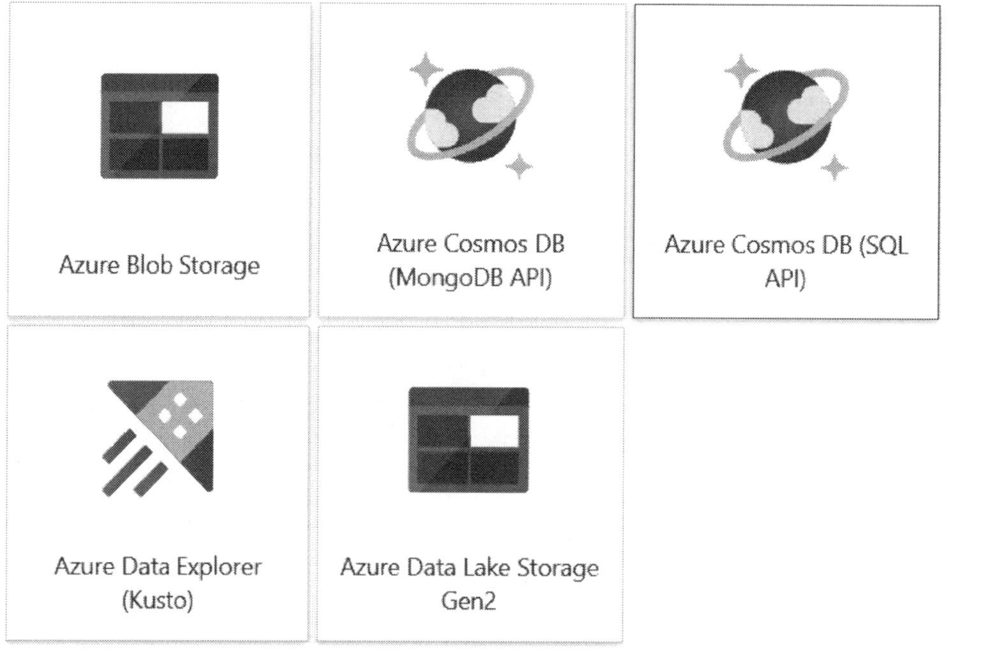


Figure 4.18 – Connect to Cosmos DB (SQL API)

6. On the **New linked service** tab, enter a name, and make a selection for **Authentication method**. Also make a selection for **Azure Cosmos DB account name** and fill in **Database Name**.

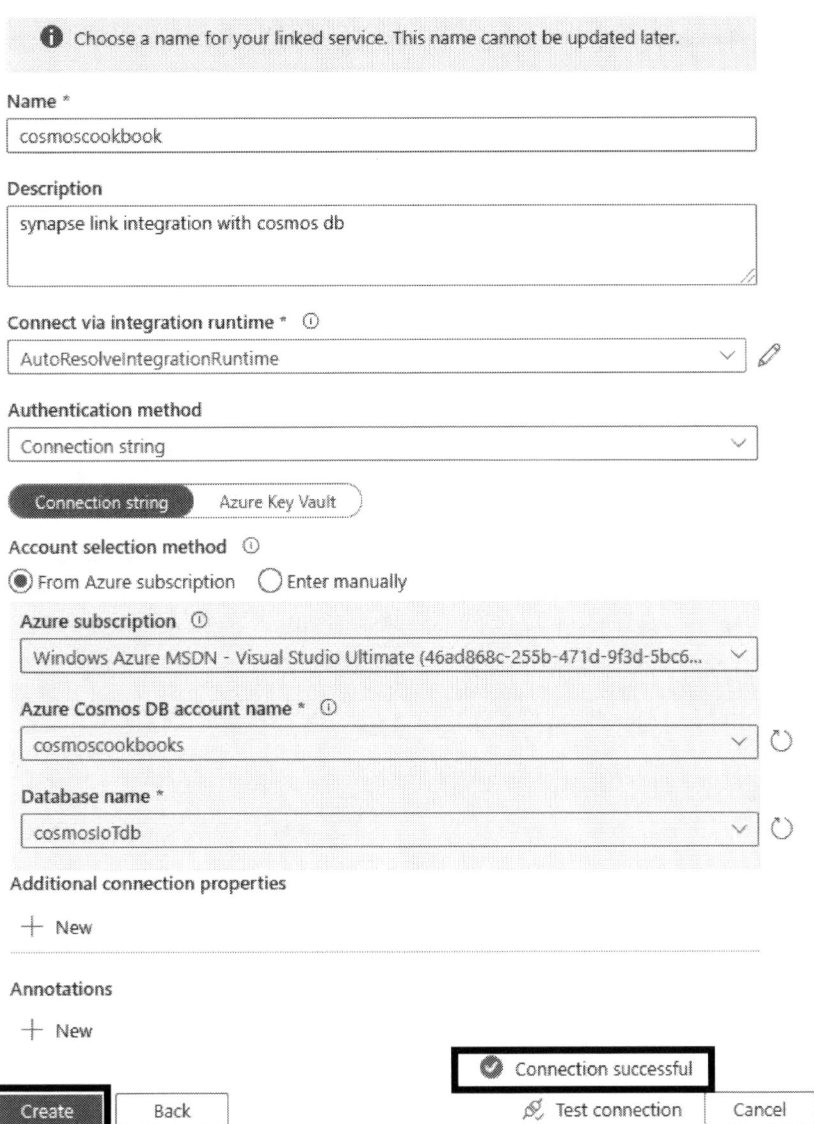


Figure 4.19 – Creating a new linked service

7. Create the linked service and publish it for us to view the linked services in the **Data** tab.

# IoT end-to-end solutions and getting real-time insights

Azure Cosmos DB analytical store allows us to perform near real-time analytics on operational data. It has both transactional and analytical stores. Before Synapse was introduced, it was really hard to get real-time analytics out of Cosmos DB. Before the release of Synapse, we needed to extract and load data in a separate analytics store to build real-time dashboards.

Now, with the introduction of Azure Synapse Link, we can integrate Cosmos DB with Synapse Analytics, serverless SQL pools, and Spark pools, thus leading the way for data analysts to analyze real-time data. Using Spark pools, Synapse, and serverless SQL, BI engineers can create real-time dashboards using Power BI. Data scientists can now use the Cosmos DB analytical store to preprocess data and create models using a Synapse Spark pool and derive critical business insights from data without disturbing the transactional store of Azure Cosmos DB.

The IoT has increased automation and performance efficiency across all industries. Capturing streaming data from IoT devices and analyzing and predicting the future state is a common scenario to improve performance efficiency in all fields.

*Figure 4.20* shows the architecture, which uses Azure Cosmos DB effectively as transactional and analytical store at near real time. It involves IoT devices installed on-premises or at the edge, streaming data at regular intervals into Azure IoT hub.

Azure IoT hub uses Azure Stream Analytics to stream data processing and ingests data into Azure Cosmos transactional store. The data is then interactively analyzed in Azure Synapse serverless SQL, which queries data from Cosmos DB analytical store using Synapse Link integration. Real time dashboards are generated in Power BI.

Data is transformed, standardized, feature engineered, and then available for predictive analytics and advanced analytics. This predicted value is used as actions for IoT devices.

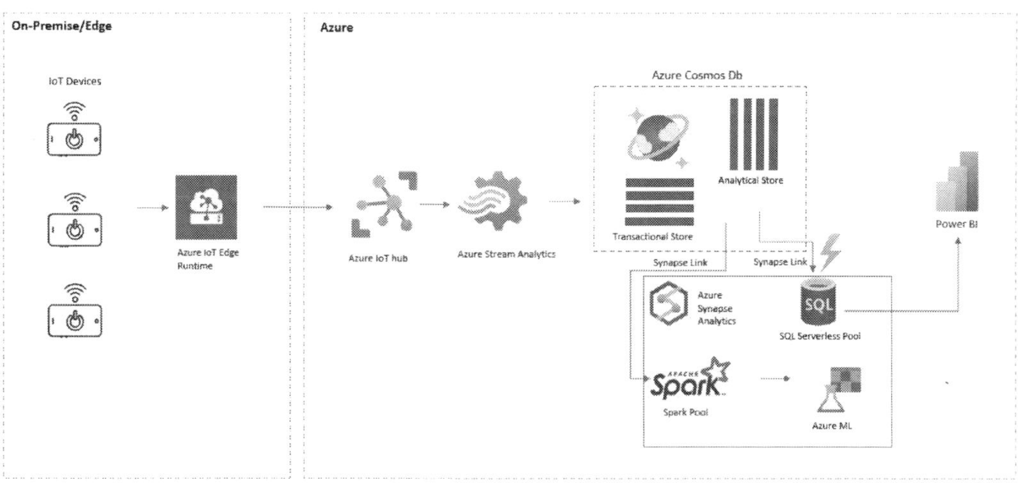


Figure 4.20 – Reference architecture for IoT real-time analytics

As we go through the recipe, we will simulate the ingestion of data from IoT devices with the help of Synapse notebooks – Spark Structured Streaming that, in the real world, can be thought of as data from IoT devices ingested through Azure IoT Hub and analyzed by Stream Analytics. Real-time insights will be created with Azure Cosmos DB by integrating with Synapse Link.

## Getting ready

We will be using an IoT temperature dataset for our scenario. This dataset will consist of temperature data for the month of October in a factory: this includes attributes such as ID, room ID, date and time, temperature, and location – whether inside or outside the set of rooms:

- To get the dataset, you can go to the following URL: `https://github.com/PacktPublishing/Analytics-in-Azure-Synapse-Simplified/Iot-Temp`.

  We will use a single item of this dataset in JSON format to simulate streaming ingestion to Azure Cosmos DB containers.

- The code for this recipe can be downloaded from the GitHub repository: `https://github.com/PacktPublishing/Analytics-in-Azure-Synapse-Simplified`.

## How to do it...

Let's get started:

1. Let's simulate stream ingestion from IoT devices to a Cosmos DB transactional store. We will use `spark.readStream` and add all columns to the data frame, which simulates the IoT temperature data. Then `writeStream` into Cosmos DB with the Synapse linked service:

```
df = (spark.readStream.format("rate").
option("rowsPerSecond", 10).load())
from pyspark.sql.functions import lit
dfIoTSignals=(df.withColumn('id', lit('1'))
              .withColumn('room_id', lit('Room Admin'))
              .withColumn('noted_
date', df["timestamp"].cast(StringType()))
              .withColumn('temp', lit('1'))
              .withColumn('location', lit('Test'))
              )
streamQuery = dfIoTSignals\
                  .writeStream\
                  .format("cosmos.oltp")\
                  .outputMode("append")\
                  .option("spark.cosmos.connection.
mode", "gateway") \
                  .option("spark.synapse.
linkedService", "cosmoscookbook")\
                  .option("spark.cosmos.
container", "cosmosIoTdb")\
                  .option("checkpointLocation", "/
writeCheckpointDir")\
                  .start()
streamQuery.awaitTermination()
```

Now, let's follow the step-by-step procedure to set up Azure Cosmos DB, analyze the data using SQL, and create real-time dashboards with Power BI.

2. Create/edit the container in Azure Cosmos DB. Fill in **Database id**, make a selection for **Database throughput**, and fill in **Container id** and **Partition key**. Click **OK**.

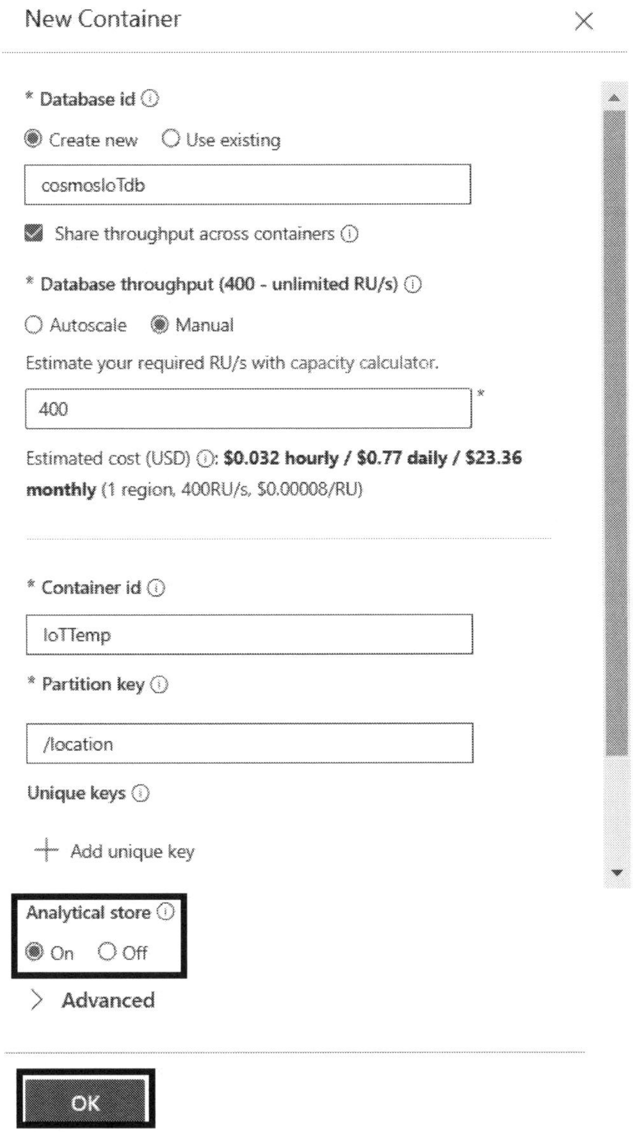

Figure 4.21 – Add a new container for Azure Cosmos DB

3. Upload a **JSON** file to Azure Cosmos DB.

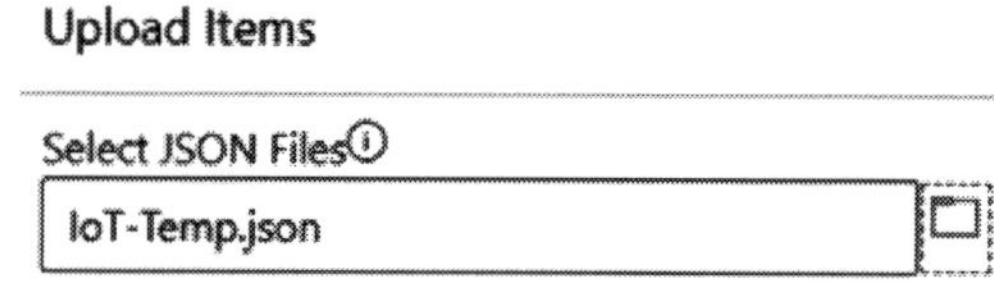


Figure 4.22 – Upload JSON to Cosmos DB

4. Create a **Serverless** SQL database in Synapse Studio.

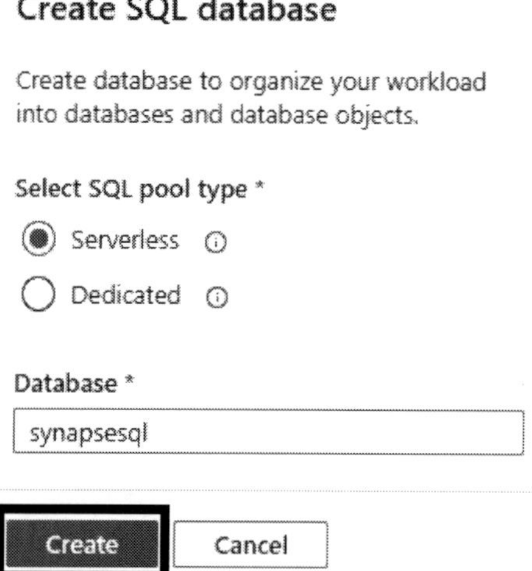


Figure 4.23 – Create a Serverless SQL database

5. Next, we will create a database in the SQL script shown as follows in *Figure 4.24* and then connect it to **Built-in**.

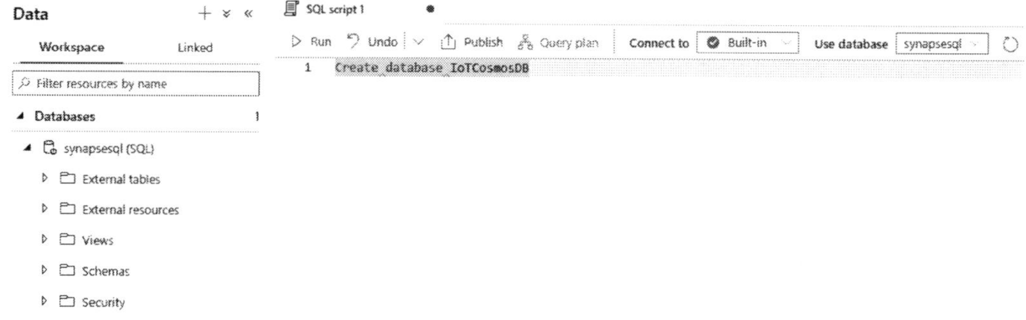


Figure 4.24 – Create a new database

6. In the next step, we will use `Create view` which access the Cosmos DB container with the account name, database name, region in lowercase, and primary read-only key:

```
CREATE VIEW IOTTEMP
AS
SELECT *
FROM OPENROWSET (
    'CosmosDB', N'account=cosmoscookbooks;database=-
cosmosIoTdb;region=westus;key=k2G5cNMSgjanJfJNv0BC-
Nyr9ydE0avGecR17WiCLJmSacs4gPiWtHklDJXKVAi7SEM9ZgjylHEPW-
EvoYFtL8Ew==',IoTTemp)
AS q1
```

7. Query the view with the `select` statement to find out how many temperatures have been recorded inside and outside the rooms:

```
select loca-
tion, count(*) as count from IOTTEMP group by location
```

The results can be viewed as follows.

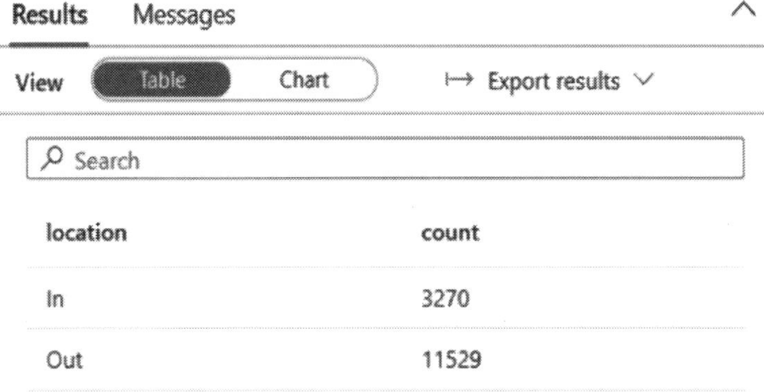


Figure 4.25 – Results window

8. Now, analyze the real-time data interactively and create charts to understand the data:

```
select DAY(CONVERT(DATETIME,noted_date,103)) AS 'Days in
October', temp from IOTTEMP order by 'Days in October'
```

9. Click **Chart** in the results and a line chart will be generated, as shown in the following screenshot of the Synapse Studio SQL script **Results** window.

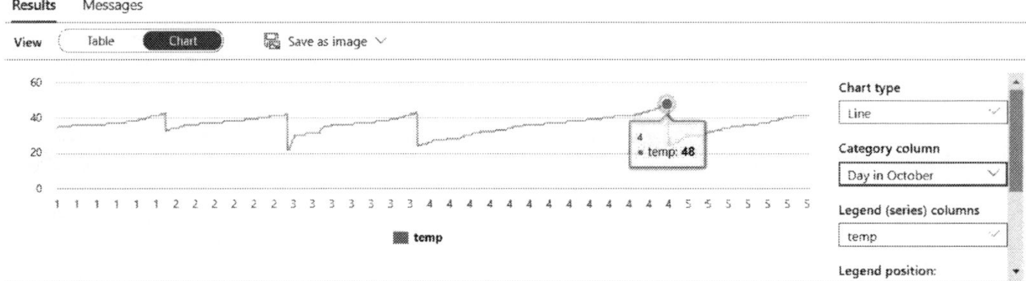


Figure 4.26 – Chart Results window

10. Let's connect the view as dataset in Power BI and create a scatter plot now. We need to first connect to the view by selecting **SQL Server** as the input data source.

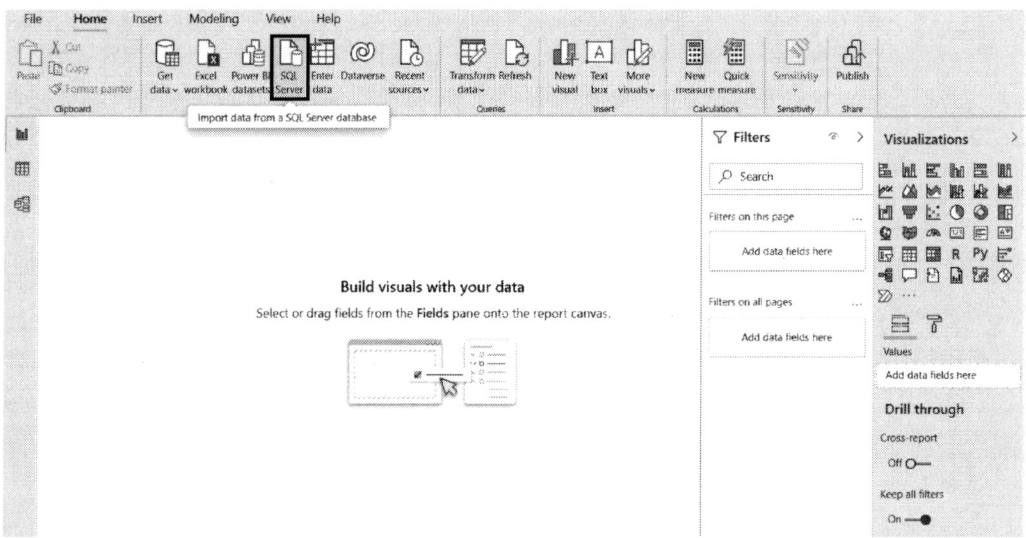


Figure 4.27 – Power BI – SQL Server data source connection

11. Go to **synapsecookbook**, click **Properties**, and copy **Serverless SQL endpoint**.

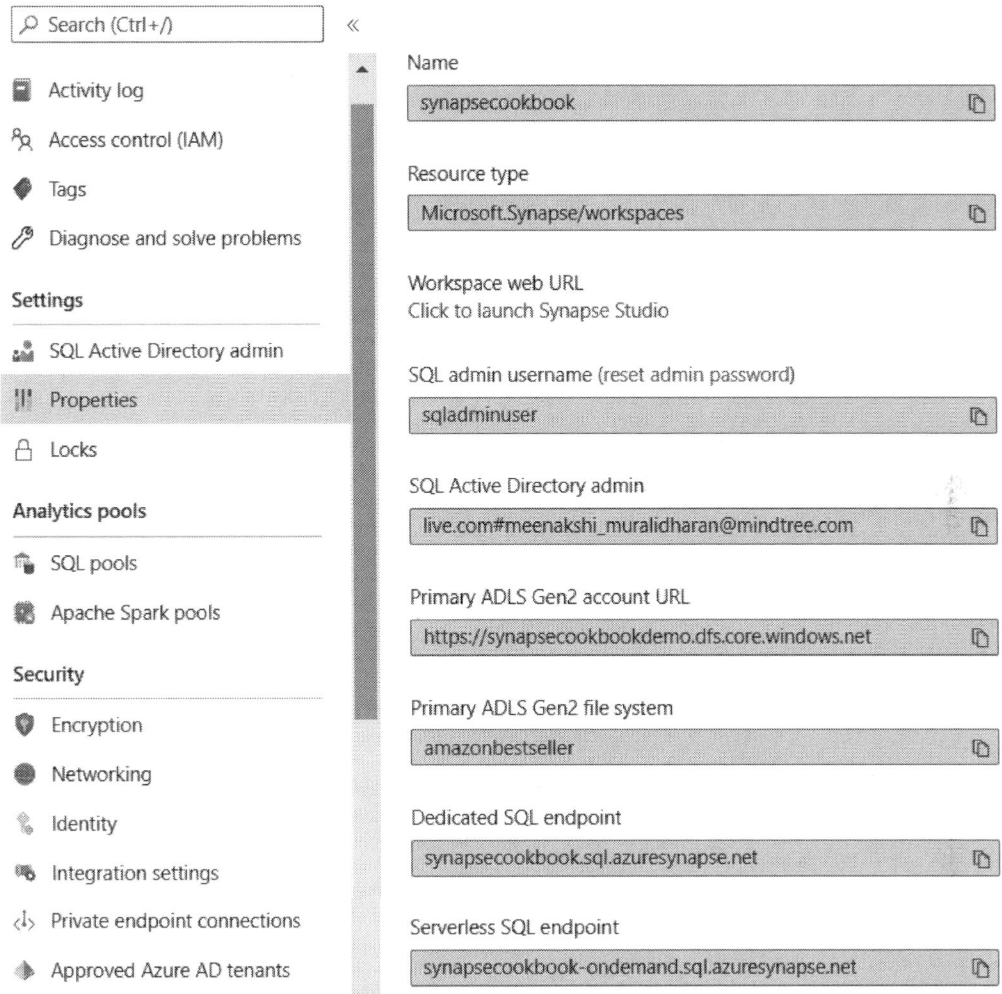


Figure 4.28 – Synapse SQL pool credentials

12. Enter the SQL Server database endpoint that was previously copied as the Power BI SQL Server data source.

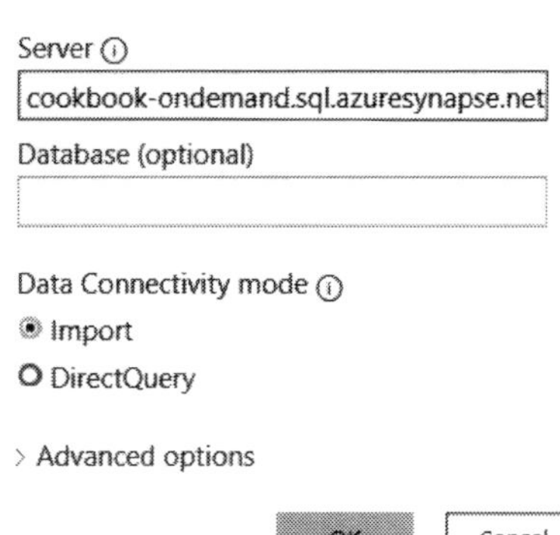


Figure 4.29 – Synapse configuration in Power BI

13. Select the view from the Synapse views as shown in the following screenshot. Select **Load**.

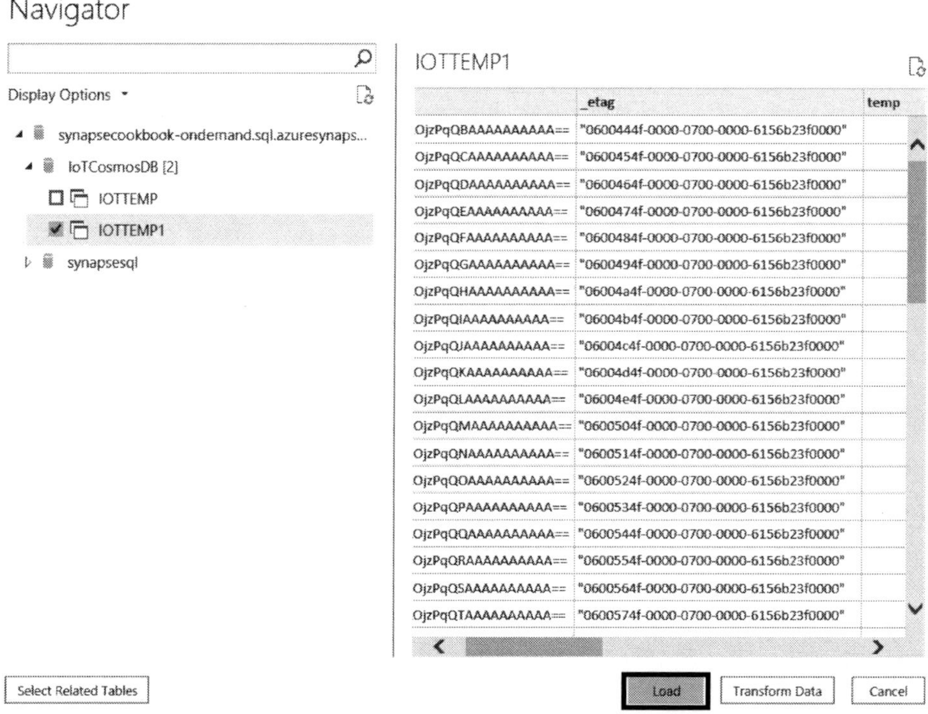


Figure 4.30 – Power BI – dataset view configuration

14. The dataset is now available in the **report** window and we can create a scatter plot visualization with **X Axis** as **Day in October** and **Y Axis** as **temp**.

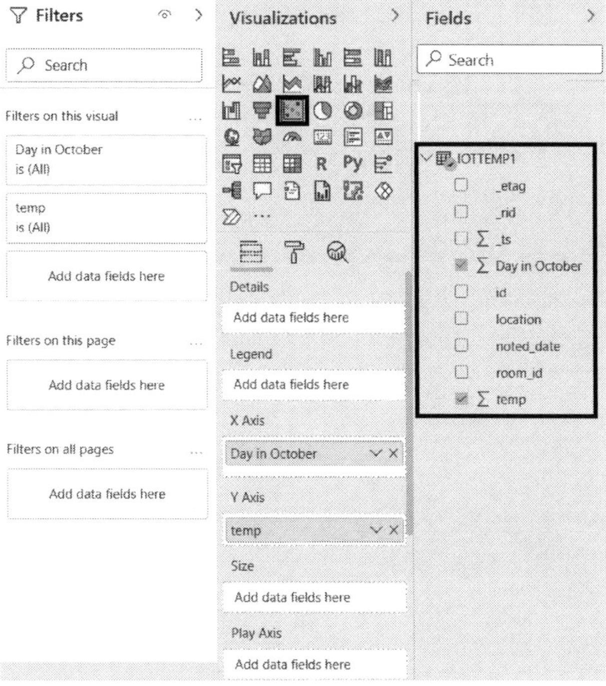


Figure 4.31 – Visualizations dataset

15. The scatter plot graph is now ready. This shows temperature data for October, broken down by day.

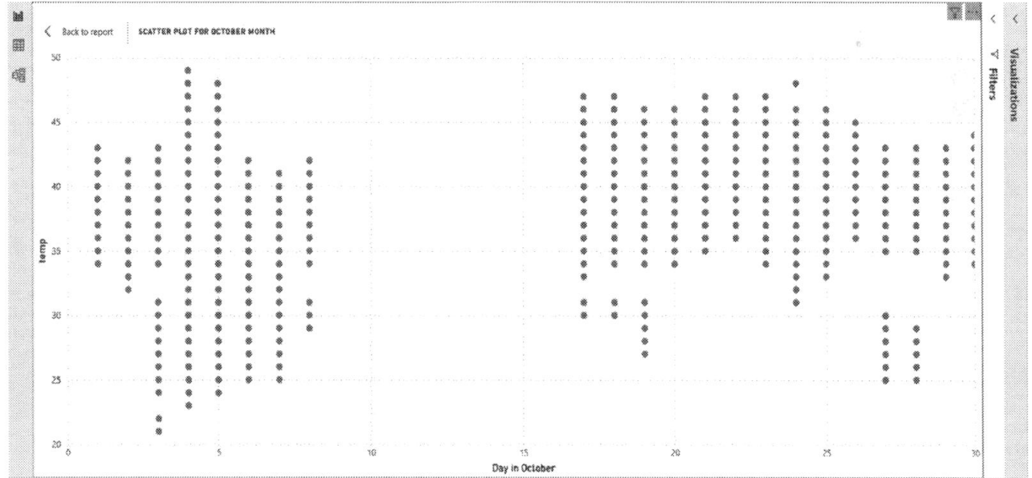


Figure 4.32 – Power BI – scatter plot

# Use cases using Synapse Link

Enterprises are leveraging real-time streaming analytics for quicker responses and near real-time analytics in several industry-standard use cases. All the following industry use cases make use of cloud-managed native HTAP integration between Azure Cosmos DB and Azure Synapse Analytics with Synapse Link:

- Detecting anomalies and fraud in real time
- Real-time personalization
- Providing healthcare, emergency, and humanitarian services
- Data-driven decision making
- Assortment optimization
- Proximity marketing
- Contextual recommendations
- Ad optimization
- Money laundering/payment fraud detection
- Risk management in rapidly changing capital markets
- Stock market surveillance
- Real-time location analytics
- Fleet management
- Analytics in sports
- Smart energy analytics
- Social media analytics
- System and network monitoring

In this section, we will learn about different pipelines for the use cases explained in the *IoT end-to-end solutions and getting real-time insights* recipe.

Smart meters and industry plants regularly sync data to Azure Event Hubs, which helps in smart energy analytics and predictive maintenance.

Immense data is generated from social media daily and it is ingested in real time for social media analytics.

Data-driven websites use end users' clicks for stream analytics to derive real-time personalization and ad optimization along with contextual recommendations.

All real-time data sources stream data in real time, which is stored in Cosmos DB Analytical store, and real-time dashboards are generated in Power BI using Synapse Link.

Based on the IoT end-to-end solution architecture in *Figure 4.20*, we have used Synapse Link along with Cosmos DB for the design of the following pipelines:

- **Data engineering pipeline** – The stream is processed with window functions and standardized and transformed to derive meaningful insights.
- **Predictive analytics** and **advanced analytics machine learning pipeline** – Synapse Link enables us to analyze quick-changing operational data in Azure Cosmos DB. Synapse Link is leveraged by data engineers and data scientists to build efficient advanced analytics machine learning and predictive pipelines.
- **Azure Cosmos DB** analytical store leverages integration with Apache Spark pools in Azure Synapse Analytics where data is queried interactively.
- Build **machine learning** (**ML**) models and deep learning models with Spark ML and Azure ML integration in Azure Synapse Analytics for batch and real-time inferencing.
- The model inference is stored in Azure Cosmos DB, which helps with near real-time operational scoring.
- Business intelligence – real-time dashboards with Power BI.

# 5
# Data Transformation and Processing with Synapse Notebooks

In this chapter, we will cover how to do data processing and transformation with Synapse notebooks. Details on using pandas DataFrames within Synapse notebooks will be covered, which will help us to explore data that is stored as Parquet files in **Azure Data Lake Storage** (**ADLS**) Gen2 as a pandas DataFrame and then write it back to ADLS Gen2 as a Parquet file.

We will be covering the following recipes:

- Landing data in ADLS Gen2
- Exploring data with ADLS Gen2 to pandas DataFrame in Synapse notebook
- Processing data from a PySpark notebook within Synapse
- Performing read-write operations to a Parquet file using Spark in Synapse
- Analytics with Spark

# Landing data in ADLS Gen2

In this recipe, we will learn how to create an ADLS Gen2 storage account and upload data as a Parquet file, where ADLS Gen2 can be considered as the landing zone before data is processed and transformed.

## Getting ready

We will be using a public dataset for our scenario. This dataset will consist of New York yellow taxi trip data; this includes attributes such as trip distances, itemized fares, rate types, payment types, pick-up and drop-off dates and times, driver-reported passenger counts, and pick-up and drop-off locations. We will be using this dataset throughout this recipe to demonstrate various use cases:

- To get the dataset, you can go to the following URL: `https://www.kaggle.com/microize/newyork-yellow-taxi-trip-data-2020-2019`.
- The code for this recipe can be downloaded from the GitHub repository: `https://github.com/PacktPublishing/Analytics-in-Azure-Synapse-Simplified`.

Let's get started.

## How to do it...

ADLS Gen2 is a data lake solution providing capabilities to store filesystems in a hierarchical namespace and low-cost object-based storage with guaranteed high availability and disaster recovery features. The **Azure Blob Filesystem** (**ABFS**) driver provides the necessary interface for ADLS Gen2 storage. Our input dataset will be stored as a Parquet file in ADLS Gen2 inside a container and subsequently used for data standardization, processing, and transformation with Synapse notebooks.

Let's create an ADLS Gen2 storage account to start:

1. Log in to the Azure portal: `https://portal.azure.com/#home`.
2. Navigate to **Storage accounts** by using the top search bar, where you can search for resources, services, and docs.

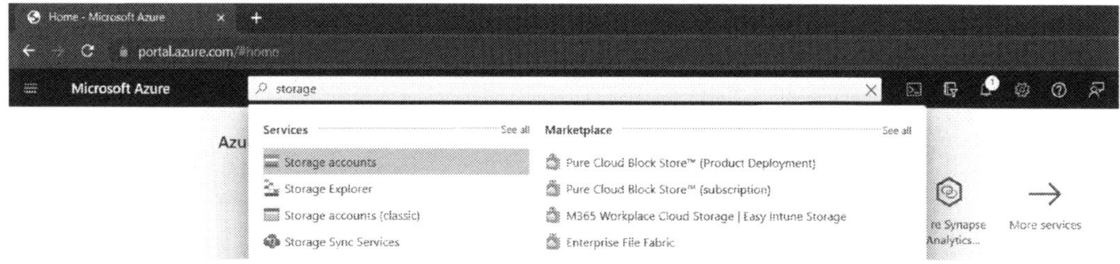


Figure 5.1 – Searching for Storage accounts

3. Click on **Create storage account**.

Figure 5.2 – Create storage account

4. On the **Basics** tab, choose the subscription and for the resource group details select **SynapseRG**, as shown in the following screenshot:

Home > Storage accounts >

Create a storage account ...

Basics Advanced Networking Data protection Tags Review + create

Azure Storage is a Microsoft-managed service providing cloud storage that is highly available, secure, durable, scalable, and redundant. Azure Storage includes Azure Blobs (objects), Azure Data Lake Storage Gen2, Azure Files, Azure Queues, and Azure Tables. The cost of your storage account depends on the usage and the options you choose below. Learn more about Azure storage accounts

Project details

Select the subscription in which to create the new storage account. Choose a new or existing resource group to organize and manage your storage account together with other resources.

Subscription * Windows Azure MSDN - Visual Studio Ultimate

Resource group * SynapseRG

Create new

Figure 5.3 – Create a storage account – Basics tab

5. Enter the storage account name as `synapsecookbookdemo`. Choose the region, but leave **Performance** as **Standard**.

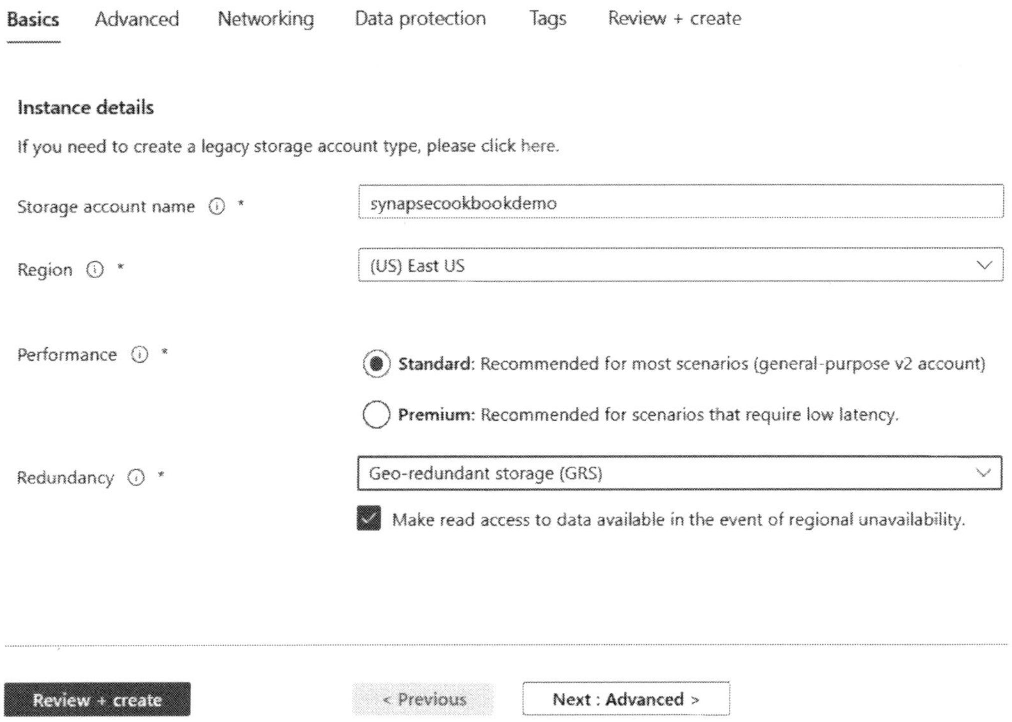

Basics Advanced Networking Data protection Tags Review + create

**Instance details**

If you need to create a legacy storage account type, please click here.

Storage account name * synapsecookbookdemo

Region * (US) East US

Performance *

**Standard:** Recommended for most scenarios (general-purpose v2 account)

**Premium:** Recommended for scenarios that require low latency.

Redundancy * Geo-redundant storage (GRS)

Make read access to data available in the event of regional unavailability.

Review + create < Previous Next : Advanced >

Figure 5.4 – Create a storage account – Basics tab

6. Go to the **Advanced** tab and configure the security settings that will impact your storage account.

Home > Storage accounts >

Create a storage account ...

Basics Advanced Networking Data protection Tags Review + create

Certain options have been disabled by default due to the combination of storage account performance, redundancy, and region.

Security

Configure security settings that impact your storage account.

Require secure transfer for REST API operations

Enable infrastructure encryption

Enable blob public access

Enable storage account key access

Default to Azure Active Directory authorization in the Azure portal

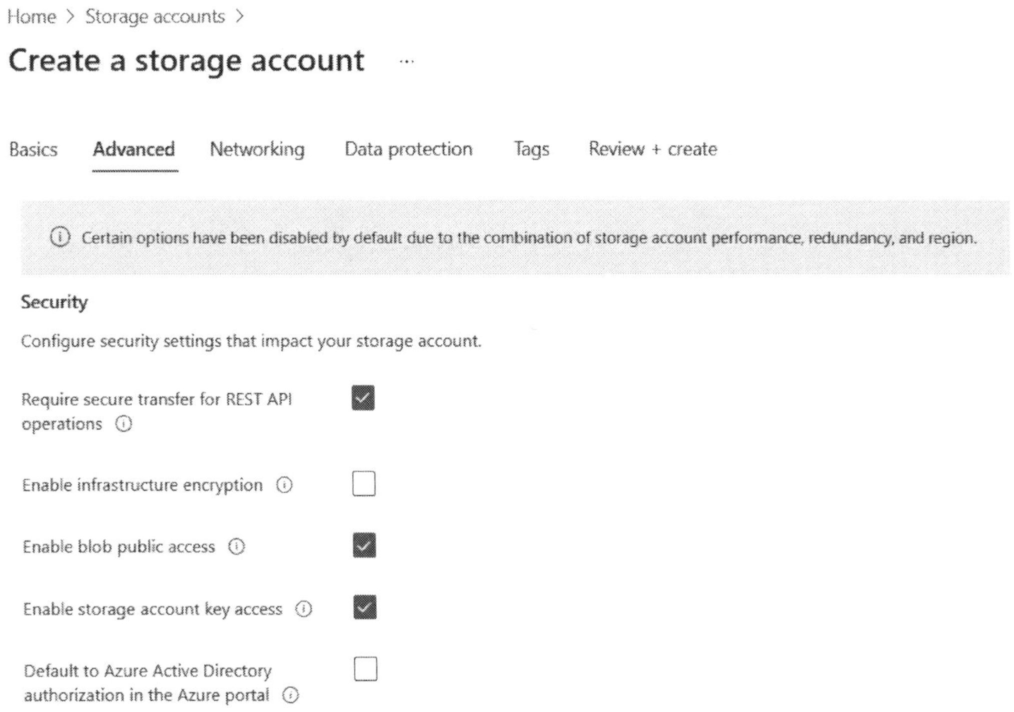

Figure 5.5 – Create a storage account – Advanced tab

7. Check **Enable hierarchical namespace**, which will accelerate the big data analytics workload and help us to enable file-level access control lists.

Basics **Advanced** Networking Data protection Tags Review + create

**Data Lake Storage Gen2**

The Data Lake Storage Gen2 hierarchical namespace accelerates big data analytics workloads and enables file-level access control lists (ACLs). Learn more

Enable hierarchical namespace ☑

**Blob storage**

Enable network file share v3 ☐

Allow cross-tenant replication ☐

Cross-tenant replication and hierarchical namespace cannot be enabled simultaneously.

Access tier

(●) **Hot:** Frequently accessed data and day-to-day usage scenarios

( ) **Cool:** Infrequently accessed data and backup scenarios

Review + create < Previous Next : Networking >

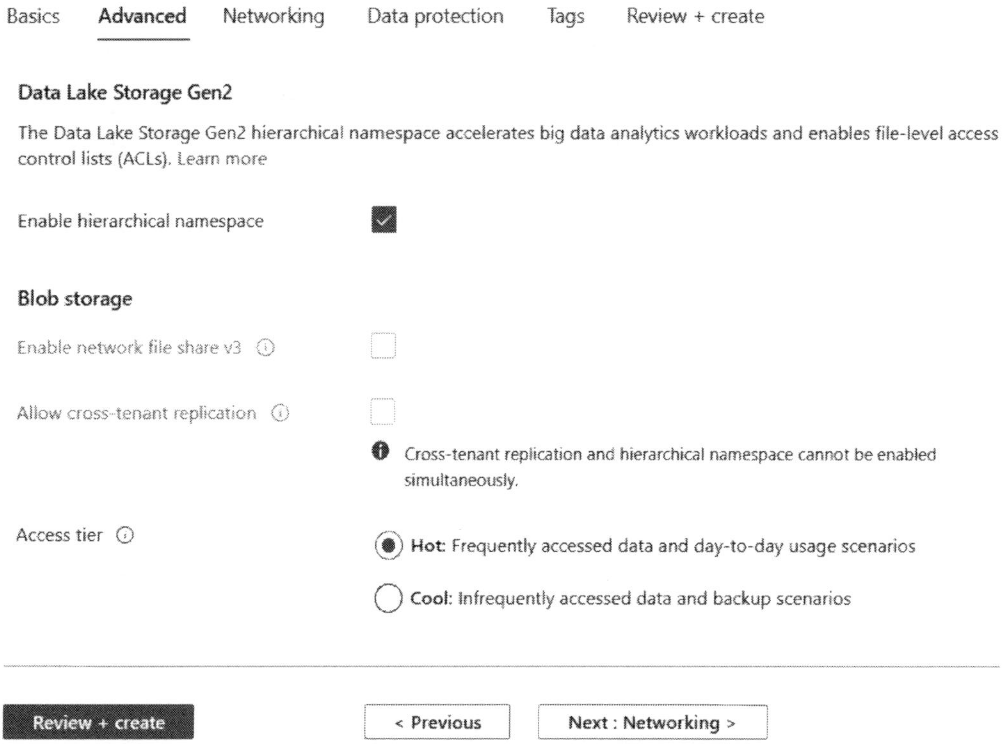

Figure 5.6 – Create a storage account – Advanced tab

8. Create the tags and review the page, then create the storage account.
9. Go to the **Access Control (IAM)** page, click **Add role assignment (Preview)**, and on the **Add role assignment** page, assign a role to the users.

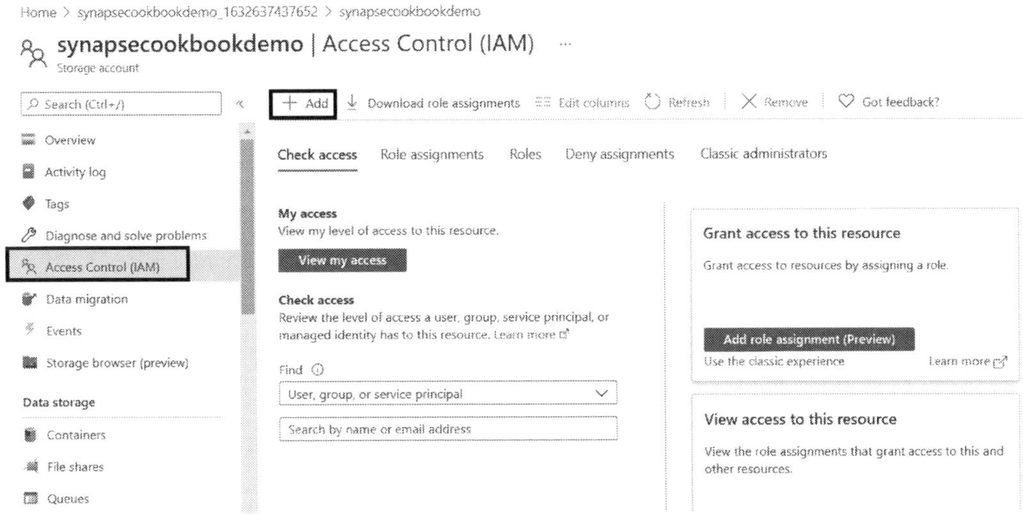


Figure 5.7 – Create a storage account – Access Control (IAM)

I. In the **Role** field, select **Reader** or **Contributor**.

II. To add or remove role assignments, we need to have write and delete permissions, such as an **Owner** role.

III. In the **Assign access to** field, select **User**, **group,** or **service principal**.

IV. In the **Select** field, select the user that requires access to the storage account.

V. Click **Save**.

If you want to add multiple users to access the storage account, you must perform the same steps for each user.



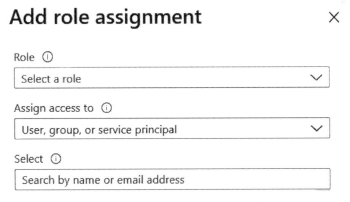

Figure 5.8 – Create a storage account – IAM role assignment

We have created a storage account in ADLS Gen2, enabled a hierarchical namespace for storage, and enabled role assignment, so we can now proceed to the next step.

Let's create a container in ADLS Gen2 now.

10. Add a container to the storage account that we created in *step 8*.

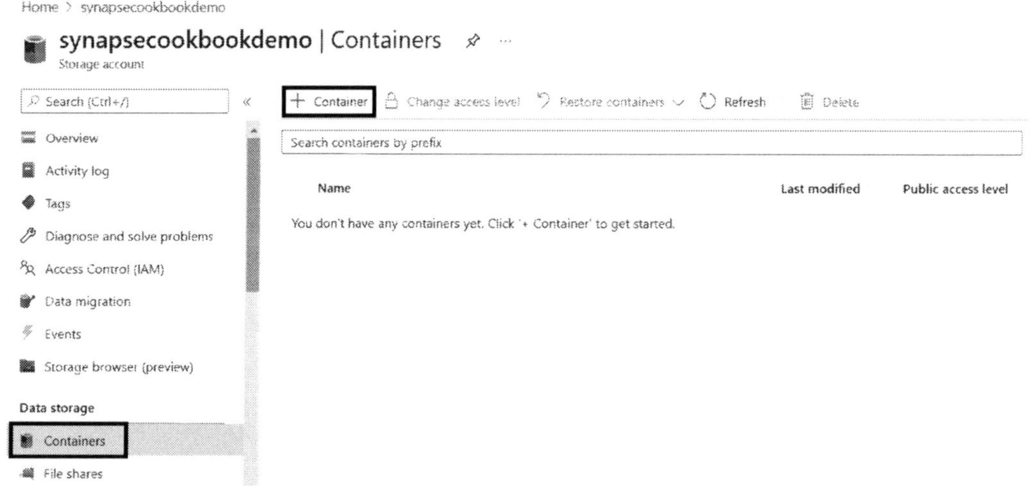


Figure 5.9 – Create a storage account – list of containers

11. Provide a name for the container and create it.

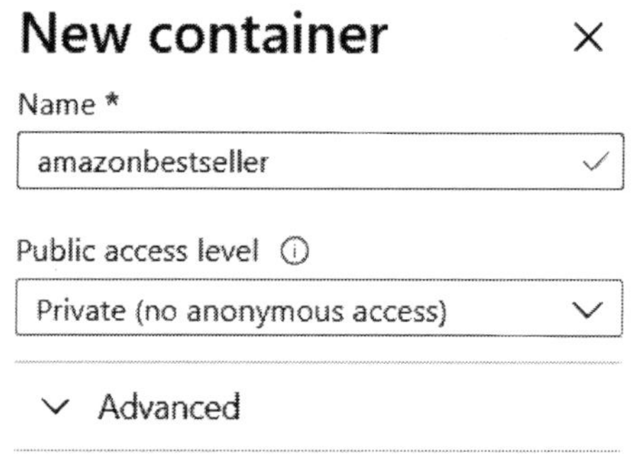


Figure 5.10 – Create a storage account – New container

12. Now is the time to upload our Parquet file.

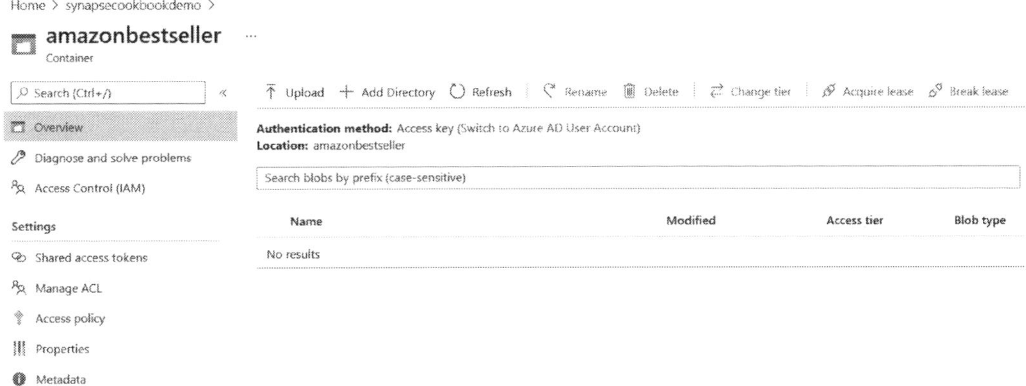


Figure 5.11 – Create a storage account – containers page

13. Upload the Parquet file to the container.

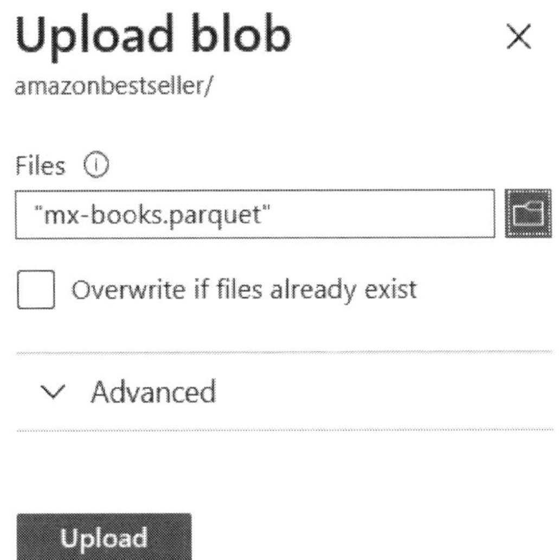


Figure 5.12 – Create a storage account – Upload blob

The data is now in our ADLS Gen2 data lake, inside a container as a Parquet file.

# Exploring data with ADLS Gen2 to pandas DataFrame in Synapse notebook

In this recipe, we will learn how to create a Synapse Analytics workspace and create Synapse notebooks so that we can load data from an ADLS Gen2 Parquet file to a pandas DataFrame. Synapse notebooks are required for us to perform a detailed analysis of data in interactive session mode.

## Getting ready

We will be using a public dataset for our scenario. This dataset will consist of New York yellow taxi trip data; this includes attributes such as trip distances, itemized fares, rate types, payment types, pick-up and drop-off dates and times, driver-reported passenger counts, and pick-up and drop-off locations. We will be using this dataset throughout this recipe to demonstrate various use cases:

- To get the dataset, you can go to the following URL: `https://www.kaggle.com/microize/newyork-yellow-taxi-trip-data-2020-2019`.
- The code for this recipe can be downloaded from the GitHub repository: `https://github.com/PacktPublishing/Analytics-in-Azure-Synapse-Simplified`.

Let's get started.

## How to do it...

Exploring an ADLS Gen2 Parquet file in a pandas DataFrame requires us to create a Synapse Analytics workspace, a Synapse Spark pool, and a Synapse notebook. The following recipe is a step-by-step guide to using the core features of Synapse Analytics.

### Creating a Synapse Analytics workspace

**Synapse Analytics workspace** creation requires us to create a resource group or have access to an existing resource group with owner permissions. Let's use an existing resource group, where you will find owner permissions for the user:

1. Log in to the Azure portal: `https://portal.azure.com/#home`.
2. Search for `Azure Synapse Analytics` by using the top search bar, where you can search for resources, services, and docs.

3. Select **Azure Synapse Analytics**.

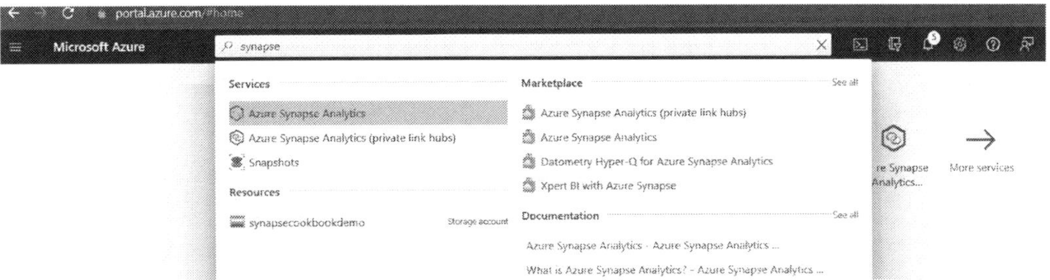


Figure 5.13 – Searching for Azure Synapse Analytics

4. Create an Azure Synapse Analytics workspace using either the **Create** button or the **Create Synapse workspace** button.

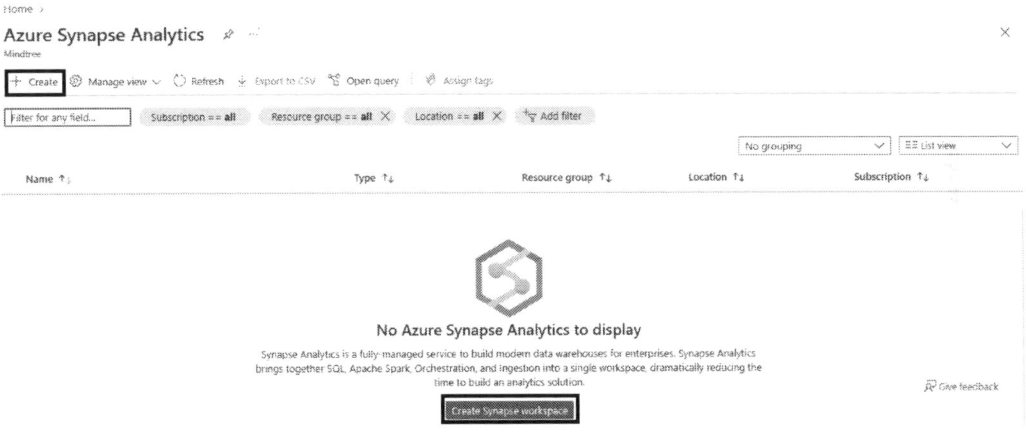


Figure 5.14 – Create Synapse workspace

5. On the **Basics** tab, enter the resource group and the workspace name as `synapsecookbook`.
6. Associate it with the ADLS Gen2 account name and the container that we created in the previous recipe.

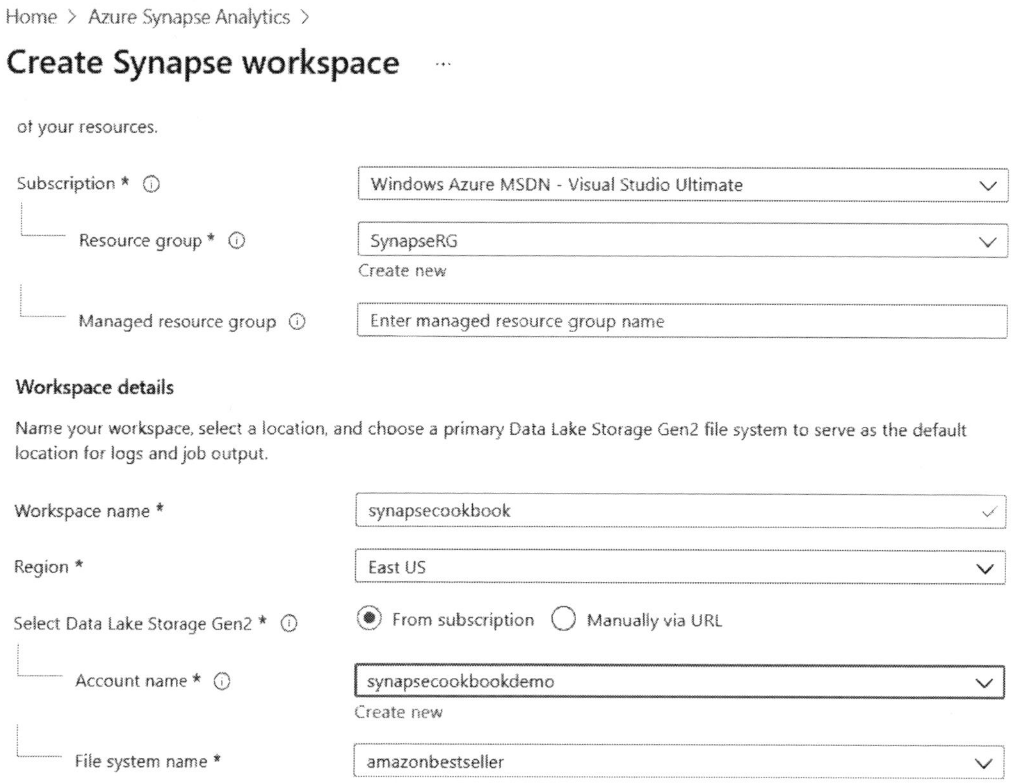

Home > Azure Synapse Analytics >

Create Synapse workspace ...

of your resources.

Subscription * ⓘ Windows Azure MSDN - Visual Studio Ultimate

Resource group * ⓘ SynapseRG

Create new

Managed resource group ⓘ Enter managed resource group name

Workspace details

Name your workspace, select a location, and choose a primary Data Lake Storage Gen2 file system to serve as the default location for logs and job output.

Workspace name * synapsecookbook

Region * East US

Select Data Lake Storage Gen2 * ⓘ From subscription Manually via URL

Account name * ⓘ synapsecookbookdemo

Create new

File system name * amazonbestseller

Figure 5.15 – Create Synapse workspace – Basics tab

7. On the **Security** tab, enter a SQL administrator password to access the Synapse workspace upon login.

* Basics * **Security** Networking Tags Review + create

Configure security options for your workspace.

**SQL administrator credentials**

Provide credentials that can be used for administrator access to the workspace's SQL pools. If you don't provide a password, one will be automatically generated. You can change the password later.

SQL Server admin login * sqladminuser

SQL Password ••••••••••

Confirm password ••••••••••

**System assigned managed identity permission**

Choose the permissions that you would like to assign to the workspace's system-assigned identity. Learn more

☑ Allow pipelines (running as workspace's system assigned identity) to access SQL pools.

☐ Allow network access to Data Lake Storage Gen2 account.

The selected Data Lake Storage Gen2 account does not restrict network access using any network access rules, or you selected a storage account manually via URL under Basics tab. Learn more

Figure 5.16 – Create Synapse workspace – Security tab

8. Review and create the workspace.

## Creating a Synapse Spark pool

**Synapse Spark pools** are the home for all Spark resources, notebooks, and clusters. When we create a Spark pool, a Spark session is created by default. This Spark pool takes care of Spark resources that will be used by the Spark session. The user can work with the Spark pool without the need to manage clusters because the Synapse workspace takes care of this, removing the overhead for users to manage it by themselves:

1. Open the Synapse workspace that we created earlier and select **Apache Spark pools**. Click **New** to create a new Synapse Spark pool.

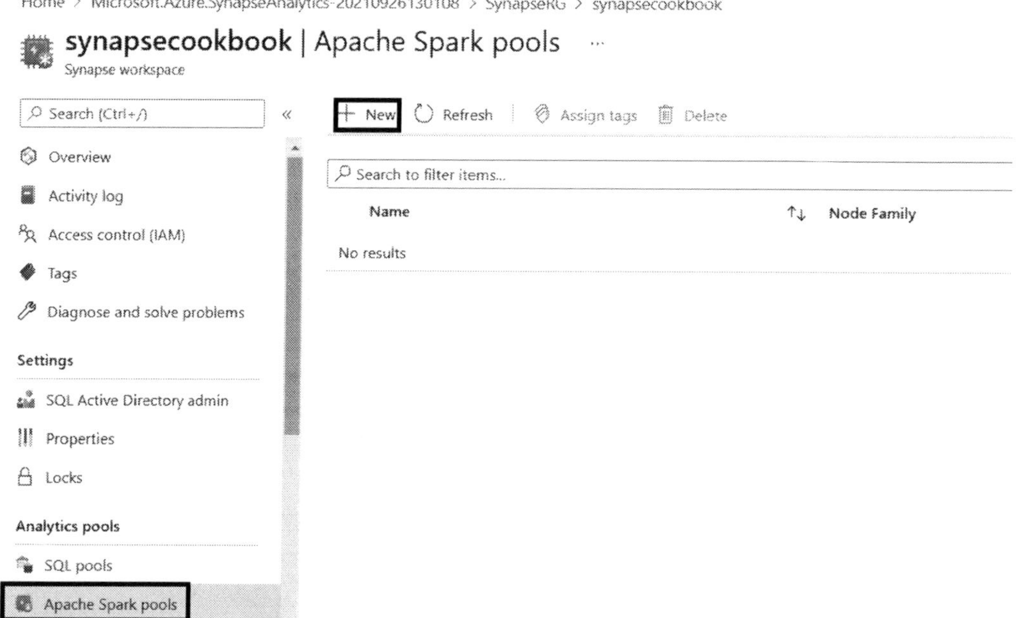


Figure 5.17 – Creating a Synapse Spark pool

2. On the **Basics** tab, enter a Spark pool name and select the desired node size. Review and create the whole setup.

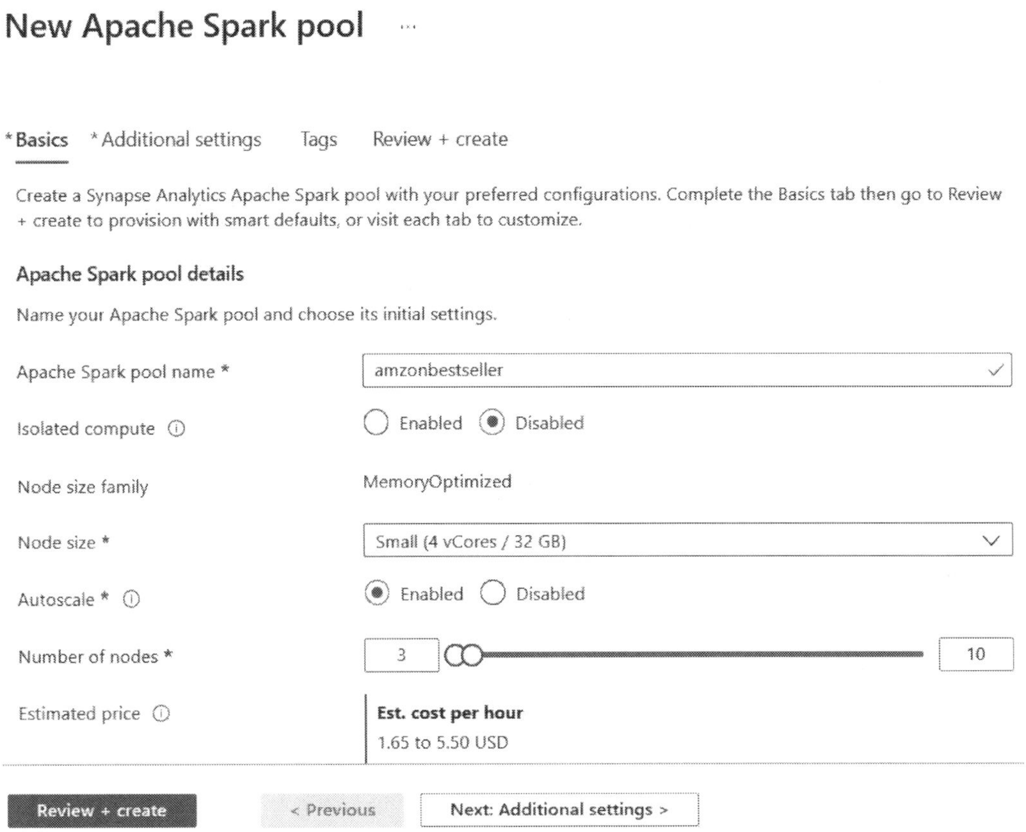

New Apache Spark pool ...

*Basics *Additional settings Tags Review + create

Create a Synapse Analytics Apache Spark pool with your preferred configurations. Complete the Basics tab then go to Review + create to provision with smart defaults, or visit each tab to customize.

Apache Spark pool details

Name your Apache Spark pool and choose its initial settings.

Apache Spark pool name * amzonbestseller

Isolated compute Enabled Disabled

Node size family MemoryOptimized

Node size * Small (4 vCores / 32 GB)

Autoscale * Enabled Disabled

Number of nodes * 3 10

Estimated price Est. cost per hour 1.65 to 5.50 USD

Review + create < Previous Next: Additional settings >

Figure 5.18 – Creating a Synapse Spark pool – Basics tab

The Spark pool is successfully created now, so we can proceed with notebook creation and execution.

## Creating a Synapse notebook

**Synapse notebooks** are interactive Spark sessions and editors for the user to work on Spark code:

1. Go to Synapse Studio and create a new notebook, as shown in the following screenshot:

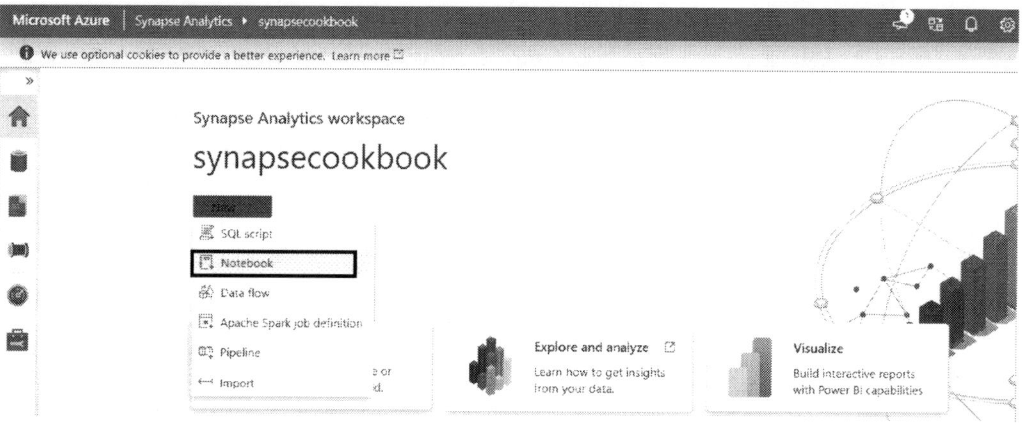


Figure 5.19 – Synapse Analytics Studio

2. Attach the notebook to the Spark pool that we created earlier and run the cell. It starts an Apache Spark session; we are now ready to code in PySpark.

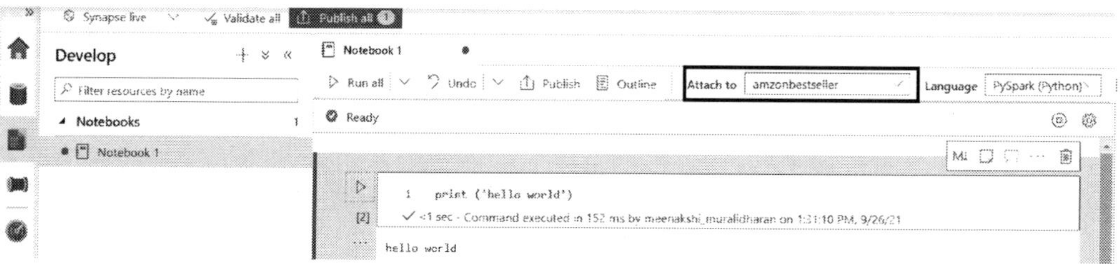


Figure 5.20 – Creating a Synapse notebook

3. Copy the ABFS path of the Parquet file from the storage account. In the code cell, copy and paste the following Python code to read the Parquet file as a DataFrame and convert it to pandas:

```
df = spark.read.parquet('abfss://amazonbestseller@
synapsecookbookdemo.dfs.core.windows.net/NYCTripSmall.
parquet')
df.show(10)
print('Converting to Pandas.')
pd = df.toPandas()
print(pd)
```

You can view the following output in pandas on a Synapse notebook screen:

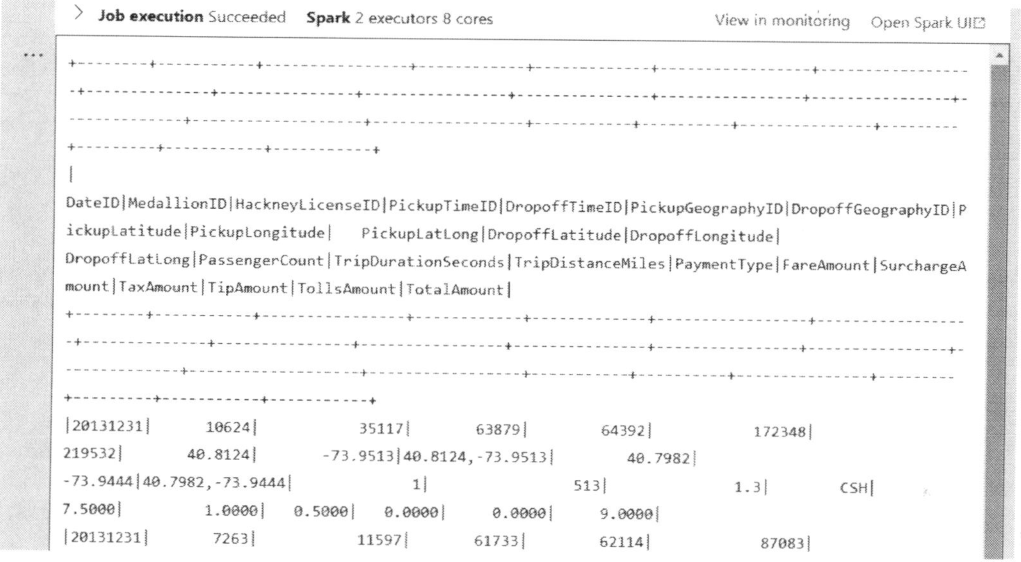


Figure 5.21 – pandas output

## There's more...

Alternatively, we can directly read Parquet files into pandas, as follows:

```
Import pandas
df = pandas.read_parquet('abfss://amazonbestseller@
synapsecookbookdemo.dfs.core.windows.net/NYCTripSmall.parquet')
print(df)
```

# Processing data from a PySpark notebook within Synapse

In this section, we will learn how to process and view data as charts with different operations of DataFrame using PySpark in Synapse notebooks. Charts are usually used to display data and help us to understand patterns between different data points. Graphs and diagrams also help to compare data.

## Getting ready

We will be using a public dataset for our scenario. This dataset will consist of New York yellow taxi trip data; this includes attributes such as trip distances, itemized fares, rate types, payment types, pick-up and drop-off dates and times, driver-reported passenger counts, and pick-up and drop-off locations. We will be using this dataset throughout this recipe to demonstrate various use cases:

- To get the dataset, you can go to the following URL: `https://www.kaggle.com/microize/newyork-yellow-taxi-trip-data-2020-2019`.
- The code for this recipe can be downloaded from the GitHub repository: `https://github.com/PacktPublishing/Analytics-in-Azure-Synapse-Simplified`.

## How to do it...

Let's get started:

1. *View the schema of the input dataset.* Read the Parquet file as a DataFrame and view the schema using the `printSchema` method of the DataFrame:

```
df = spark.read.parquet('abfss://amazonbestseller@synapsecookbookdemo.dfs.core.windows.net/NYCTripSmall.parquet')
```

```
df.printSchema()
```

The output is shown in the following screenshot:

```
> Job execution Succeeded    Spark 2 executors 8 cores
root
 |-- DateID: integer (nullable = true)
 |-- MedallionID: integer (nullable = true)
 |-- HackneyLicenseID: integer (nullable = true)
 |-- PickupTimeID: integer (nullable = true)
 |-- DropoffTimeID: integer (nullable = true)
 |-- PickupGeographyID: integer (nullable = true)
 |-- DropoffGeographyID: integer (nullable = true)
 |-- PickupLatitude: double (nullable = true)
 |-- PickupLongitude: double (nullable = true)
 |-- PickupLatLong: string (nullable = true)
 |-- DropoffLatitude: double (nullable = true)
 |-- DropoffLongitude: double (nullable = true)
 |-- DropoffLatLong: string (nullable = true)
 |-- PassengerCount: integer (nullable = true)
 |-- TripDurationSeconds: integer (nullable = true)
 |-- TripDistanceMiles: double (nullable = true)
 |-- PaymentType: string (nullable = true)
 |-- FareAmount: decimal(19,4) (nullable = true)
 |-- SurchargeAmount: decimal(19,4) (nullable = true)
 |-- TaxAmount: decimal(19,4) (nullable = true)
 |-- TipAmount: decimal(19,4) (nullable = true)
 |-- TollsAmount: decimal(19,4) (nullable = true)
 |-- TotalAmount: decimal(19,4) (nullable = true)
```

Figure 5.22 – Reading from a Parquet file

2. *View the records in a DataFrame.* The DataFrame's `show` method, applied to a number of records, helps us to view the records in the DataFrame. Disable truncation with the `truncate` statement to view all the records fully:

```
df.show(5, truncate=false)
```

*Figure 5.23* shows the output:

```
1    df.show(5, truncate = False)
[3]  ✓ <1 sec - Command executed in 1 sec 64 ms by meenakshi_muralidharan on 2:31:55 PM, 9/26/21
> Job execution Succeeded   Spark 2 executors 8 cores                     View in monitoring   Open Spark UI
+--------+------------+----------------+------------+-------------+-------------------+--------------------+---------------+----------------+--------------------
---------+---------------+----------------+-------------+--------------------+-----------------+-------------+------------+-----------------+---------+----------+-
----------+-----------+
|DateID  |MedallionID|HackneyLicenseID|PickupTimeID|DropoffTimeID|PickupGeographyID|DropoffGeographyID|PickupLatitude|PickupLongitude|PickupLatLong
|DropoffLatitude|DropoffLongitude|DropoffLatLong
|PassengerCount|TripDurationSeconds|TripDistanceMiles|PaymentType|FareAmount|SurchargeAmount|TaxAmount|TipAmount|TollsAmount|TotalAmount|
+--------+------------+----------------+------------+-------------+-------------------+--------------------+---------------+----------------+--------------------
---------+---------------+----------------+-------------+--------------------+-----------------+-------------+------------+-----------------+---------+----------+-
----------+-----------+
|20131231|10624      |35117           |63879       |64392        |172348             |219532              |40.8124        |-73.9513
|40.8124,-73.9513|40.7982        |-73.9444         |40.7982,-73.9444|1           |513               |1.3             |CSH         |7.5000      |1.0000
|0.5000    |0.0000    |0.0000     |9.0000      |
|20131231|7263       |11597           |61733       |62114        |87083              |137768              |40.7352        |-73.9857        |40.7352,-73.9857|40.751
|-73.9789        |40.751,-73.9789 |1            |380              |1.3             |CSH         |7.0000    |1.0000         |0.5000    |0.0000    |0.0000
|8.5000    |
|20131231|1899       |5301            |59488       |59815        |82160              |146431              |40.7699        |-73.9483        |40.7699,-73.9483|40.763
|-73.962         |40.763,-73.962  |1            |326              |1.0             |CSH         |6.0000    |1.0000         |0.5000    |0.0000    |0.0000
|7.5000    |
|20131231|9471       |28727           |69093       |69548        |276342             |43408               |40.7507        |-73.9746
|40.7507,-73.9746|40.7428        |-73.9823         |40.7428,-73.9823|1           |454               |1.0             |CSH         |7.0000      |1.0000
|0.5000    |0.0000    |0.0000     |8.5000      |
|20131231|2556       |16124           |51720       |52440        |155260             |211054              |40.7138        |-74.0119
|40.7138,-74.0119|40.7494        |-73.9694         |40.7494,-73.9694|1           |720               |6.11            |CSH         |19.5000     |0.0000
|0.5000    |0.0000    |0.0000     |20.0000     |
+--------+------------+----------------+------------+-------------+-------------------+--------------------+---------------+----------------+--------------------
---------+---------------+----------------+-------------+--------------------+-----------------+-------------+------------+-----------------+---------+----------+-
----------+-----------+
```

Figure 5.23 – Output of the DataFrame

3. *View selected columns of the DataFrame.* Select the desired columns using the `select` method and view the results with the `show` method:

```
df.select('PassengerCount', 'DateID').show(10)
```

The output is shown in the following screenshot:

```
[4]  1   df.select('PassengerCount','DateID').show(10)
     ✓ 1 sec - Command executed in 1 sec 835 ms by meenakshi_muralidharan on 2:33:10 PM, 9/26/21

  > Job execution Succeeded   Spark 2 executors 8 cores          View in monitoring   Open Spark UI

+--------------+--------+
|PassengerCount|  DateID|
+--------------+--------+
|             1|20131231|
|             1|20131231|
|             1|20131231|
|             1|20131231|
|             1|20131231|
|             1|20131231|
|             1|20131231|
|             1|20131231|
|             1|20131231|
|             1|20131231|
+--------------+--------+
only showing top 10 rows
```

Figure 5.24 – Passenger output

4. *Use the* `groupBy` *clause and sort the records in a DataFrame.* Group by any of the desired columns and sort the results in ascending order:

```
df.groupBy("DateID").count().sort("count",
ascending=True).show()
```

The following screenshot shows the output:

```
[5]  1   df.groupBy("DateID").count().sort("count",ascending=True).show()
     ✓ 4 sec - Command executed in 4 sec 358 ms by meenakshi_muralidharan on 2:33:52 PM, 9/26/21

  > Job execution Succeeded   Spark 2 executors 8 cores          View in monitoring   Open Spark UI

+--------+-----+
|  DateID|count|
+--------+-----+
|20131217| 3992|
|20131225| 4776|
|20131226| 5149|
|20131228| 6104|
|20131222| 6186|
|20131227| 6205|
|20131223| 6433|
|20131230| 6513|
|20131224| 6789|
|20131229| 7048|
|20131231| 7449|
|20131221| 7664|
|20131218| 8307|
|20131219| 8577|
|20131220| 8808|
+--------+-----+
```

Figure 5.25 – Datewise count of trips

5. *View descriptive statistical results of the DataFrame.* Descriptive or summary statistics of a DataFrame can be viewed using the `count`, `min`, `max`, `mean`, and `stddev` functions supported by PySpark. `describe` will perform all summary statistics and show the results of the DataFrame:

```
df.describe().show()
```

The following screenshot shows the results:

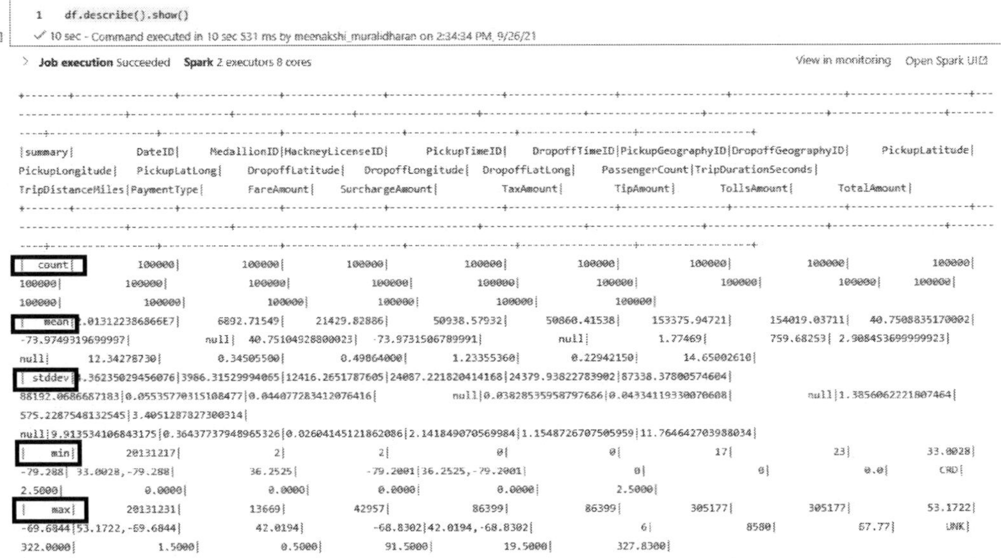


Figure 5.26 – Statistical results of the DataFrame

6. *Filter a column in the DataFrame.* Filter the results of a column using the `filter` function. The following code filters the DataFrame where `TripDistanceMiles` is greater than 1.5 miles and displays all the records:

```
df.filter(df.TripDistanceMiles > 1.5).count()
```

*Figure 5.27* displays the result:

```
[8]  1  df.filter(df.TripDistanceMiles > 1.5).count()
     ✓ 1 sec - Command executed in 1 sec 72 ms by meenakshi_muralidharan on 2:37:20 PM, 9/26/21
   > Job execution Succeeded  Spark 2 executors 8 cores        View in monitoring  Open Spark UI
   57418
```

Figure 5.27 – Filter trip distance greater than 1.5 miles

- *Add a column to the DataFrame.* A new column can be added to the DataFrame using `withColumn`. The following code shows a column named `Longtrip` being added to the DataFrame:

```
from pyspark.sql.functions import *
df=df.withColumn("Longtrip", col("TripDistanceMiles"))
df.show(5)
```

The output is shown in the following screenshot:

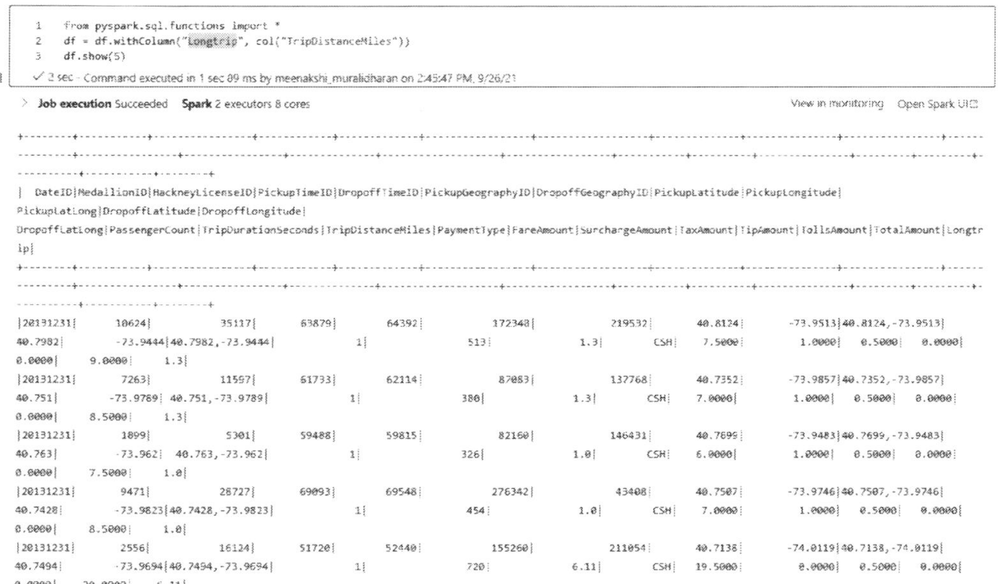

Figure 5.28 – Adding a new column to the DataFrame

7. *Filter trip data to trips between 1 and 3 miles.* We can filter the trip data to where the travel distance is within 1 to 3 miles and display the records:

```
df.filter(df["Longtrip"].between(1,3)).show(5)
```

The following screenshot shows the results:

```
1   df.filter(df["Longtrip"].between(1, 3)).show(5)
[29]  ✓ 1 sec - Command executed in 1 sec 76 ms by meenakshi_muralidharan on 3:03:11 PM, 9/26/21
> Job execution Succeeded   Spark 2 executors 8 cores                    View in monitoring   Open Spark UI

+--------+-----------+----------------+------------+-------------+-------------------+--------------------+--------------+---------------+------
--------+---------------+---------------+-------------+------------------+-----------------+----------+----------+---------------+---------+--------+-
----------+----------+--------+
| DateID|MedallionID|HackneyLicenseID|PickupTimeID|DropoffTimeID|PickupGeographyID|DropoffGeographyID|PickupLatitude|PickupLongitude|
PickupLatLong|DropoffLatitude|DropoffLongitude|
DropoffLatLong|PassengerCount|TripDurationSeconds|TripDistanceMiles|PaymentType|FareAmount|SurchargeAmount|TaxAmount|TipAmount|TollsAmount|TotalAmount|Longtr
ip|
+--------+-----------+----------------+------------+-------------+-------------------+--------------------+--------------+---------------+------
--------+---------------+---------------+-------------+------------------+-----------------+----------+----------+---------------+---------+--------+-
----------+----------+--------+
|20131231|      10624|           35117|       63879|        64392|           172348|            219532|       40.8124|       -73.9513|40.8124,-73.9513|
40.7982|        -73.9444|40.7982,-73.9444|             1|                513|              1.3|        CSH|    7.5000|         1.0000|   0.5000|   0.0000|
0.0000|    9.0000|     1.3|
|20131231|       7263|           11597|       61733|        62114|            87083|            137768|       40.7352|       -73.9857|40.7352,-73.9857|
40.751|        -73.9789| 40.751,-73.9789|             1|                380|              1.3|        CSH|    7.0000|         1.0000|   0.5000|   0.0000|
0.0000|    8.5000|     1.3|
|20131231|       1899|            5301|       59488|        59815|            82160|            146431|       40.7699|       -73.9483|40.7699,-73.9483|
40.763|         -73.962| 40.763,-73.962|              1|                326|              1.0|        CSH|    6.0000|         1.0000|   0.5000|   0.0000|
0.0000|    7.5000|     1.0|
|20131231|       9471|           28727|       69093|        69548|           276342|             43408|       40.7507|       -73.9746|40.7507,-73.9746|
40.7428|        -73.9823|40.7428,-73.9823|             1|                454|              1.0|        CSH|    7.0000|         1.0000|   0.5000|   0.0000|
0.0000|    8.5000|     1.0|
|20131231|       1433|           33809|       31260|        32100|           263305|             80576|        40.726|       -73.9773| 40.726,-73.9773|
40.749|         -73.9838| 40.749,-73.9838|             1|                840|             2.16|        CSH|   11.5000|         0.0000|   0.5000|   0.0000|
0.0000|   12.0000|    2.16|
```

Figure 5.29 – Filtering to trips between 1 and 3 miles

8. *View in a chart*. We can select the **Chart** option in the Synapse notebook and view the data in a bar chart:

```
df=df.groupby("DateID").agg({'TotalAmount':"sum"})
display(df)
```

The following screenshot shows the output:

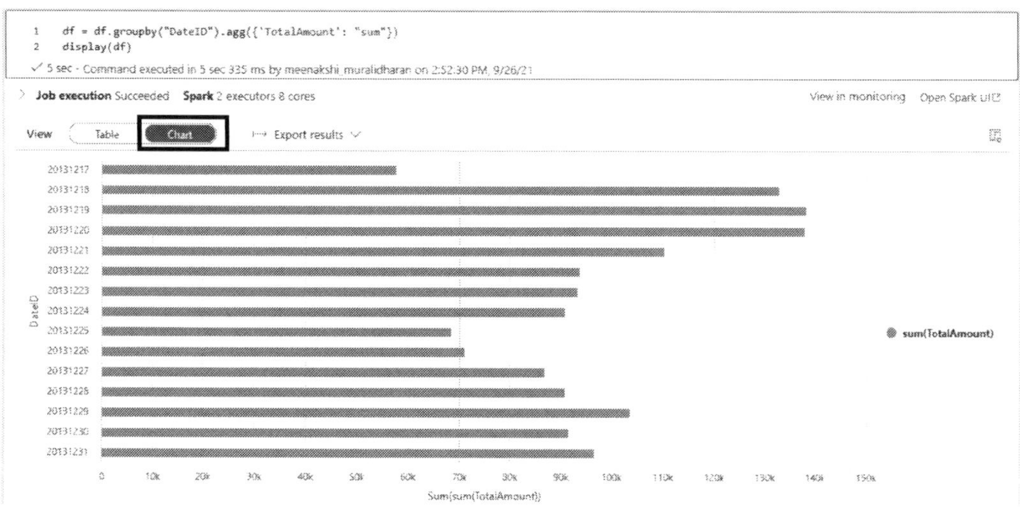


Figure 5.30 – Viewing a bar chart

Select the chart settings with the following code and change to a pie chart to get a clear picture of the data:

```
df=df.groupby("DateID").agg({'TotalAmount':"sum"})
display(df)
```

The result is shown in the following screenshot:

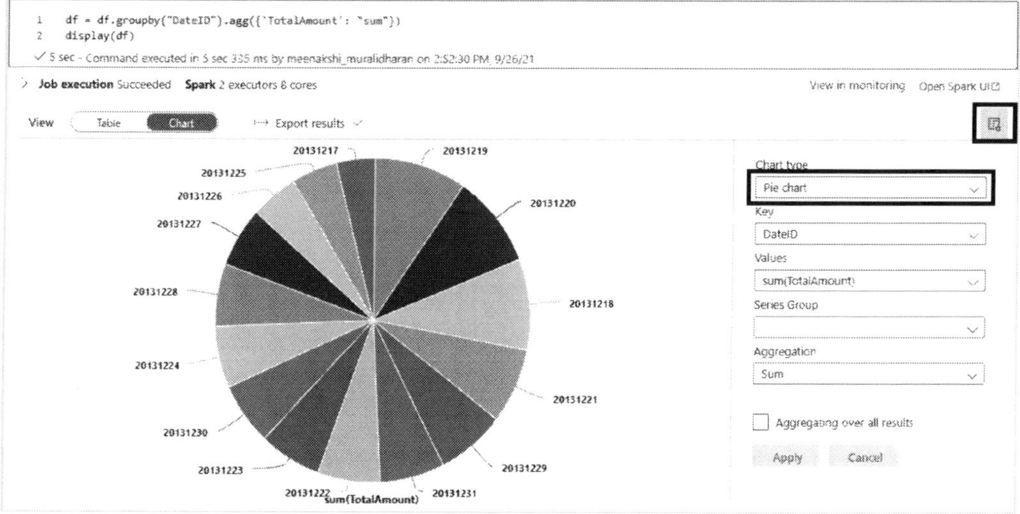


Figure 5.31 – Viewing the pie chart

# Performing read-write operations to a Parquet file using Spark in Synapse

Apache Parquet is a columnar file format that is supported by many big data processing systems and is the most efficient file format for storing data. Most of the Hadoop and big data world uses Parquet to a large extent. The advantage is the efficient data compression support, which enhances the performance of complex data.

Spark supports both reading and writing Parquet files because it reduces the underlying data storage. Since it occupies less storage, it actually reduces I/O operations and consumes less memory.

In this section, we will learn about reading Parquet files and writing to Parquet files. Reading and writing to a Parquet file with PySpark code is straightforward.

## Getting ready

We will be using a public dataset for our scenario. This dataset will consist of New York yellow taxi trip data; this includes attributes such as trip distances, itemized fares, rate types, payment types, pick-up and drop-off dates and times, driver-reported passenger counts, and pick-up and drop-off locations. We will be using this dataset throughout this recipe to demonstrate various use cases:

- To get the dataset, you can go to the following URL: `https://www.kaggle.com/microize/newyork-yellow-taxi-trip-data-2020-2019`.
- The code for this recipe can be downloaded from the GitHub repository: `https://github.com/PacktPublishing/Analytics-in-Azure-Synapse-Simplified`.

## How to do it...

Let's get started:

1. Use `spark.read.parquet` to read Parquet files from ABFS storage in ADLS Gen2. The files are read as a DataFrame. Use the DataFrame's `write.parquet` method to write Parquet files and specify the ABFS storage path.

The following code snippet performs the operation of reading and writing to Parquet files:

```
df = spark.read.parquet('abfss://amazonbestseller@
synapsecookbookdemo.dfs.core.windows.net/NYCTripSmall.
parquet')
from pyspark.sql.functions import *
df = df.withColumn("Longtrip", col("TripDistanceMiles"))
df.write.parquet('abfss://amazonbestseller@
synapsecookbookdemo.dfs.core.windows.net/
NYCTripSmallwrite.parquet')
dfwrite = spark.read.parquet('abfss://amazonbestseller@
synapsecookbookdemo.dfs.core.windows.net/
NYCTripSmallwrite.parquet')
dfwrite.show(5)
```

2. Go to Synapse Studio, choose **storage**, and navigate to the **Linked** tab server, where the storage account can be accessed.

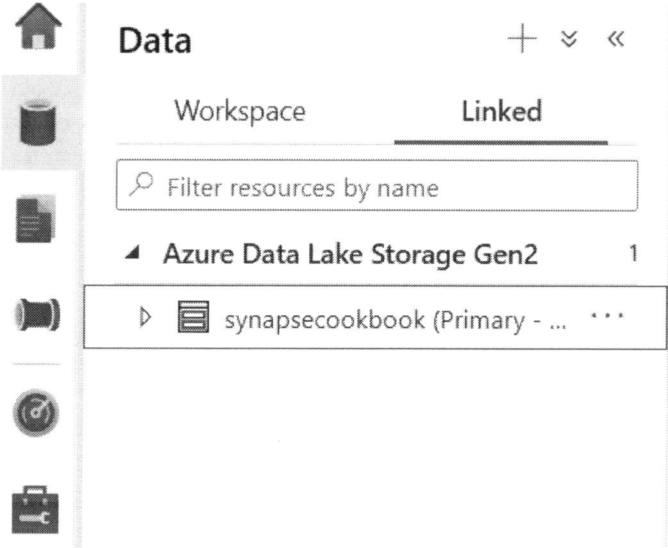


Figure 5.32 – Storage account from Synapse Studio

3. The New York taxi Parquet file has `write` in the filename for identification in our code, as you can see in the following screenshot, stored in the ADLS Gen2 filesystem:

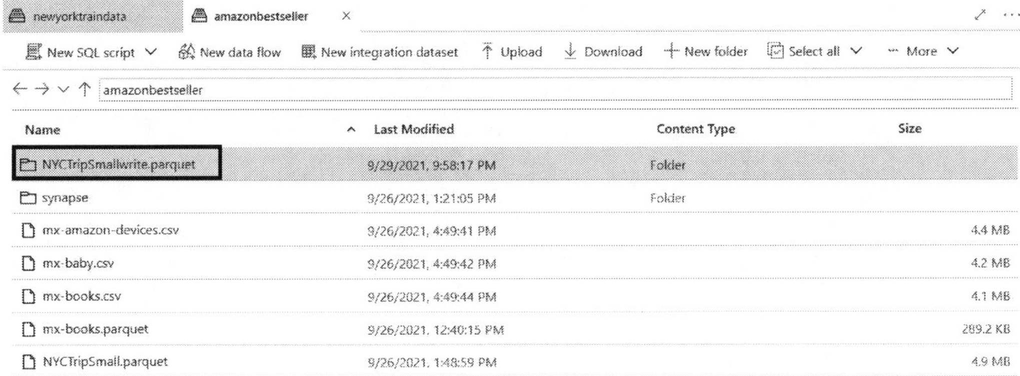


Figure 5.33 – Viewing the Parquet file written in code in the storage account

# Analytics with Spark

In this section, we will learn how to do exploratory analysis with a dataset using PySpark in Synapse notebooks.

## Getting ready

We will be using a public dataset for our scenario. This dataset will consist of New York yellow taxi trip data; this includes attributes such as trip distances, itemized fares, rate types, payment types, pick-up and drop-off dates and times, driver-reported passenger counts, and pick-up and drop-off locations. We will be using this dataset throughout this recipe to demonstrate various use cases:

- To get the dataset, you can go to the following URL: `https://www.kaggle.com/microize/newyork-yellow-taxi-trip-data-2020-2019`.
- The code for this recipe can be downloaded from the GitHub repository: `https://github.com/PacktPublishing/Analytics-in-Azure-Synapse-Simplified`.

## How it works...

Let's get started and try to find out the busiest day of the week with the most trips:

1. Read the Parquet file in the Synapse notebook. The trip data is read from ADLS Gen2 into a DataFrame using `spark.read.parquet`:

```
dftrip = spark.read.parquet('abfss://amazonbestseller@
synapsecookbookdemo.dfs.core.windows.net/NYCTripSmall.
parquet')
```

2. Add a new date column to analyze the data. A `trip_date` date column is added and the existing `DateID` column, which is a string, is converted to date format, `yyyyMMdd`. The schema is analyzed to check whether the new column is added:

```
from pyspark.sql import functions as F
```

```
dftrip=dftrip.withColumn("trip_date", F.to_date(F.
col("DateID").cast("string"),\'yyyyMMdd'))
```

```
dftrip.printSchema()
```

The following screenshot shows the results:

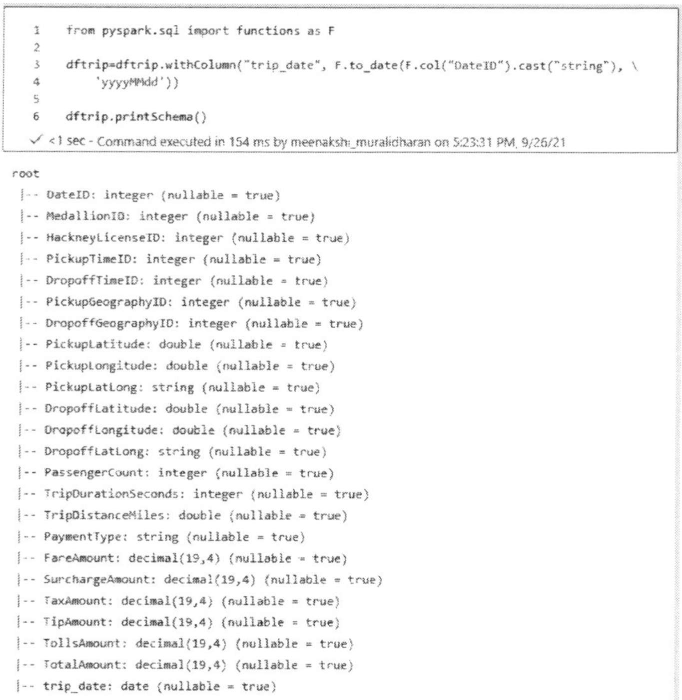

```
from pyspark.sql import functions as F

dftrip=dftrip.withColumn("trip_date", F.to_date(F.col("DateID").cast("string"), \
    'yyyyMMdd'))

dftrip.printSchema()
```

✓ <1 sec - Command executed in 154 ms by meenakshi_muralidharan on 5:23:31 PM, 9/26/21

```
root
 |-- DateID: integer (nullable = true)
 |-- MedallionID: integer (nullable = true)
 |-- HackneyLicenseID: integer (nullable = true)
 |-- PickupTimeID: integer (nullable = true)
 |-- DropoffTimeID: integer (nullable = true)
 |-- PickupGeographyID: integer (nullable = true)
 |-- DropoffGeographyID: integer (nullable = true)
 |-- PickupLatitude: double (nullable = true)
 |-- PickupLongitude: double (nullable = true)
 |-- PickupLatLong: string (nullable = true)
 |-- DropoffLatitude: double (nullable = true)
 |-- DropoffLongitude: double (nullable = true)
 |-- DropoffLatLong: string (nullable = true)
 |-- PassengerCount: integer (nullable = true)
 |-- TripDurationSeconds: integer (nullable = true)
 |-- TripDistanceMiles: double (nullable = true)
 |-- PaymentType: string (nullable = true)
 |-- FareAmount: decimal(19,4) (nullable = true)
 |-- SurchargeAmount: decimal(19,4) (nullable = true)
 |-- TaxAmount: decimal(19,4) (nullable = true)
 |-- TipAmount: decimal(19,4) (nullable = true)
 |-- TollsAmount: decimal(19,4) (nullable = true)
 |-- TotalAmount: decimal(19,4) (nullable = true)
 |-- trip_date: date (nullable = true)
```

Figure 5.34 – Adding a date column

3. Analyze the day, month, and year of the date column. Date functions are effectively used to analyze the day of the week, day of the month, and day of the year so that the whole DataFrame provides more information:

```
dftrip.select(col("trip_date"),
dayofweek(col("trip_date")).alias("dayofweek"),
dayofmonth(col("trip_date")).alias("dayofmonth"),
dayofyear(col("trip_date")).alias("dayofyear"),
      ).show()
```

The output is shown in the following screenshot:

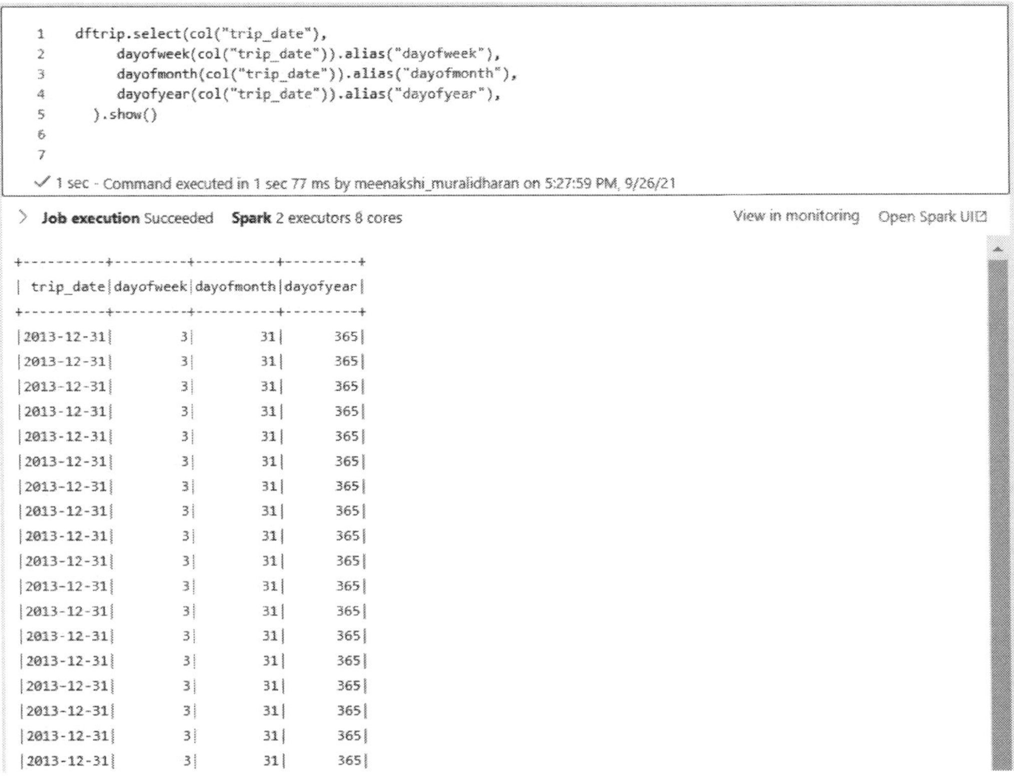


Figure 5.35 – Viewing the day of the week, month, and year

4. Add a day column and find out the day of the trip. A day column is added and the `trip_date` column is used to derive the day of the week. The `date_format` function helps to display the day of the week, which will be used for our calculation:

```
import pyspark.sql.functions as f
dftrip=dftrip.withColumn('Day', f.date_format('trip_
date', 'E'))
dftrip.show(5)
```

The following screenshot shows the result:

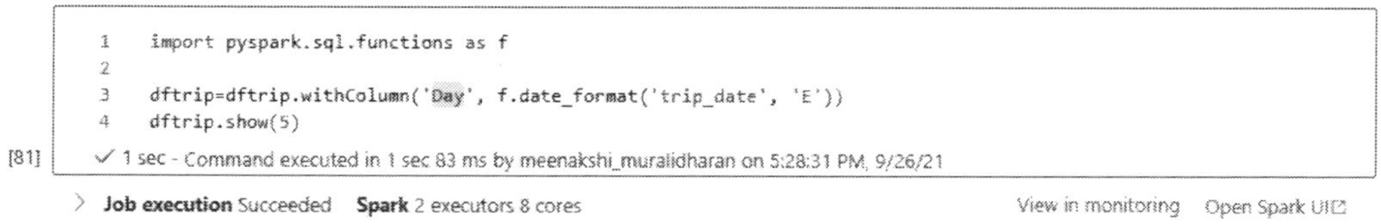

```
import pyspark.sql.functions as f

dftrip=dftrip.withColumn('Day', f.date_format('trip_date', 'E'))
dftrip.show(5)
```

[81] ✓ 1 sec - Command executed in 1 sec 83 ms by meenakshi_muralidharan on 5:28:31 PM, 9/26/21

> **Job execution** Succeeded **Spark** 2 executors 8 cores View in monitoring Open Spark UI

Figure 5.36 – Adding a new Day column

5. Analyze the most trips in a day of the week. The DataFrame is grouped by the `Day` column and the overall count is displayed to find out the most trips in a day of the week. Tuesdays are the day of the week when the most trips take place:

```
dftrip.groupBy("Day").count().orderBy("count").show(7)
```

The following screenshot shows the output:

```
dftrip.groupBy("Day").count().orderBy("count").show(7)
```

[88] ✓ 2 sec - Command executed in 1 sec 867 ms by meenakshi_muralidharan on 5:32:17 PM, 9/26/21

> **Job execution** Succeeded **Spark** 2 executors 8 cores View in monitoring Open Spark UI

```
+---+-----+
|Day|count|
+---+-----+
|Mon|12946|
|Wed|13083|
|Sun|13234|
|Thu|13726|
|Sat|13768|
|Fri|15013|
|Tue|18230|
+---+-----+
```

Figure 5.37 – Finding the most trips in a week

6. Display a chart showing trips on a day of the week. The chart displayed clearly indicates that Tuesdays are the busiest day of the week:

```
dftrip=dftrip.agg({'Day':"count"})
display(dftrip)
```

*Figure 5.38* shows the result:

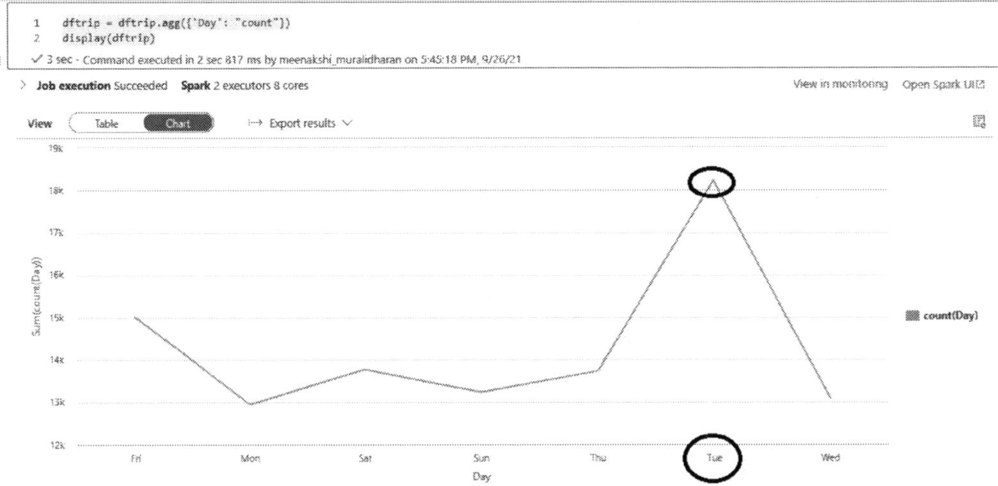


Figure 5.38 – View in a line chart

# 6
# Enriching Data Using the Azure ML AutoML Regression Model

In this chapter, we will cover how to train and enrich your data using a no-code, UI-based machine learning approach with Synapse Studio. We will learn how to configure and use an AutoML and cloud-based service of Azure ML to build your machine learning model with ease. Using AutoML, you will be able to develop a highly scalable, efficient, and robust model with a code-free experience. You will learn how to connect to an existing data source and train the model without writing a single line of code, using machine learning techniques within Synapse Studio.

You will also learn something very interesting – how to integrate Azure Cognitive Services so that you can bring the power of AI along with predictive analytics.

Apart from this, you will also get to learn how to use scalable machine learning models using SparkML and **Machine Learning Library** (**MLlib**). The Synapse runtime consists of many open source libraries, which you can leverage to build the Azure Machine Learning SDK.

We will cover the following recipes:

- Training a model using AutoML in Synapse
- Building a regression model from Azure Machine Learning in Synapse Studio
- Modeling and scoring using SQL pools
- An overview of Spark MLlib and Azure Synapse
- Integrating AI and Cognitive Service

# Training a model using AutoML in Synapse

Azure Synapse Studio gives you the flexibility to develop a machine learning model on top of your dataset. In this recipe, you will learn how you can use the AutoML feature to train your model on the existing Spark tables. You can select the Spark table that you want to train the dataset on with the code-free experience of machine learning models using AutoML.

We will be using the **regression** model in this recipe. However, it is completely dependent on the problem that you are trying to solve, and you can choose from models including regression, **classification**, or **Time Series Insights** to fit your need.

## Getting ready

We will be using the same Spark tables that we created in *Chapter 2, Creating Robust Data Pipelines and Data Transformation.*

We will need to do some setup to prepare for this recipe:

- We need to do this to get ready for the next steps. For more on how to create the Azure Machine Learning workspace, you can refer to `https://docs.microsoft.com/en-us/azure/machine-learning/quickstart-create-resources:`

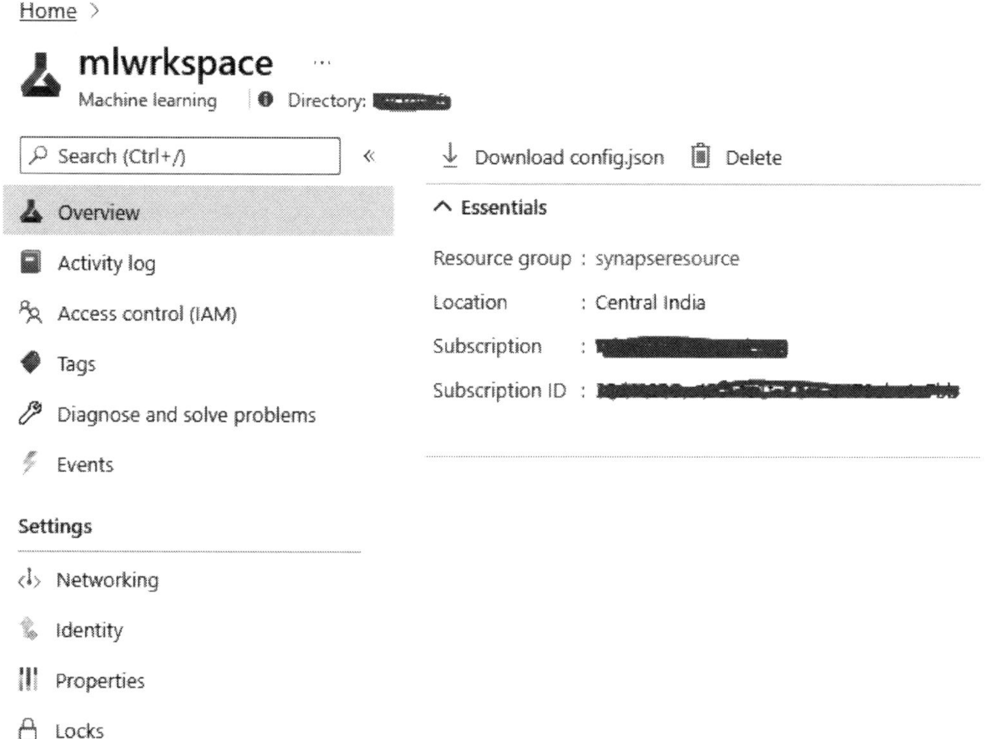


Figure 6.1 – The Azure Machine Learning workspace

- Make sure you have created the Azure Machine Learning linked service in the Azure Synapse workspace:

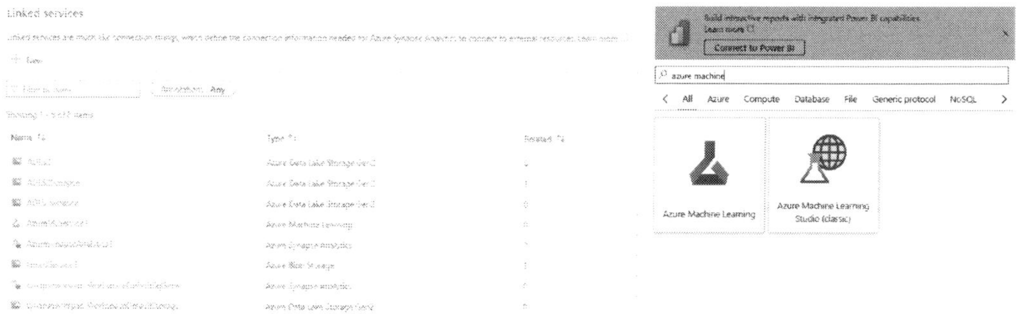


Figure 6.2 – Select Azure Machine Learning to link the service

- Ensure that you have provided the right permission to the Azure Synapse workspace, choosing either the **Managed Identity** or **Service Principal** authentication method:
  - If you have set the authentication method as **Managed Identity**, make sure that you have provided the **Managed Service Identity** (**MSI**) role access control in the Synapse workspace to the Machine Learning workspace.
  - If you have set the authentication method as **Service Principal**, you need to follow the standard procedure of app registration and role assignment for the Azure Machine Learning workspace:

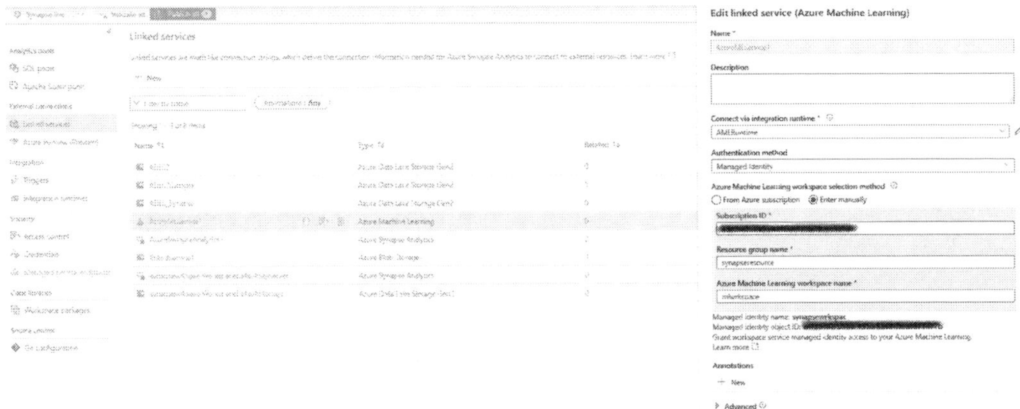


Figure 6.3 – The Azure Machine Learning linked service

## How to do it...

Let's begin this recipe and see how we can create the AutoML model with Azure Synapse Studio. We will be leveraging the existing Spark table to build the Azure Machine Learning model using AutoML:

1. Create a new machine learning model under the **Data** tab by selecting the **default (Spark)** database and then **Train a new model**, as shown in *Figure 6.4*:

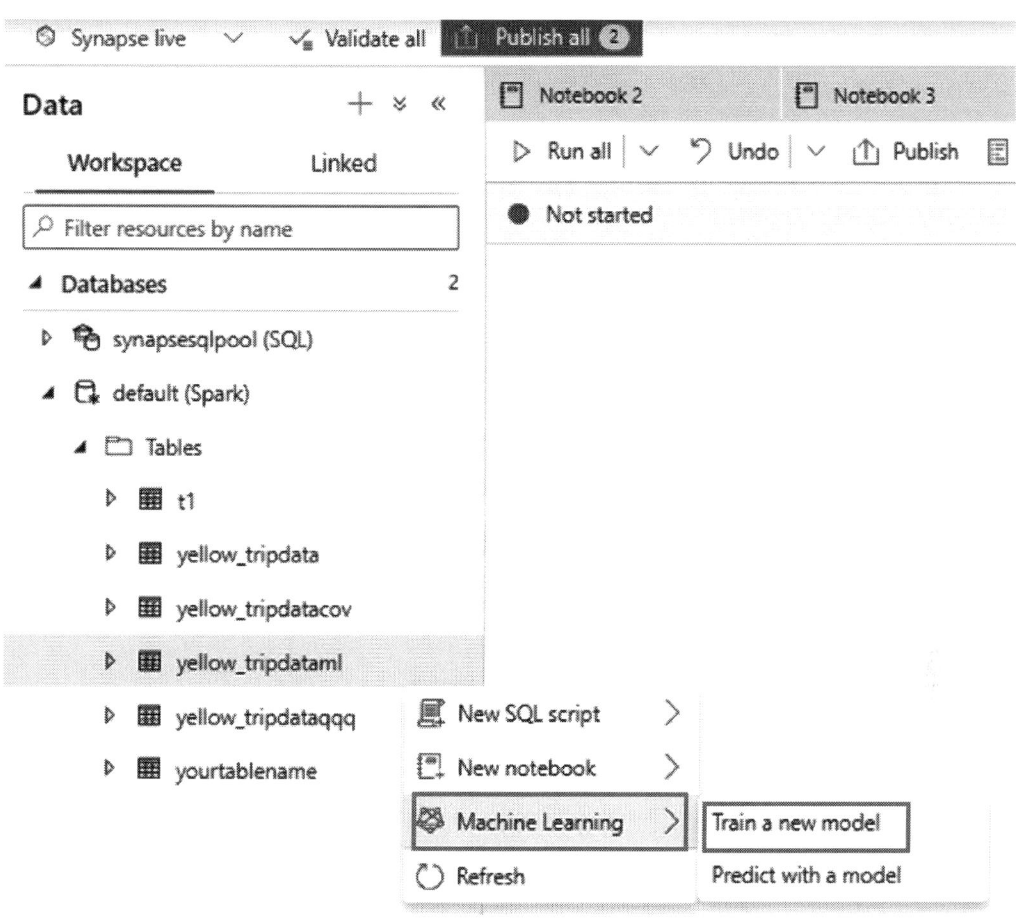


Figure 6.4 – Create a new machine learning model

2. You now get to choose an automated machine learning model – **Classification**, **Regression**, or **Time series forecasting.** For our recipe, we will be choosing **Regression**, as shown in *Figure 6.5*:

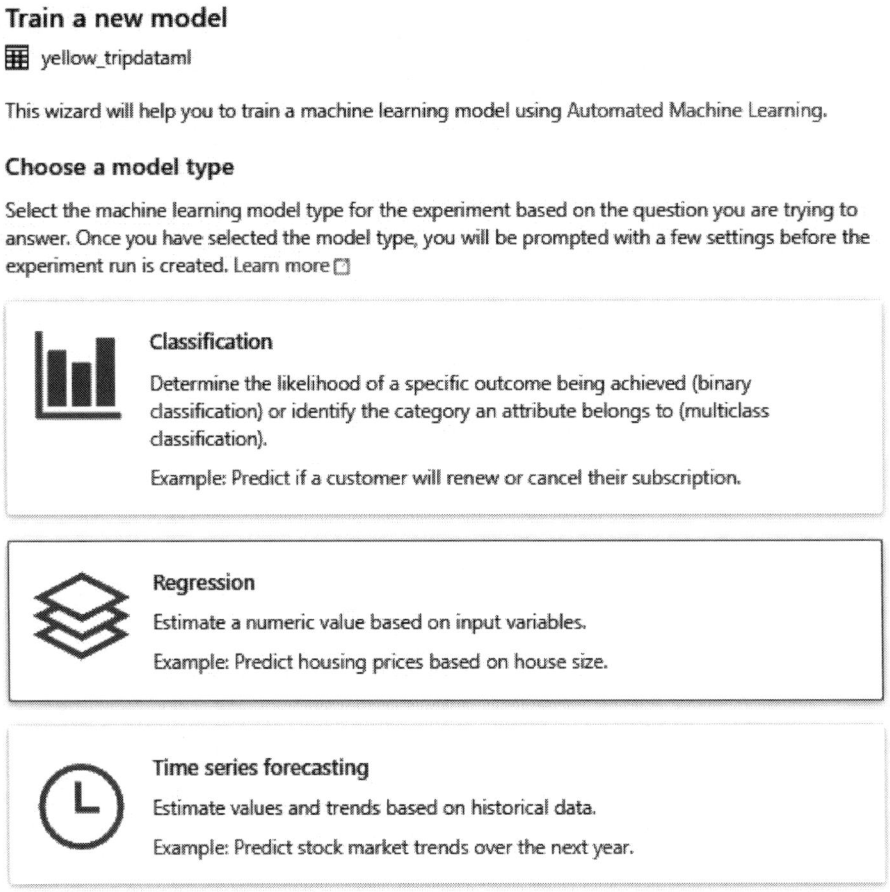

**Train a new model**

yellow_tripdataml

This wizard will help you to train a machine learning model using Automated Machine Learning.

**Choose a model type**

Select the machine learning model type for the experiment based on the question you are trying to answer. Once you have selected the model type, you will be prompted with a few settings before the experiment run is created. Learn more

**Classification**

Determine the likelihood of a specific outcome being achieved (binary classification) or identify the category an attribute belongs to (multiclass classification).

Example: Predict if a customer will renew or cancel their subscription.

**Regression**

Estimate a numeric value based on input variables.

Example: Predict housing prices based on house size.

**Time series forecasting**

Estimate values and trends based on historical data.

Example: Predict stock market trends over the next year.

Figure 6.5 – Choosing an automated ML model

You can now configure the experiment-related parameters in the UI. Make sure you set **Target column** as an integer; otherwise, you will not be able to create the experiment:

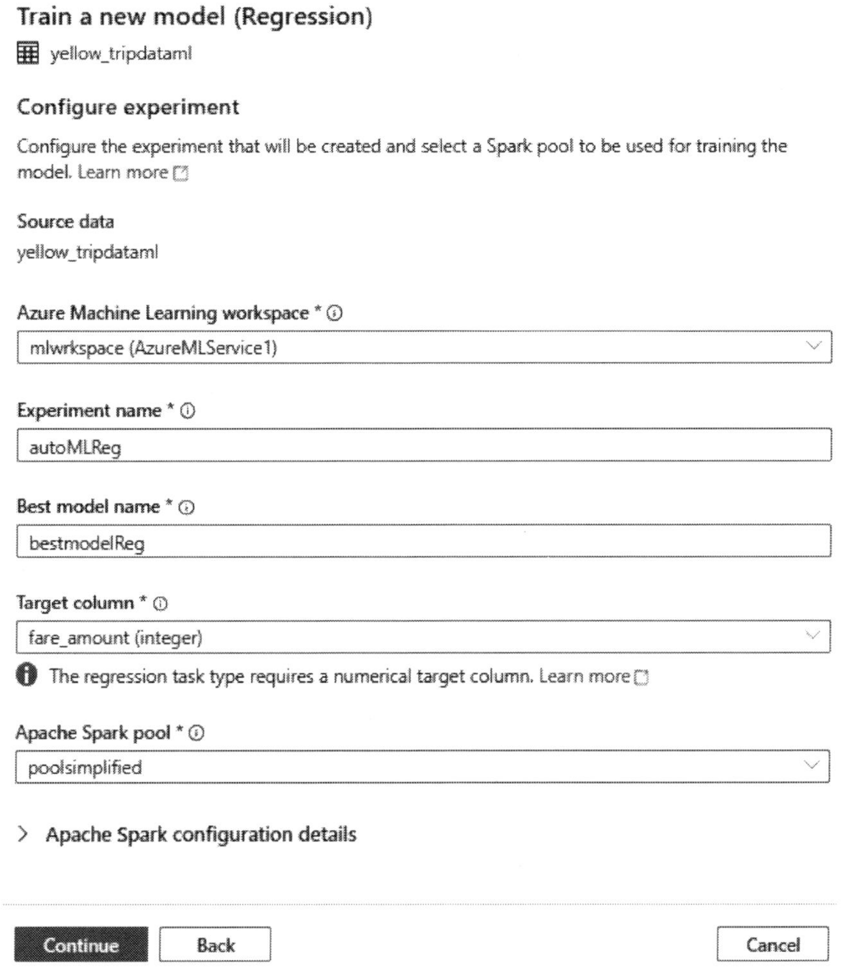

Train a new model (Regression)

yellow_tripdataml

Configure experiment

Configure the experiment that will be created and select a Spark pool to be used for training the model. Learn more

Source data

yellow_tripdataml

Azure Machine Learning workspace *

mlwrkspace (AzureMLService1)

Experiment name *

autoMLReg

Best model name *

bestmodelReg

Target column *

fare_amount (integer)

The regression task type requires a numerical target column. Learn more

Apache Spark pool *

poolsimplified

> Apache Spark configuration details

Continue Back Cancel

Figure 6.6 – Configure the experiment

3. Choose the primary metric. The model will estimate a numeric value based on the input variable you provide. Make sure you have set the **Open Neural Network Exchange** (**ONNX**) model compatibility to **Enable** so that you can call the trained model for scoring in a Synapse Spark pool. Click **Create run** to submit the experiment:

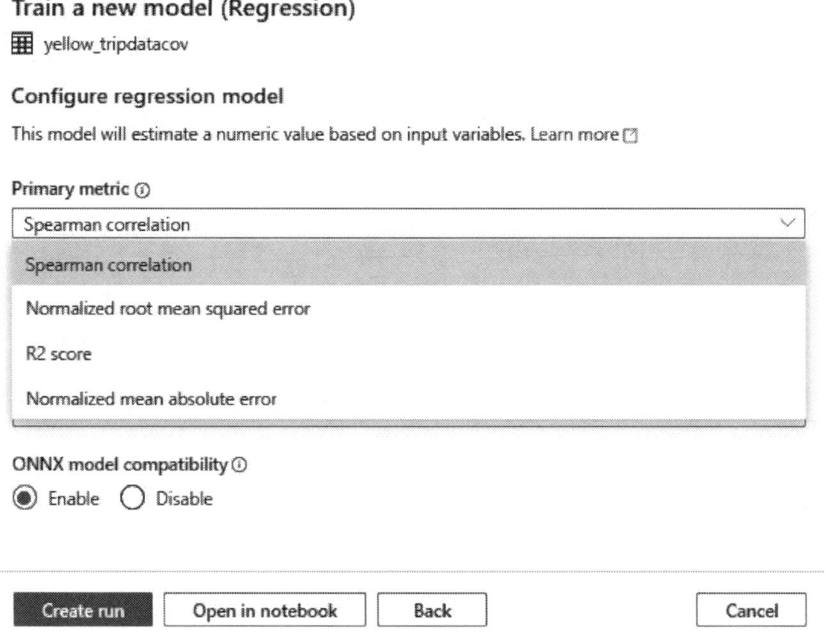


Figure 6.7 – The model variable input

## How it works...

The AutoML run will be executed in the Azure Machine Learning workspace once you have submitted the experiment for execution. You can monitor the model execution from the Azure Machine Learning portal:

**Notifications**

Dismiss all

**AutoML run started**

An AutoML run 'synpasebookwks-yellow_tripdataml-20210927045140' has been started on Spark pool 'synapsebookpool'.

View in Azure Machine Learning portal

3 hours ago

Figure 6.8 – The AutoML run started

The model training will be leveraging the existing Spark pool that you have created in Synapse Analytics as part of the Spark compute. However, for monitoring the Automated ML model training, you can go directly to the Azure Machine Learning portal to check the experiment execution and monitor it from there:

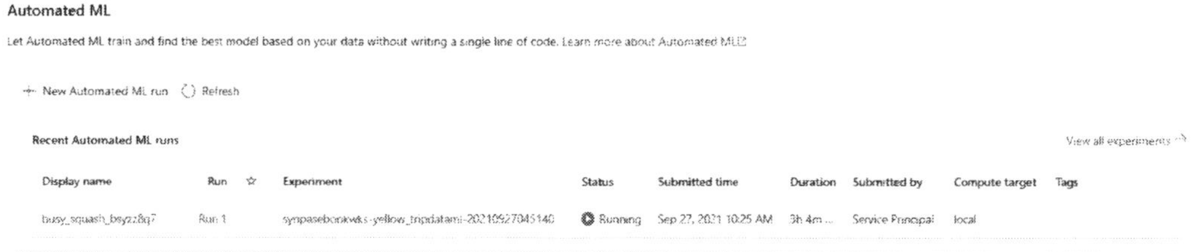


Figure 6.9 – View the experiment status in the Azure Machine Learning portal

You should be able to see all the child runs and their statuses from the Azure Machine Learning portal, along with other details such as the run name, the submitted time, and the run duration, as shown in *Figure 6.10*:

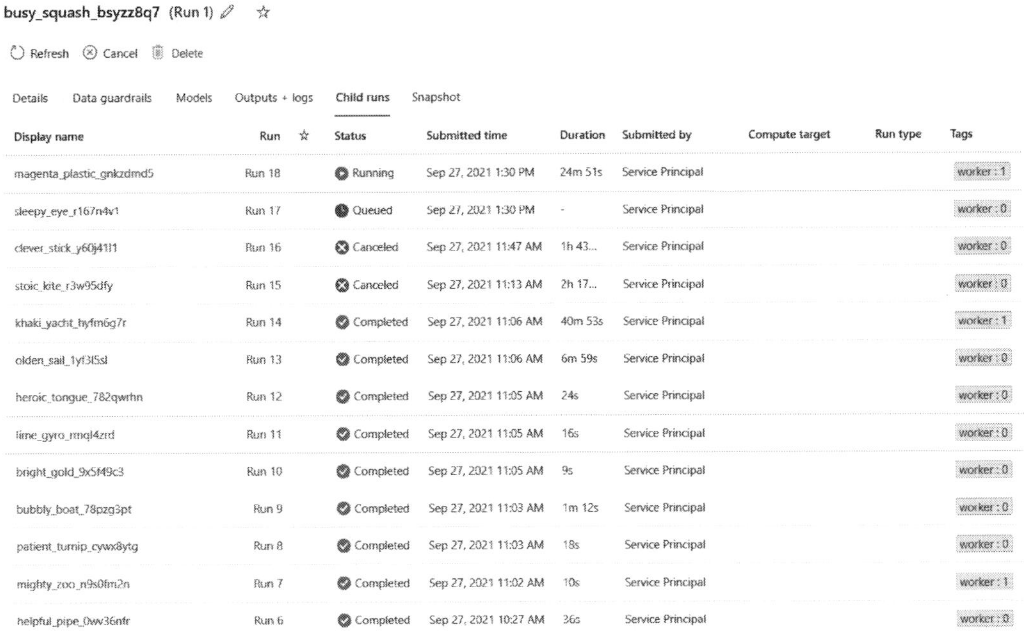

busy_squash_bsyzz8q7 (Run 1)

Refresh Cancel Delete

Details | Data guardrails | Models | Outputs + logs | **Child runs** | Snapshot

| Display name | Run | Status | Submitted time | Duration | Submitted by | Compute target | Run type | Tags |
|---|---|---|---|---|---|---|---|---|
| magenta_plastic_gnkzdmd5 | Run 18 | Running | Sep 27, 2021 1:30 PM | 24m 51s | Service Principal | | | worker : 1 |
| sleepy_eye_r167n4v1 | Run 17 | Queued | Sep 27, 2021 1:30 PM | - | Service Principal | | | worker : 0 |
| clever_stick_y60j41l1 | Run 16 | Canceled | Sep 27, 2021 11:47 AM | 1h 43... | Service Principal | | | worker : 0 |
| stoic_kite_r3w95dfy | Run 15 | Canceled | Sep 27, 2021 11:13 AM | 2h 17... | Service Principal | | | worker : 0 |
| khaki_yacht_hyfm6g7r | Run 14 | Completed | Sep 27, 2021 11:06 AM | 40m 53s | Service Principal | | | worker : 1 |
| olden_sail_1yf3l5sl | Run 13 | Completed | Sep 27, 2021 11:06 AM | 6m 59s | Service Principal | | | worker : 0 |
| heroic_tongue_782qwrhn | Run 12 | Completed | Sep 27, 2021 11:05 AM | 24s | Service Principal | | | worker : 0 |
| lime_gyro_rnql4zrd | Run 11 | Completed | Sep 27, 2021 11:05 AM | 16s | Service Principal | | | worker : 0 |
| bright_gold_9x5f49c3 | Run 10 | Completed | Sep 27, 2021 11:05 AM | 9s | Service Principal | | | worker : 0 |
| bubbly_boat_78pzg3pt | Run 9 | Completed | Sep 27, 2021 11:03 AM | 1m 12s | Service Principal | | | worker : 0 |
| patient_turnip_cywx8ytg | Run 8 | Completed | Sep 27, 2021 11:03 AM | 18s | Service Principal | | | worker : 0 |
| mighty_zoo_n9s0fm2n | Run 7 | Completed | Sep 27, 2021 11:02 AM | 10s | Service Principal | | | worker : 1 |
| helpful_pipe_0wv36nfr | Run 6 | Completed | Sep 27, 2021 10:27 AM | 36s | Service Principal | | | worker : 0 |

Figure 6.10 – The model training status run view

# Building a regression model from Azure Machine Learning in Synapse Studio

Let's now look at how you can build a regression model with Azure Synapse Studio using a Jupyter notebook and then deploy the same on the Azure Machine Learning workspace. In the previous recipe, we saw how we can build and train a machine learning model with code-less experience.

It's time to explore how we can build the regression model with Synapse Studio using the notebook experience and deploy the Studio on the Azure Machine Learning workspace.

We will be leveraging the same Spark pool to build and train the model and deploy it from the Azure Synapse workspace to the Azure Machine Learning workspace, which is linked to Synapse.

We will perform this within the same notebook experience.

## Getting ready

Make sure the following have been completed before you begin:

- The Azure Machine Learning workspace in the Azure Machine Learning service in Azure, as we did in the *Training a model using AutoML in Synapse recipe.*
- You will need to create the Azure Machine Learning linked service in the Azure Synapse workspace if not created already. For more details on how to create an Azure Machine Learning linked service, refer to this link: `https://github.com/MicrosoftDocs/azure-docs/blob/main/articles/synapse-analytics/machine-learning/quickstart-integrate-azure-machine-learning.md`.
- Ensure that you have provided the right permission to the Azure Synapse workspace, choosing either **Managed Identity** or **Service Principal**:
    - If you have set the authentication method as **Managed Identity**, make sure you have provided the MSI role access control in the Synapse workspace to the Azure Machine Learning workspace.
    - If you have set the authentication method as **Service Principal**, you need to follow the standard procedure of app registration and role assignment for the Azure Machine Learning workspace.

## How to do it...

Let's get back to the same Synapse workspace, and under **Develop**, create a new notebook with the name `AMLSparkNotebook`:

1. Import `azureml.core`, which includes the core package, classes, and module for Azure Machine Learning:

```
import azureml.core
from azureml.core import Experiment, Workspace, Dataset, Datastore
from azureml.train.automl import AutoMLConfig
```

```
from notebookutils import mssparkutils
from azureml.data.dataset_factory import
TabularDatasetFactory
```

The notebook view is shown in *Figure 6.11*:

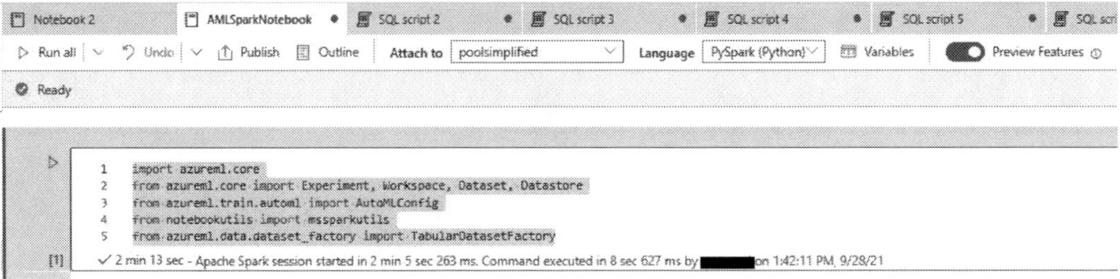


Figure 6.11 – The azureml.core import

2. Link the Azure Machine Learning service using the `linkedService_name` function and define the experiment name and workspace. This will take the Azure Machine Learning workspace, which you have linked earlier, as the parameter. You can refer to the following code:

```
linkedService_name = "AzureMLService"
experiment_name = "synapsewrkspac-mybookexperiement"
ws = mssparkutils.azureML.getWorkspace(linkedService_
name)
experiment = Experiment(ws, experiment_name)
```

*Figure 6.12* shows the notebook:

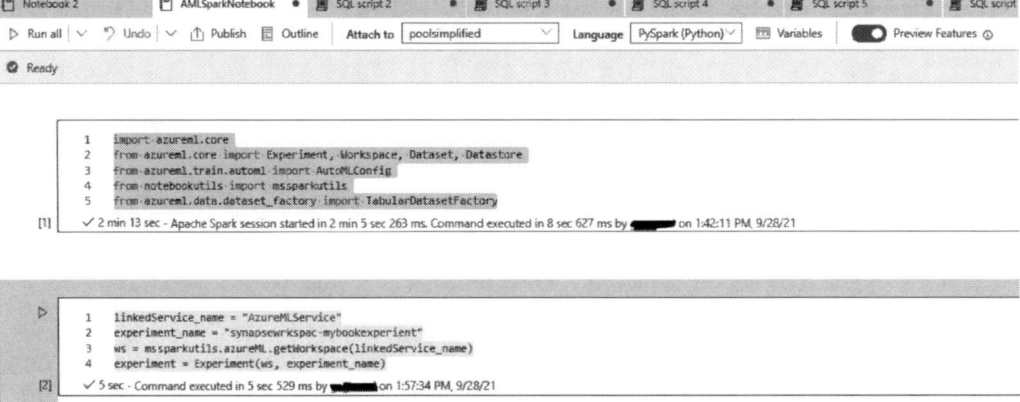


Figure 6.12 – Defining the experiment

3. Define the dataset and specify the Spark table that you want to use to build the regression model and define the `dataframe`. Finally, the dataset will consist of the `dataframe`, `datastore`, and `experiment name` parameters:

```
df = spark.sql("SELECT * FROM default.yellow_tripdataml")
datastore = Datastore.get_default(ws)
dataset = TabularDatasetFactory.register_spark_
dataframe(df, datastore, name = experiment_name +
"-dataset")
```

Please refer to *Figure 6.13* for dataset definition:

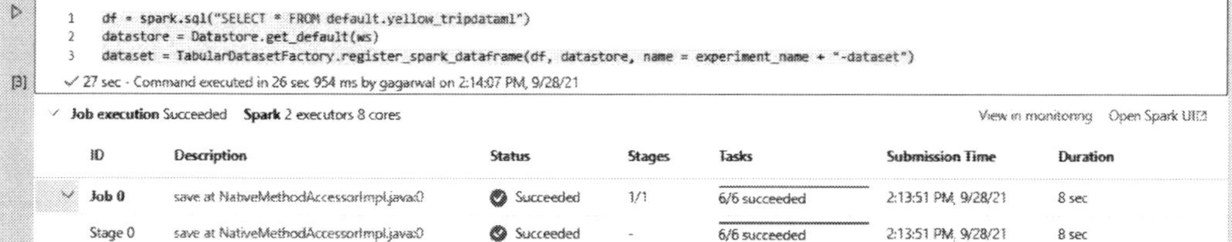

Figure 6.13 – Defining the dataset

4. Define the AutoML configuration for your experiment. This will actually define what model you want to apply and the primary metric you wanted to use. Please make sure that you set `enable_onnx_compatible_model` as `True` so that you can call this model with the Synapse workspace for the SQL pool:

```
automl_config = AutoMLConfig(spark_context = sc,
                             task = "regression",
                             training_data = dataset,
                             label_column_name = "fare_
amount",
                             primary_metric = "spearman_
correlation",
                             experiment_timeout_
hours = 1,
                             max_concurrent_
iterations = 1,
                             enable_onnx_compatible_
models = True)
```

You can refer to *Figure 6.14* to understand how to define the `automl` configuration:

```
automl_config = AutoMLConfig(spark_context = sc,
                             task = "regression",
                             training_data = dataset,
                             label_column_name = "fare_amount",
                             primary_metric = "spearman_correlation",
                             experiment_timeout_hours = 1,
                             max_concurrent_iterations = 1,
                             enable_onnx_compatible_models = True)
```

[4] ✓ <1 sec - Command executed in 153 ms by on 2:18:24 PM, 9/28/21

Figure 6.14 – The AutoML configuration

5. You can now submit and run the experiment:

```
run = experiment.submit(automl_config)
displayHTML("<a href={} target='_
blank'>Your experiment in Azure Machine Learning portal:
{}</a>".format(run.get_portal_url(), run.id))
```

After you submit the Spark job, you will see the following output. You can click on the link generated by the run, as shown in *Figure 6.15*:

```
run = experiment.submit(automl_config)
displayHTML("<a href={} target='_blank'>Your experiment in Azure Machine Learning portal: {}</a>".format(run.get_portal_url(), run.id))
```

[5] ✓ 45 sec - Command executed in 45 sec 432 ms by on 2:27:05 PM, 9/28/21

Submitting spark run.

Your experiment in Azure Machine Learning portal: AutoML_db701cc4-056b-4f17-a7cf-df9b68724875

Figure 6.15 – Submit and run the experiment

6. Finally, you can monitor the experiment run, model training, and the process of navigating to the Azure Machine Learning portal, as shown in *Figure 6.16*.

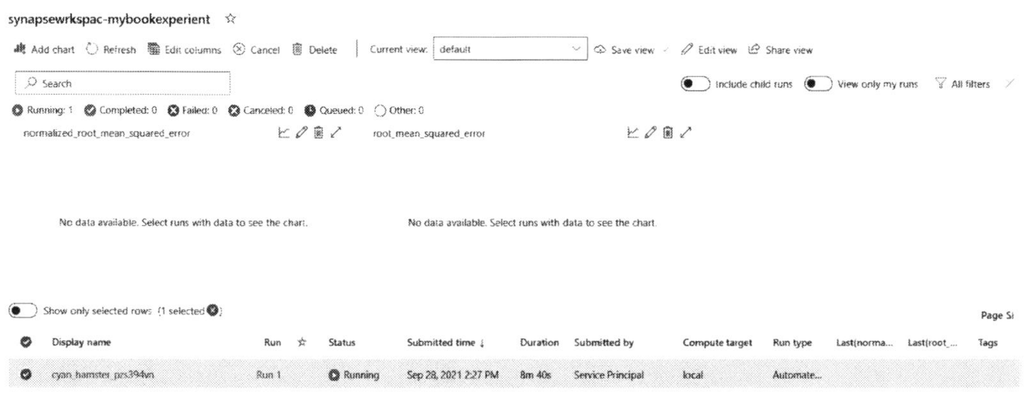

Figure 6.16 – The experiment run status

## How it works...

This recipe leverages the power of the Spark pool that you have created to perform the data exploration and train your machine learning model. The notebook experience within Synapse makes it a one-stop shop for the developer and the data analyst to collaborate and perform their respective activities; this empowers the data scientist to create the AutoML model:

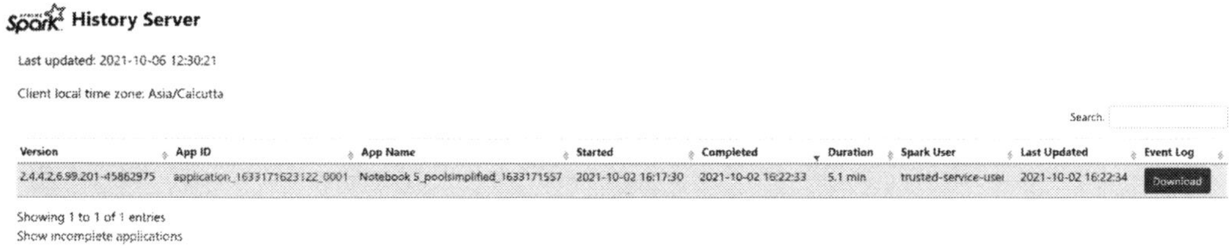

Figure 6.17 – The Spark history run status

The takeaway from this recipe is that you can combine a notebook and UI-based approach to build the machine learning model. The notebook can be published to the Synapse workspace, and you can load it anytime and customize the model as per your need.

# Modeling and scoring using SQL pools

In this recipe, you will learn how to enrich your data, which is under SQL dedicated pools, and apply the existing machine learning model that we created in the *Training a model using AutoML in Synapse* section. This will help the data analyst and the data professional to directly select and run the existing machine learning model without worrying about writing the actual model.

This is the best way to utilize the model that you trained in the *Training a model using AutoML in Synapse* recipe and leverage it to predict the existing SQL pool tables with the help of the predict model wizard in the Synapse workspace.

## Getting ready

To complete this recipe:

- Make sure you have created the Azure Machine Learning workspace in the Azure Machine Learning Service in Azure as we did in the *Training a model using AutoML in Synapse recipe.*
- You will need to have created the Azure Machine Learning linked service in the Azure Synapse workspace.
- Ensure that you have provided the right permission to the Azure Synapse workspace, choosing either **Managed Identity** or **Service Principal**:
    - If you have set the authentication method as **Managed Identity**, make sure you have provided the MSI role access control in the Synapse workspace to the Azure Machine Learning workspace.
    - If you have set the authentication method as **Service Principal**, you need to follow the standard procedure of app registration and role assignment for the Azure Machine Learning workspace.
- The model is trained and deployed in the Azure Machine Learning workspace, which we have already done in the *Training a model using AutoML in Synapse recipe.*

Now, let's begin the actual recipe.

## How to do it...

Let's get back to the same Synapse workspace, and under **Data** tab, expand the SQL pool database and navigate to the `table` folder:

1. Click on the action dots on the SQL pool table that you want to use to make a prediction with the model. Select **Machine Learning | Predict with a model**, as shown in *Figure 6.17*:

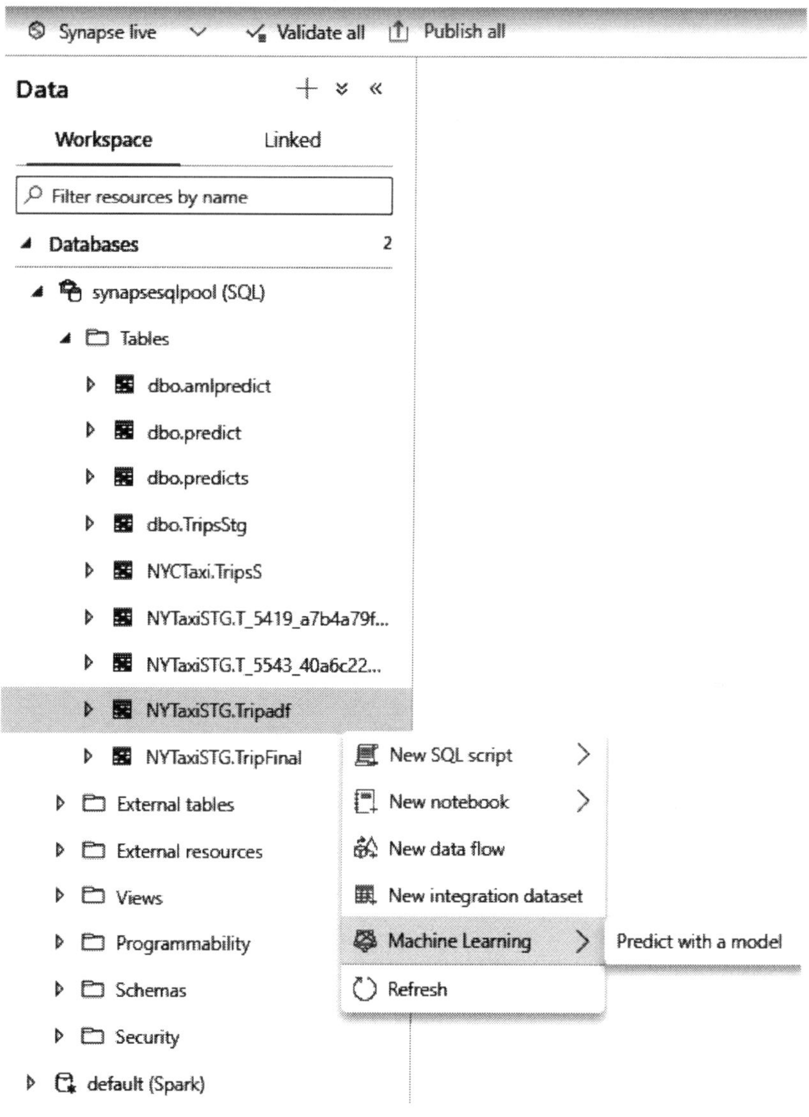


Figure 6.18 – Machine Learning – Predict with a model

2. Once you select **Predict with a model**, it will take you to another blade where you need to select the Azure Machine Learning workspace from the drop-down box. This will show you the models that you have previously created in the same Azure Machine Learning workspace. Select and click **Continue**, as shown in *Figure 6.19*:

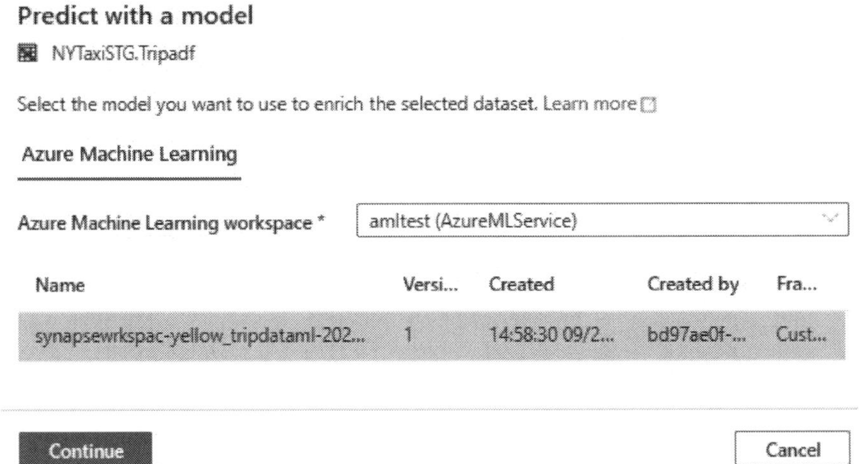


Figure 6.19 – Select a model from the linked Azure Machine Learning workspace

You need to map the `table` column with the machine learning model and define the model output as `variable1`. The mappings are mostly pre-populated, since the model is already deployed in the Azure Machine Learning workspace. Click **Continue**:

**Predict with a model**

NYTaxiSTG.Tripadf

Map the source table columns to the expected model inputs. Learn more

**Input mapping** *

+ New | Delete

| Source column | | Model input | Input type |
|---|---|---|---|
| VendorID | → | VendorID | varchar |
| tpep_pickup_datetim | → | tpep_pickup_date... | varchar |
| tpep_dropoff_datetin | → | tpep_dropoff_dat... | varchar |
| passenger_count | → | passenger_count | varchar |
| trip_distance | → | trip_distance | varchar |
| RateCodeID | → | RatecodeID | varchar |
| store_and_fwd_flag | → | store_and_fwd_flag | varchar |
| PULocationID | → | PULocationID | varchar |
| DOLocationID | → | DOLocationID | varchar |
| payment_type | → | payment_type | varchar |
| extra | → | extra | varchar |
| mta_tax | → | mta_tax | varchar |
| tip_amount | → | tip_amount | varchar |
| tolls_amount | → | tolls_amount | varchar |
| improvement_surcha | → | improvement_sur... | varchar |
| total_amount | → | total_amount | varchar |
| congestion_surcharg | → | congestion_surch... | varchar |

**Output mapping** *

+ New | Delete

| Model output | Output type |
|---|---|
| variable1 | real |

Continue | Back | Cancel

Figure 6.20 – Define the model output mapping

3. You need to now define the stored procedure name, which will be created once you generate the SQL script. You also need to specify the target table for storing the machine learning model, and then click **Deploy model + open script**, as shown in *Figure 6.21*:

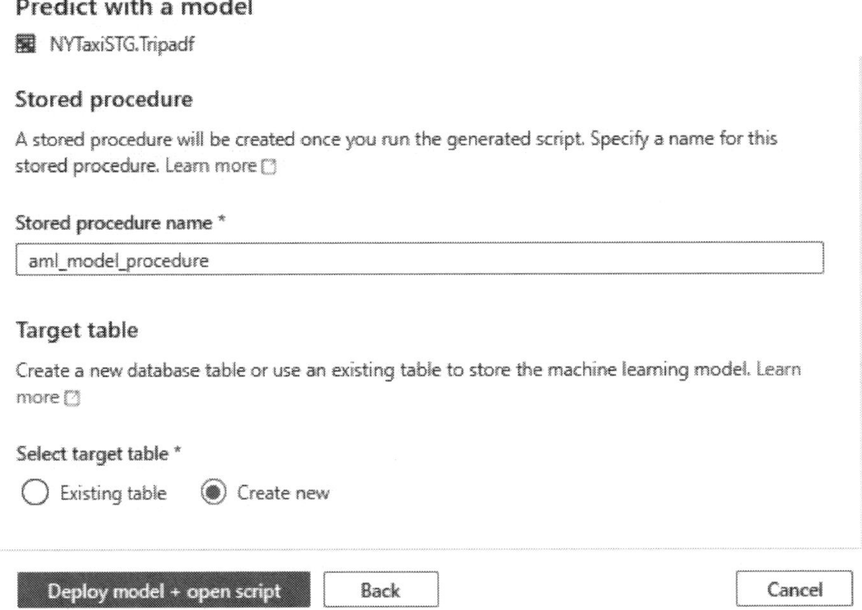


Figure 6.21 – Define the model output mapping

4. This will generate the SQL script that will create the stored procedure. The stored procedure will internally call the predict Azure Machine Learning scoring model that you created previously in the linked Azure Machine Learning workspace:

```
CREATE PROCEDURE aml_model_procedure
AS
BEGIN
SELECT
    CAST([VendorID] AS [varchar]) AS [VendorID],
    CAST([tpep_pickup_datetime] AS [varchar]) AS [tpep_
pickup_datetime],
```

```
    CAST([tpep_dropoff_datetime] AS [varchar]) AS [tpep_
dropoff_datetime],
    CAST([passenger_count] AS [varchar]) AS [passenger_
count],
    CAST([trip_distance] AS [varchar]) AS [trip_
distance],
    CAST([RateCodeID] AS [varchar]) AS [RatecodeID],
    CAST([store_and_fwd_flag] AS [varchar]) AS [store_
and_fwd_flag],
    CAST([PULocationID] AS [varchar]) AS [PULocationID],
    CAST([DOLocationID] AS [varchar]) AS [DOLocationID],
    CAST([payment_type] AS [varchar]) AS [payment_type],
    CAST([extra] AS [varchar]) AS [extra],
    CAST([mta_tax] AS [varchar]) AS [mta_tax],
    CAST([tip_amount] AS [varchar]) AS [tip_amount],
    CAST([tolls_amount] AS [varchar]) AS [tolls_amount],
    CAST([improvement_
surcharge] AS [varchar]) AS [improvement_surcharge],
    CAST([total_amount] AS [varchar]) AS [total_amount],
    CAST([congestion_
surcharge] AS [varchar]) AS [congestion_surcharge]
INTO [NYTaxiSTG].[#Tripadf]
FROM [NYTaxiSTG].[Tripadf];
SELECT *
FROM PREDICT (MODEL = (SELECT [model] FROM aml_
models WHERE [ID] = 'synapsewrkspac-yellow_tripdataml-
20210927014551-Best:1'),
              DATA = [NYTaxiSTG].[#Tripadf],
              RUNTIME = ONNX) WITH ([variable1] [real])
END
GO
EXEC aml_model_procedure
```

You can refer to *Figure 6.22* to check the output of the stored procedure:

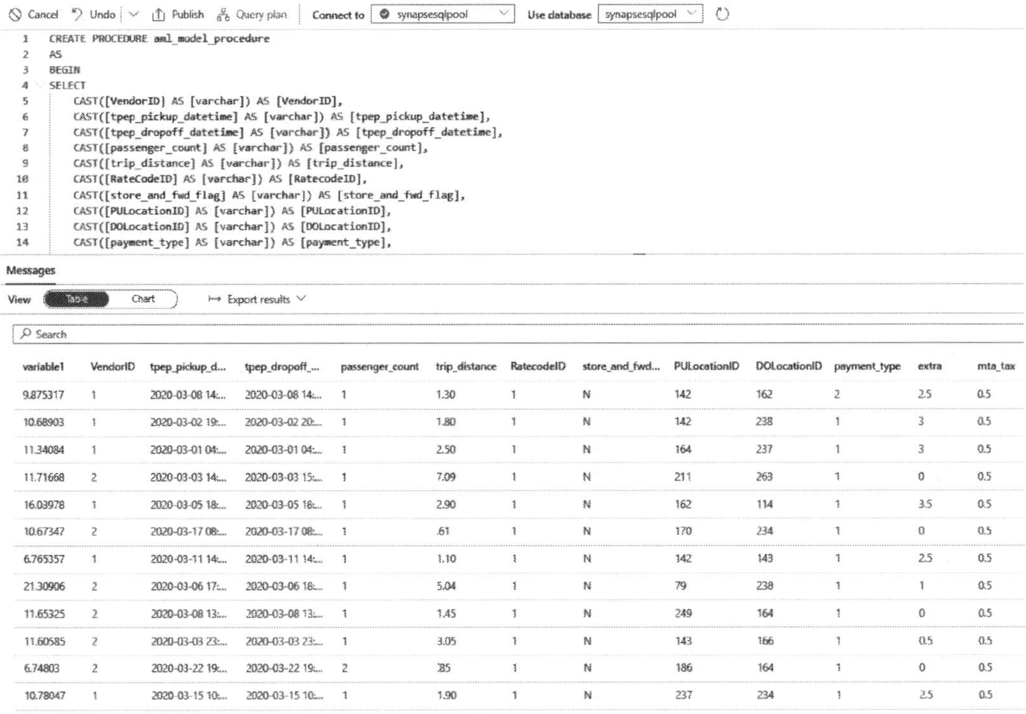

Cancel | Undo | Publish | Query plan | Connect to synapsesqlpool | Use database synapsesqlpool

```
CREATE PROCEDURE aml_model_procedure
AS
BEGIN
SELECT
    CAST([VendorID] AS [varchar]) AS [VendorID],
    CAST([tpep_pickup_datetime] AS [varchar]) AS [tpep_pickup_datetime],
    CAST([tpep_dropoff_datetime] AS [varchar]) AS [tpep_dropoff_datetime],
    CAST([passenger_count] AS [varchar]) AS [passenger_count],
    CAST([trip_distance] AS [varchar]) AS [trip_distance],
    CAST([RateCodeID] AS [varchar]) AS [RatecodeID],
    CAST([store_and_fwd_flag] AS [varchar]) AS [store_and_fwd_flag],
    CAST([PULocationID] AS [varchar]) AS [PULocationID],
    CAST([DOLocationID] AS [varchar]) AS [DOLocationID],
    CAST([payment_type] AS [varchar]) AS [payment_type],
```

Messages

View Table Chart | Export results

Search

| variable1 | VendorID | tpep_pickup_d... | tpep_dropoff_... | passenger_count | trip_distance | RatecodeID | store_and_fwd... | PULocationID | DOLocationID | payment_type | extra | mta_tax |
|---|---|---|---|---|---|---|---|---|---|---|---|---|
| 9.875317 | 1 | 2020-03-08 14:... | 2020-03-08 14:... | 1 | 1.30 | 1 | N | 142 | 162 | 2 | 2.5 | 0.5 |
| 10.68903 | 1 | 2020-03-02 19:... | 2020-03-02 20:... | 1 | 1.80 | 1 | N | 142 | 238 | 1 | 3 | 0.5 |
| 11.34084 | 1 | 2020-03-01 04:... | 2020-03-01 04:... | 1 | 2.50 | 1 | N | 164 | 237 | 1 | 3 | 0.5 |
| 11.71668 | 2 | 2020-03-03 14:... | 2020-03-03 15:... | 1 | 7.09 | 1 | N | 211 | 263 | 1 | 0 | 0.5 |
| 16.03978 | 1 | 2020-03-05 18:... | 2020-03-05 18:... | 1 | 2.90 | 1 | N | 162 | 114 | 1 | 3.5 | 0.5 |
| 10.67347 | 2 | 2020-03-17 08:... | 2020-03-17 08:... | 1 | .61 | 1 | N | 170 | 234 | 1 | 0 | 0.5 |
| 6.765357 | 1 | 2020-03-11 14:... | 2020-03-11 14:... | 1 | 1.10 | 1 | N | 142 | 143 | 1 | 2.5 | 0.5 |
| 21.30906 | 2 | 2020-03-06 17:... | 2020-03-06 18:... | 1 | 5.04 | 1 | N | 79 | 238 | 1 | 1 | 0.5 |
| 11.65325 | 2 | 2020-03-08 13:... | 2020-03-08 13:... | 1 | 1.45 | 1 | N | 249 | 164 | 1 | 0 | 0.5 |
| 11.60585 | 2 | 2020-03-03 23:... | 2020-03-03 23:... | 1 | 3.05 | 1 | N | 143 | 166 | 1 | 0.5 | 0.5 |
| 6.74803 | 2 | 2020-03-22 19:... | 2020-03-22 19:... | 2 | .85 | 1 | N | 186 | 164 | 1 | 0 | 0.5 |
| 10.78047 | 1 | 2020-03-15 10:... | 2020-03-15 10:... | 1 | 1.90 | 1 | N | 237 | 234 | 1 | 2.5 | 0.5 |

Figure 6.22 – Running the stored procedure

## How it works...

Let's understand what we have done so far and how this works. The SQL dedicated pool has the capability to run and score with the existing machine learning model with a historical dataset. You can predict and score with familiar T-SQL scripts and call the model with the script. You saw how we can create a stored procedure and define a table output for scoring using the existing machine learning model.

You can refer to the following architecture to understand how exactly the overall recipe works and what we have done. However, this functionality is currently not supported in SQL serverless pool:

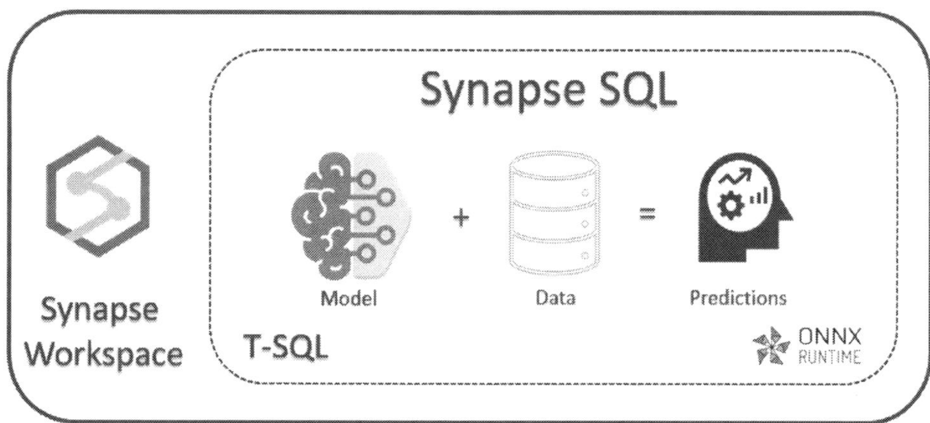


Figure 6.23 – Model, score, and predict

# An overview of Spark MLlib and Azure Synapse

Azure Synapse Analytics provides you with a single collaborative platform for data processing in memory, leveraging the power of Apache Spark. This is an in-memory distributed platform in which you have the option to run scalable machine learning algorithms.

MLlib and Spark ML are two highly distributed and scalable environments for machine learning libraries. Some of the default machine learning libraries that are included are TensorFlow, scikit-learn, PyTorch, and XGBoost.

SynapseML (previously MMLSpark) is the Microsoft machine learning library for Apache Spark, which includes many distributed frameworks for Spark and provides seamless integration between the **Microsoft Cognitive Toolkit** (**CNTK**) or OpenCV. This enables high throughput with extraordinary performance because of the Spark cluster running behind.

# Integrating AI and Cognitive Services

In this recipe, we will learn how we can integrate Azure Cognitive Services into the Synapse workspace.

With Azure Cognitive Services, we are now bringing together the power of AI to enrich our data with pre-trained AI models.

## Getting ready

For this recipe, you will need the following:

- You need to have a linked service created for Azure Cognitive Services with the Synapse workspace.
- Either Anomaly Detector or Text Analytics Azure resources should be created.
- Key Vault configuration and a secrets access policy should be defined.

## How to do it...

Let's go through the step-by-step process of integrating Cognitive Services with the Synapse workspace:

1. Create a new Anomaly Detector resource, which we will be leveraging within the Synapse workspace:

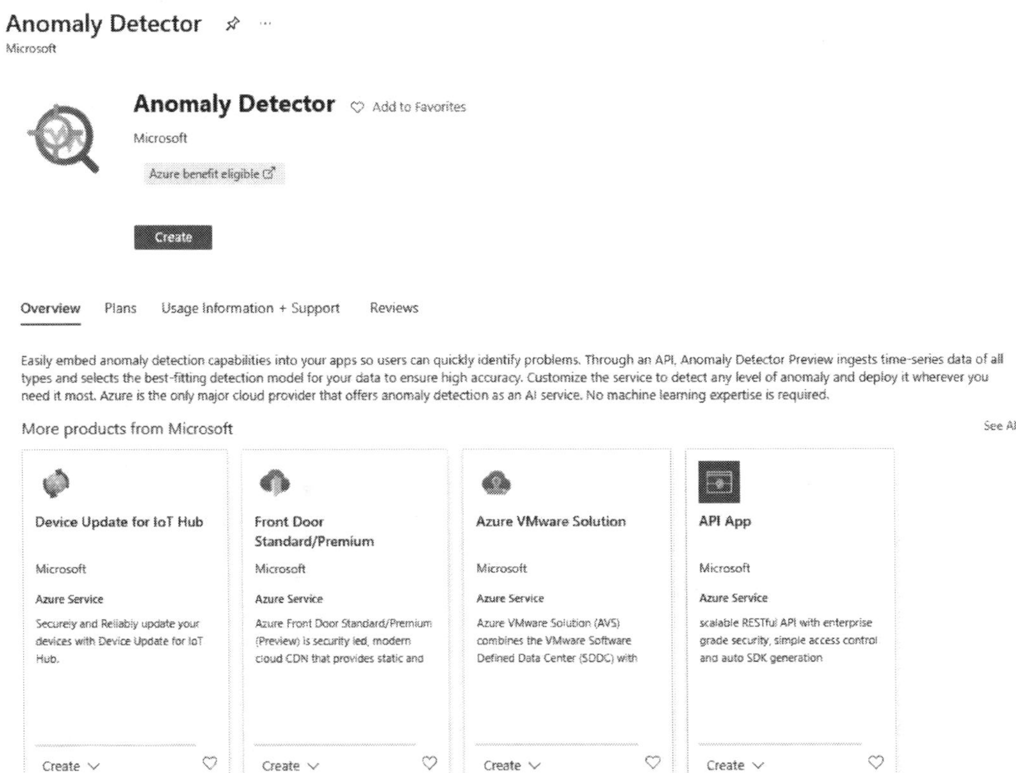


Figure 6.24 – Create Anomaly Detector

2. Create a new Key Vault instance and add the access policy so that you can grant access to the Azure Synapse workspace under **Principal**, as shown in *Figure 6.25*:

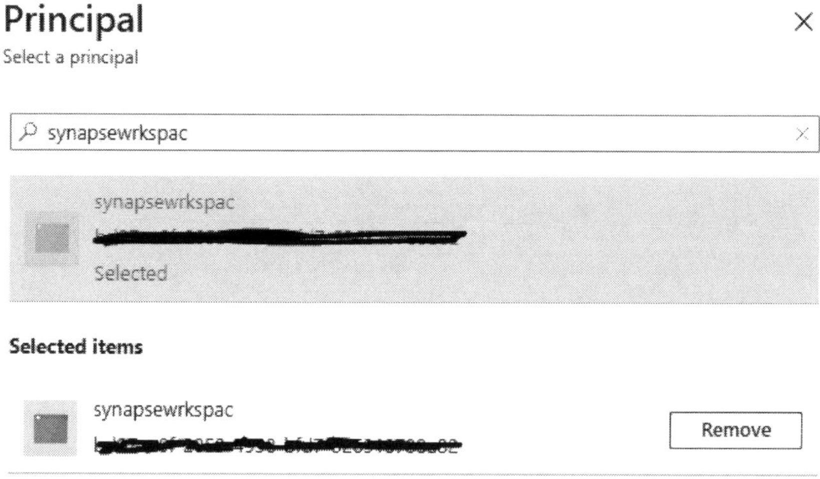


Figure 6.25 – The Key Vault access policy

3. Create a new secret under Key Vault from the Anomaly Detector endpoint keys and keep the secret name handy for future reference, as shown in *Figure 6.26*:

Dashboard > synapsebookkeyv > synapseresource > synapsebookkeyv >

Create a secret ...

Upload options Manual

Name * synapsebooksecret

Value * ••••••••••••••••••••••••••••••••

Content type (optional)

Set activation date

Set expiration date

Enabled Yes No

Tags 0 tags

Figure 6.26 – A Key Vault secret

4. Create a new linked service for Key Vault in the Synapse Analytics workspace, and specify the same Key Vault name that we created in the previous steps, as shown in *Figure 6.27*:

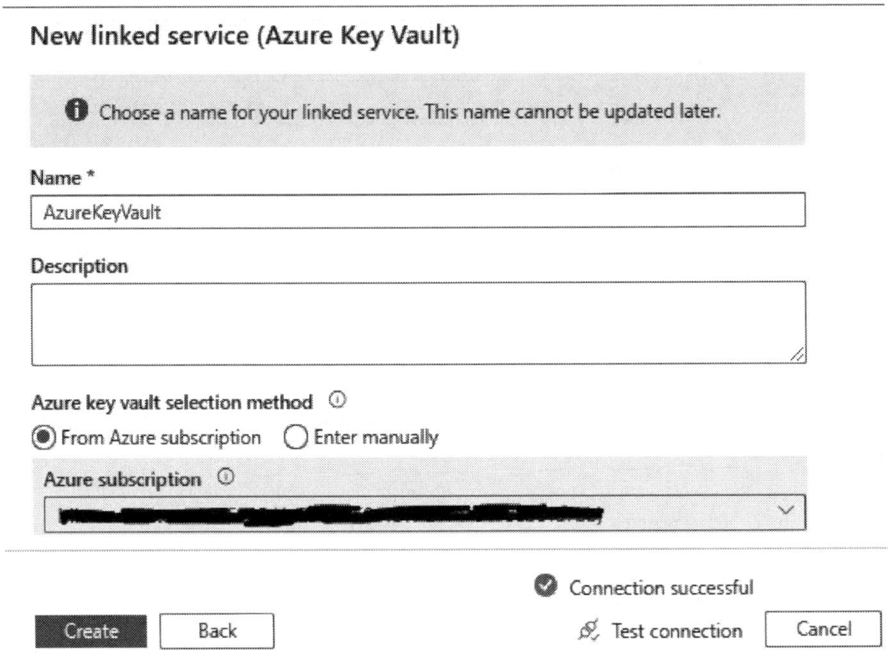

New linked service (Azure Key Vault)

Choose a name for your linked service. This name cannot be updated later.

Name *

AzureKeyVault

Description

Azure key vault selection method

From Azure subscription  Enter manually

Azure subscription

Connection successful

Create  Back  Test connection  Cancel

Figure 6.27 – The Key Vault linked service

5. Create a new linked service for Cognitive Services in the Synapse Analytics workspace; select the existing Cognitive service, **Azure Key Vault** (**AKV**), which we created earlier, and the name of the secret, as shown in *Figure 6.28*:

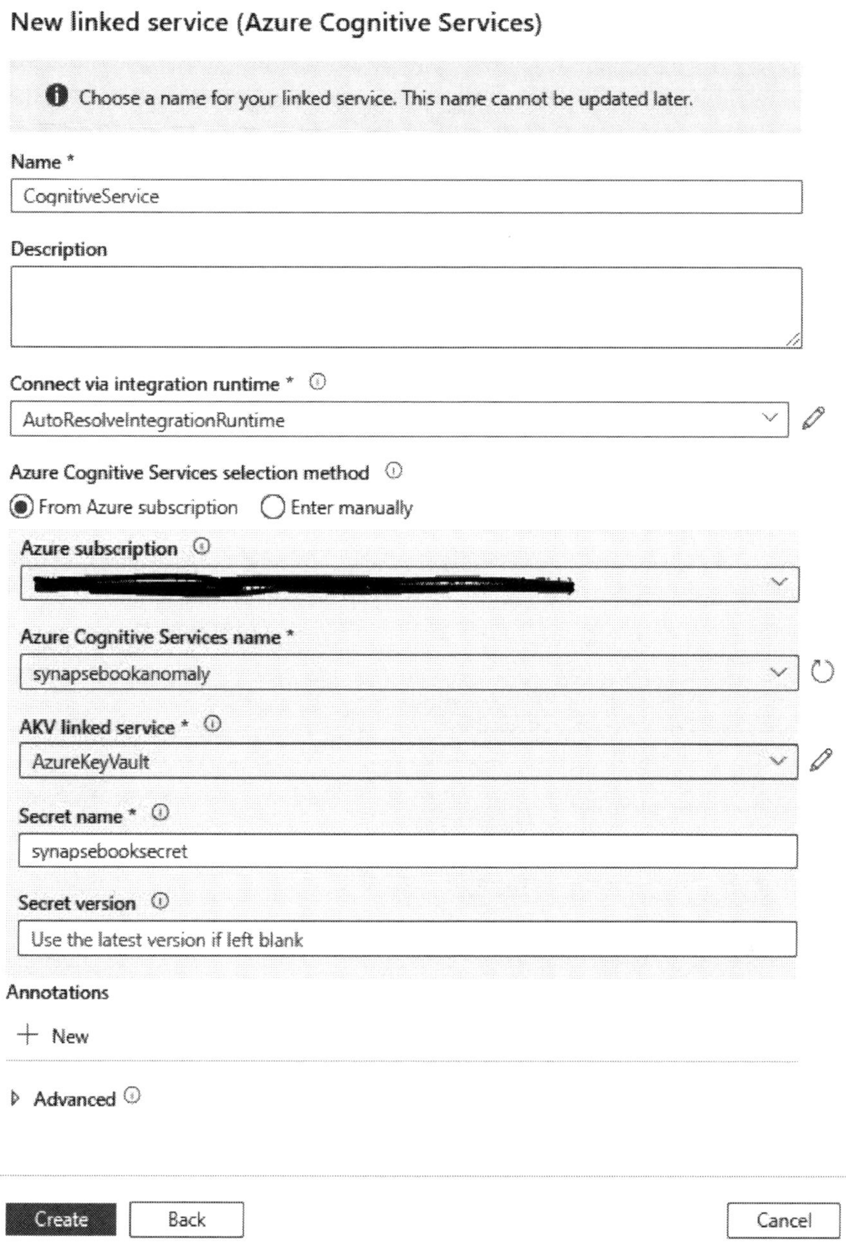

New linked service (Azure Cognitive Services)

Choose a name for your linked service. This name cannot be updated later.

Name *

CognitiveService

Description

Connect via integration runtime *

AutoResolveIntegrationRuntime

Azure Cognitive Services selection method

From Azure subscription   Enter manually

Azure subscription

Azure Cognitive Services name *

synapsebookanomaly

AKV linked service *

AzureKeyVault

Secret name *

synapsebooksecret

Secret version

Use the latest version if left blank

Annotations

+ New

Advanced

Create   Back   Cancel

Figure 6.28 – The Cognitive linked service

## How it works...

Let's understand how we will leverage the Anomaly Detector Cognitive Service on the Spark pool table to predict with the model. Azure Cognitive Services is a cloud-based service for the REST API that will help you to build various cognitive intelligence.

Here, we are leveraging the existing Cognitive Service, which we created in the *How to do it...* section.

You need to create a machine learning prediction model on the Spark table that you want to run the anomaly detection:

1. Right-click and select the Spark table so that you can run the predict with the model, as shown in *Figure 6.29*:

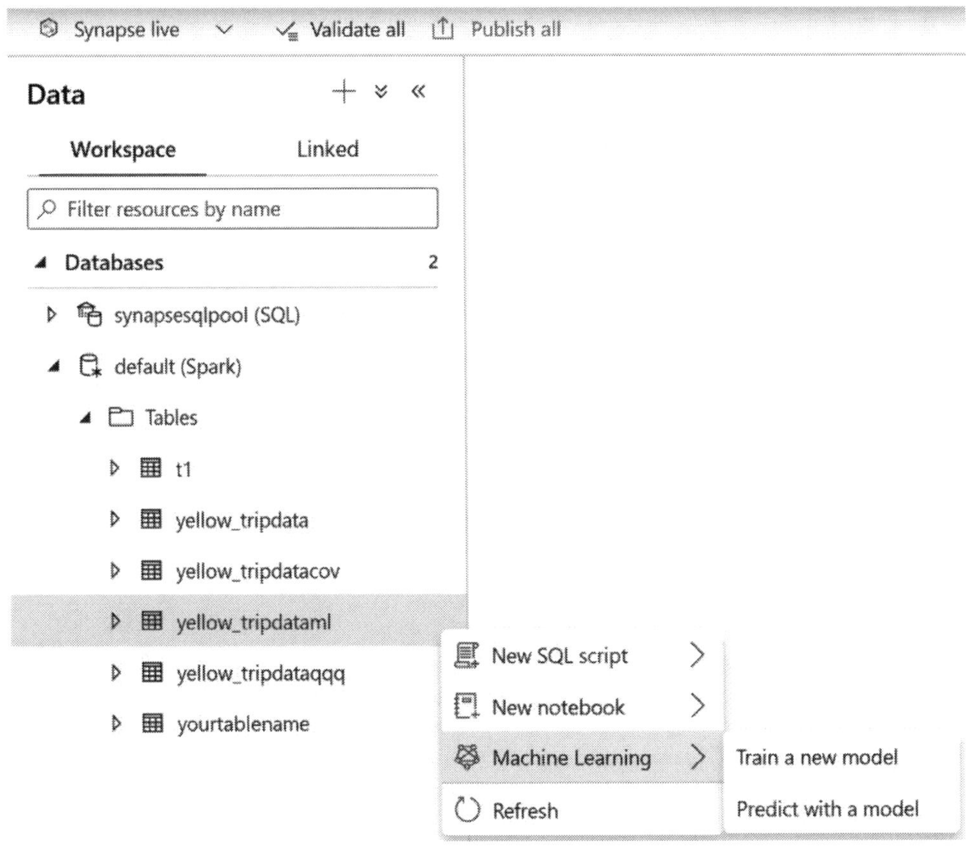


Figure 6.29 – Select the Spark table to predict with the model

2. Select **Anomaly Detector**, which will allow you to enrich the selected dataset with the pre-trained Azure Cognitive Services, as shown in *Figure 6.30*:

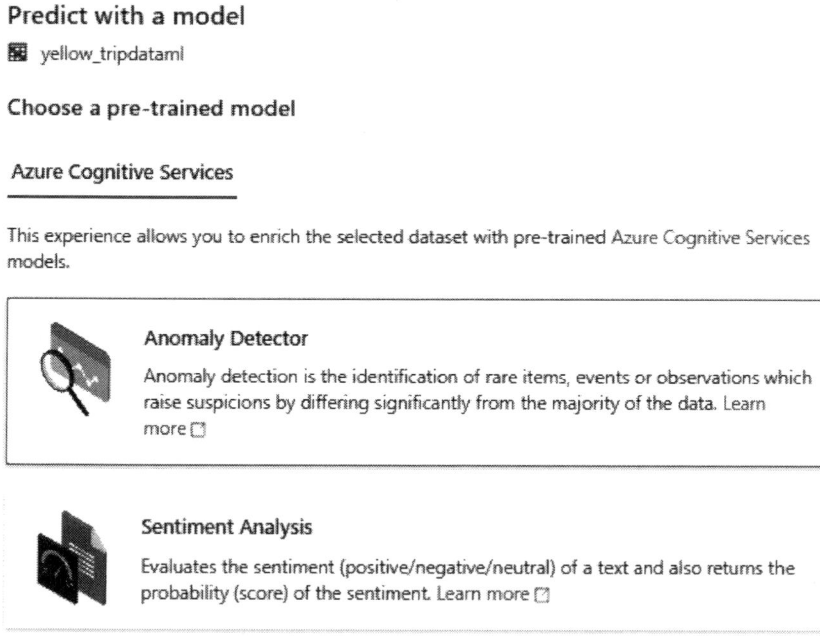

**Predict with a model**

yellow_tripdataml

**Choose a pre-trained model**

Azure Cognitive Services

This experience allows you to enrich the selected dataset with pre-trained Azure Cognitive Services models.

**Anomaly Detector**

Anomaly detection is the identification of rare items, events or observations which raise suspicions by differing significantly from the majority of the data. Learn more

**Sentiment Analysis**

Evaluates the sentiment (positive/negative/neutral) of a text and also returns the probability (score) of the sentiment. Learn more

Figure 6.30 – Predict with Anomaly Detector

This will eventually connect with the existing Cognitive Service that we created in the *Getting ready* section in this recipe:

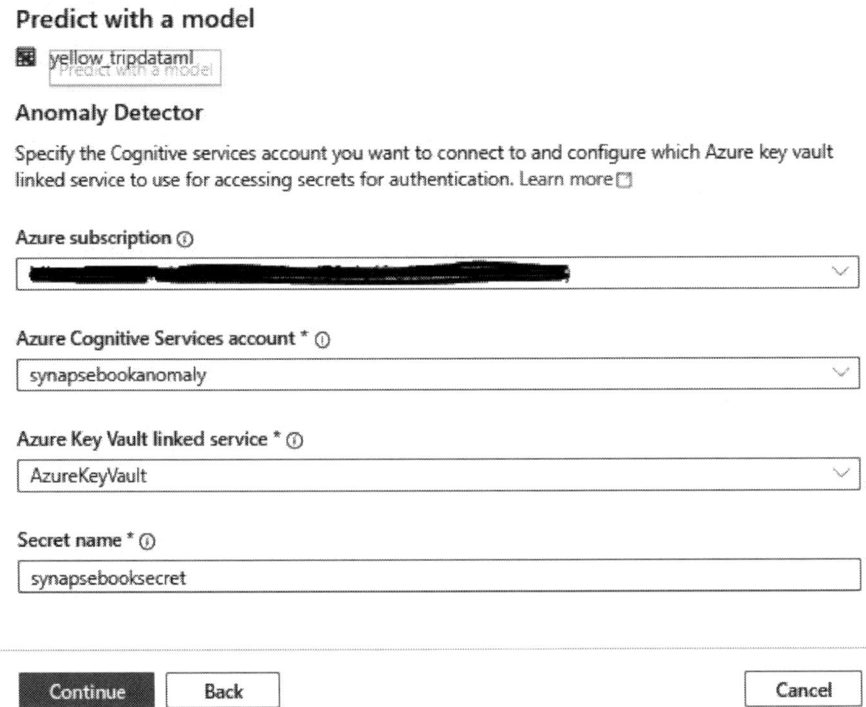


Figure 6.31 – The Anomaly Detector parameters

This will eventually generate the code for calling the Anomaly Detector pre-trained model, which you can run and modify as required:

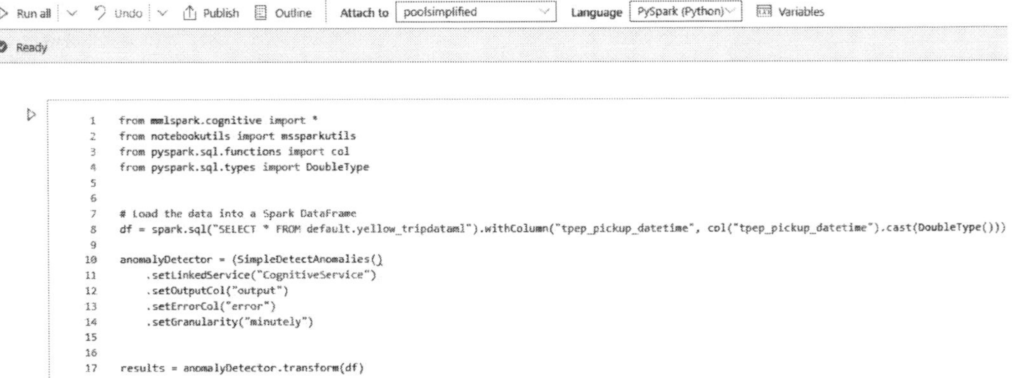


Figure 6.32 – The Anomaly Detector code generated

# 7
# Visualizing and Reporting Petabytes of Data

In this chapter, we will cover how to visualize data and create reports using **Power BI**. You will be learning how to develop reports within a **Synapse workspace** and link Power BI to an existing dataset.

You will also learn something very interesting – how to integrate existing Power BI reports into the Synapse workspace and visualize the data in the same place without any difficulty.

Apart from this, you will also learn performance best practices for developing your Power BI reports with a very large dataset.

We will be covering the following recipes:

- Combining Power BI and a serverless  SQL pool
- Working on a composite model
- Using materialized views to improve performance

# Combining Power BI and aserverless SQL pool

Azure Synapse Studio gives you the flexibility to connect to the Power BI workspace and provides you with seamless integration between data sources and reports. You can work within the Synapse workspace to create Power BI reports independently in the Power BI service.

You have the flexibility to combine multiple data sources to create a single Power BI dataset. This helps you to analyze disparate data sources and create insight by referring to a single data model. We refer to this as a **Power BI linked service**.

## Getting ready

We will be using the same Synapse workspace that we have used throughout the book for this recipe.

The prerequisites for this recipe are as follows:

- Make sure you have Power BI Desktop downloaded and installed. You can download it from this link: `https://www.microsoft.com/en-in/download/details.aspx?id=58494`.
- You need to have a Power BI Pro license to develop reports and get all the benefits of Power BI features.
- We will be using the `BoxOfficeMojo` dataset.

## How to do it...

Let's begin this recipe and see how we can bring the Power BI service into the Synapse workspace and leverage it for creating reports.

You need to link the Power BI service to the existing Synapse workspace:

1. Go to the **Home** tab on the Synapse Studio portal and click the **Visualize** tab to create a Power BI linked service, as shown in *Figure 7.1*:

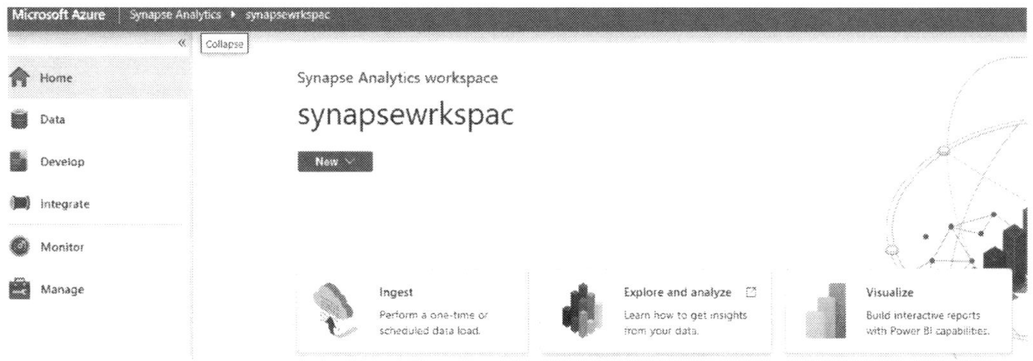


Figure 7.1 – Create a Power BI linked service

2. You can now get the option blade to provide the details that are required to create the Power BI linked service for the Synapse workspace. Please fill in all the details, as shown in *Figure 7.2*. You need to sign in to the Power BI account to get the Power BI **Tenant** and **Workspace name** details:

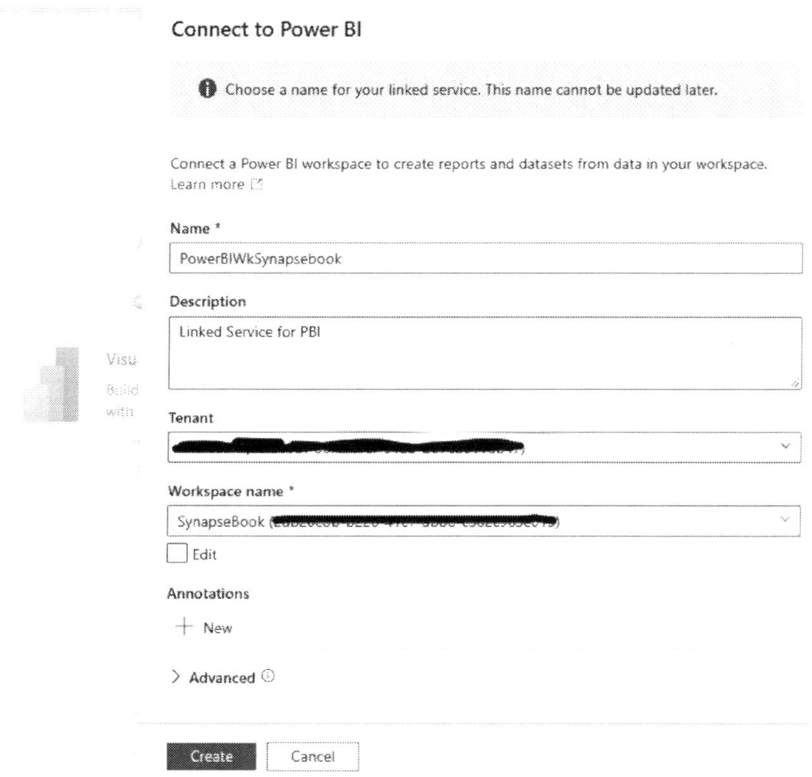


Figure 7.2 – Choose the name of your linked service

3. Go to the **Manage** tab in Synapse Studio and publish the Power BI linked service name `PowerBIWkSynapsebook` under **Linked services**, as shown in *Figure 7.3*:

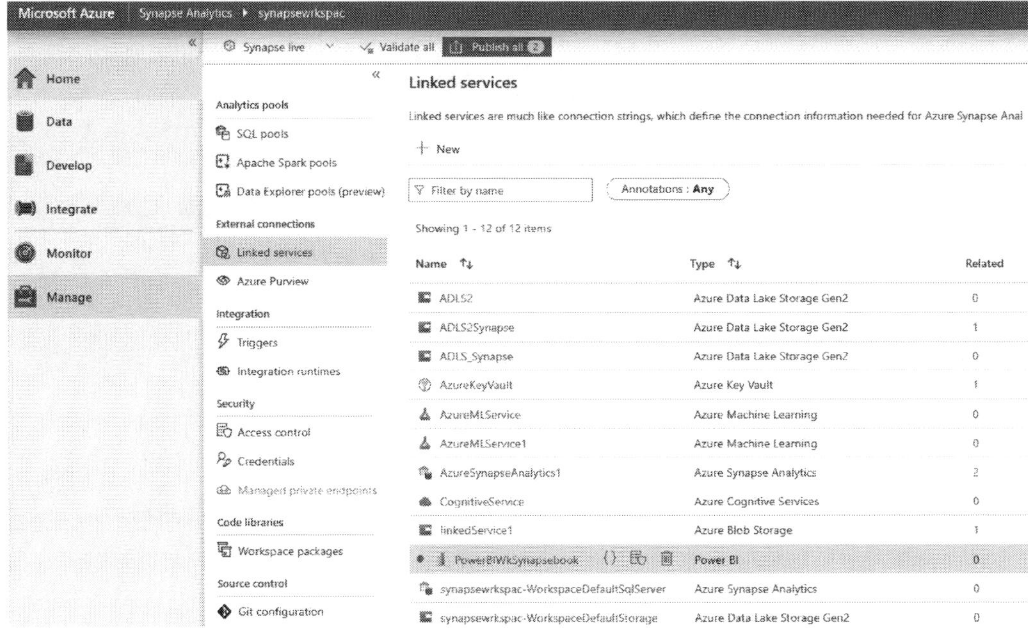


Figure 7.3 – Manage the linked service

4. Finally, you need to click on the **Publish all** button at the top to publish the Power BI linked service, as shown in *Figure 7.4*:

## Publish all

You are about to publish all pending changes to the live environment. Learn more

**Pending changes (2)**

| NAME | CHANGE | EXISTING |
|---|---|---|
| ∨ Linked services | | |
| PowerBIWkSynapsebook | (New) | - |
| > SQL script | | |

Publish Cancel

Figure 7.4 – Publishing the linked service

Now, how does it work?

## How it works...

The Power BI linked service will link to the Synapse workspace, which gives you the ability to work directly and access the existing Power BI reports within Synapse Studio.

Go to the **Develop** tab, where you will be able to see the **Power BI** folder, which contains the **PowerBIWkSynapsebook** Power BI workspace that we have created in this recipe, as shown in *Figure 7.5*:

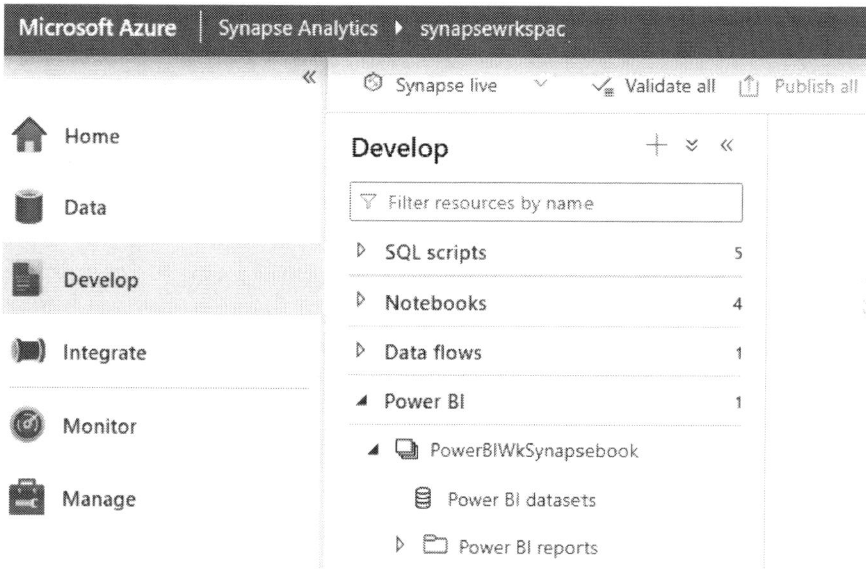


Figure 7.5 – Navigating to Power BI Workspace

You can see **Power BI datasets** and **Power BI reports**, and you can access the existing Power BI reports from the Synapse workspace directly.

In *Figure 7.6*, you can see that we have already an existing report name, **BoxofficeMojo**, in the Power BI workspace. You can access it in Synapse Studio. You can even edit the existing report and directly save it from Synapse Studio:

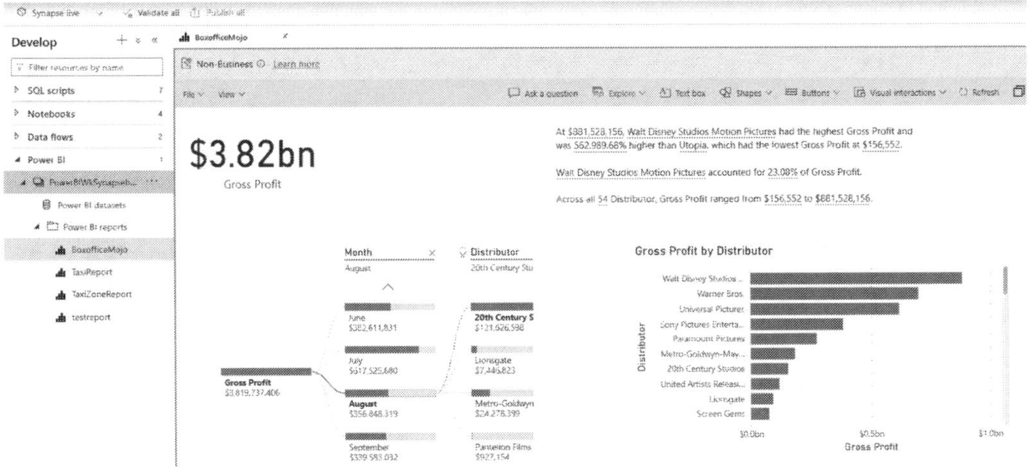


Figure 7.6 – Accessing the existing Power BI report

You can now even create a Power BI report using the SQL pool dataset and visualize it; you need to build the Power BI dataset and connect it to the Synapse pool.

Follow the following steps:

1. Click on **Power BI datasets** and then **New Power BI dataset**, as shown in *Figure 7.7*:

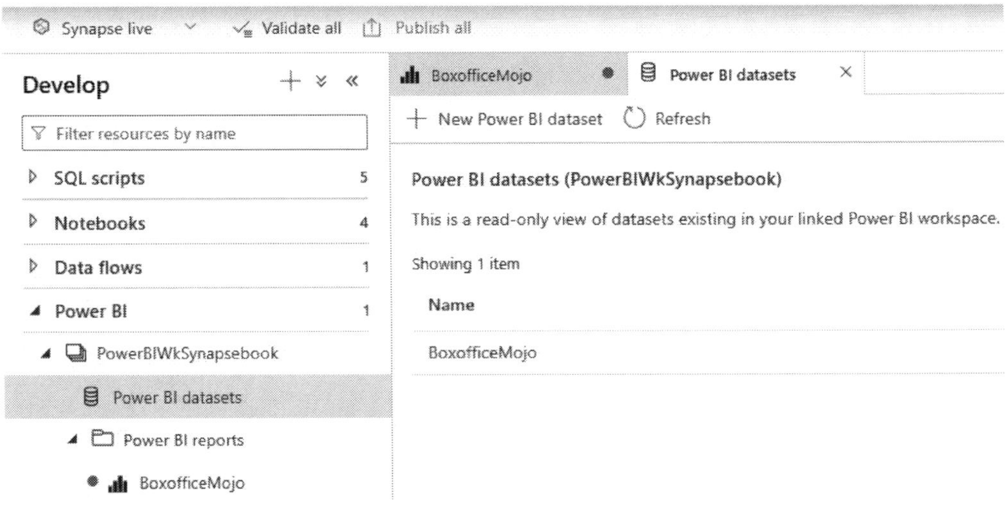


Figure 7.7 – Create a Power BI dataset

2. You need to select the data source. In our case, this will be **synapsesqlpool**. Click **Continue**:

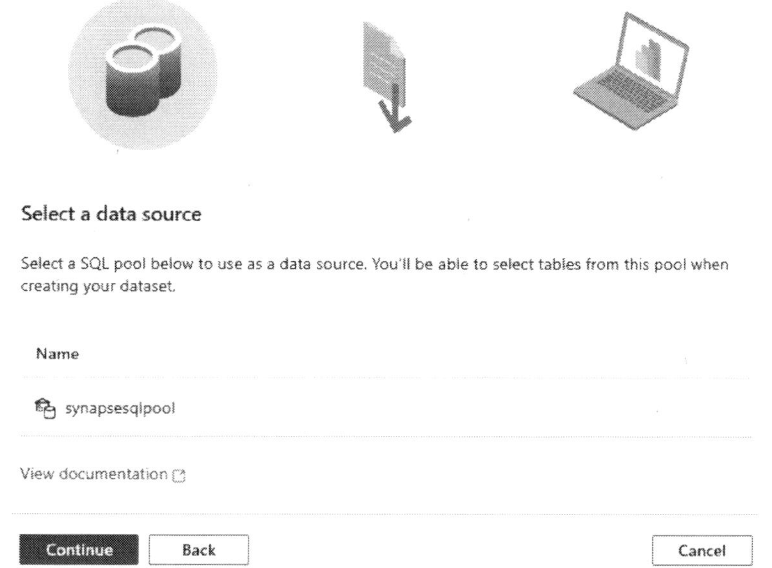


Figure 7.8 – Select the data source for creating the dataset

This will give you the option to download the `.pbids` (the Power BI data source) Power BI desktop file, as shown in *Figure 7.9*:

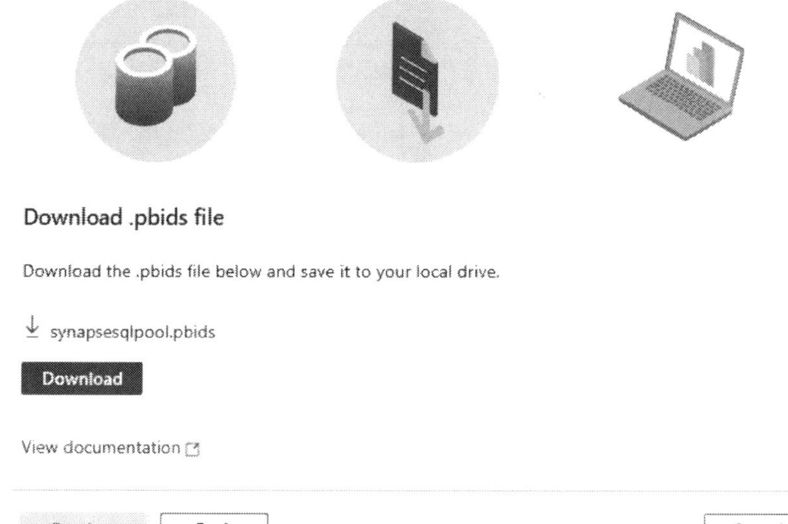


Figure 7.9 – Download the .pbids file

3. After you download the `.pbids` file, this will provide the connection information you need to authenticate the data source, as shown in *Figure 7.10*:

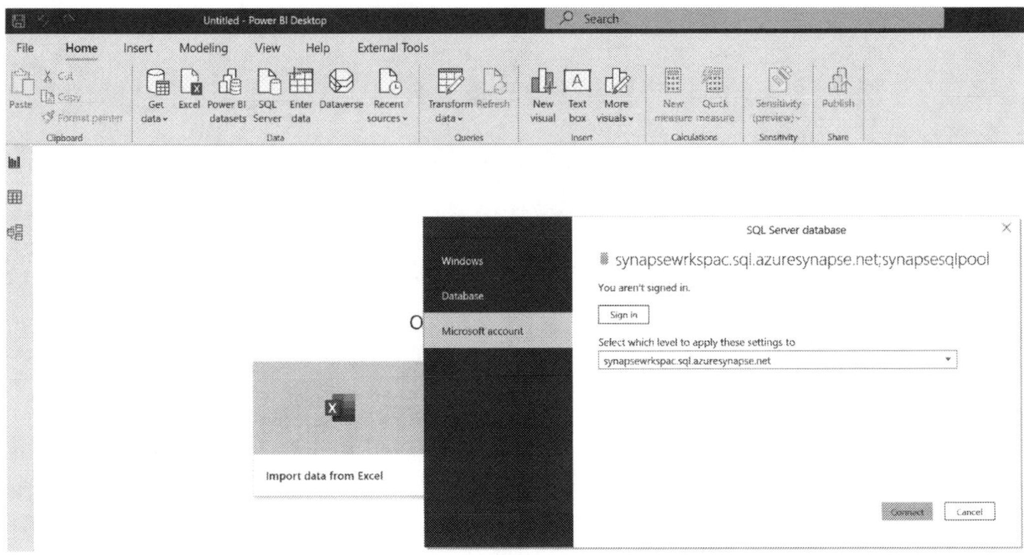


Figure 7.10 – Authenticate the data source connection

4. Once you have signed in, you can create Power BI reports using Power BI Desktop and deploy them to the same workspace, **Synapsebook**, in the Power BI service, as shown in *Figure 7.11*:

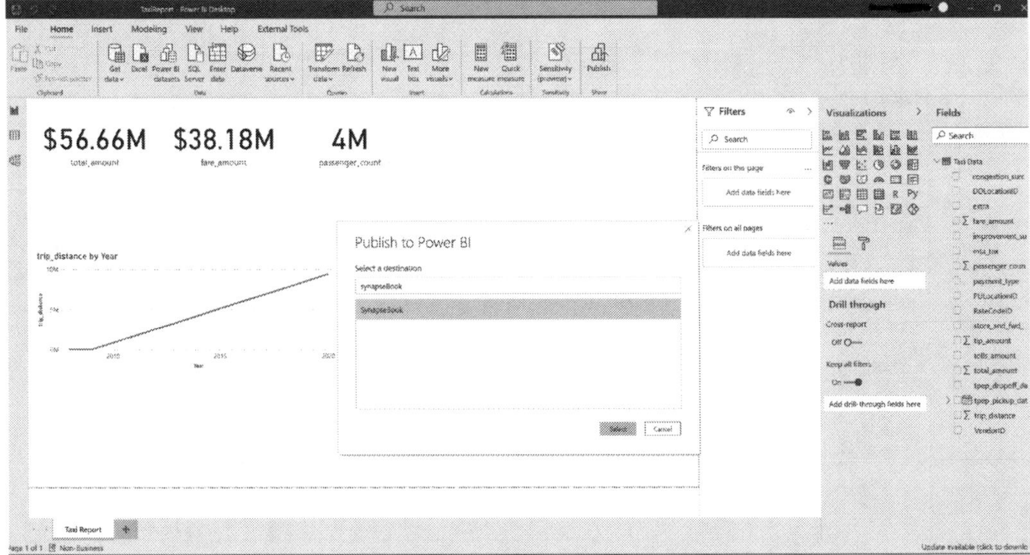


Figure 7.11 – Publish a report using Power BI Desktop

5. Finally, you should be able to access the same report from Synapse Studio, which is integrated as shown in *Figure 7.12*:

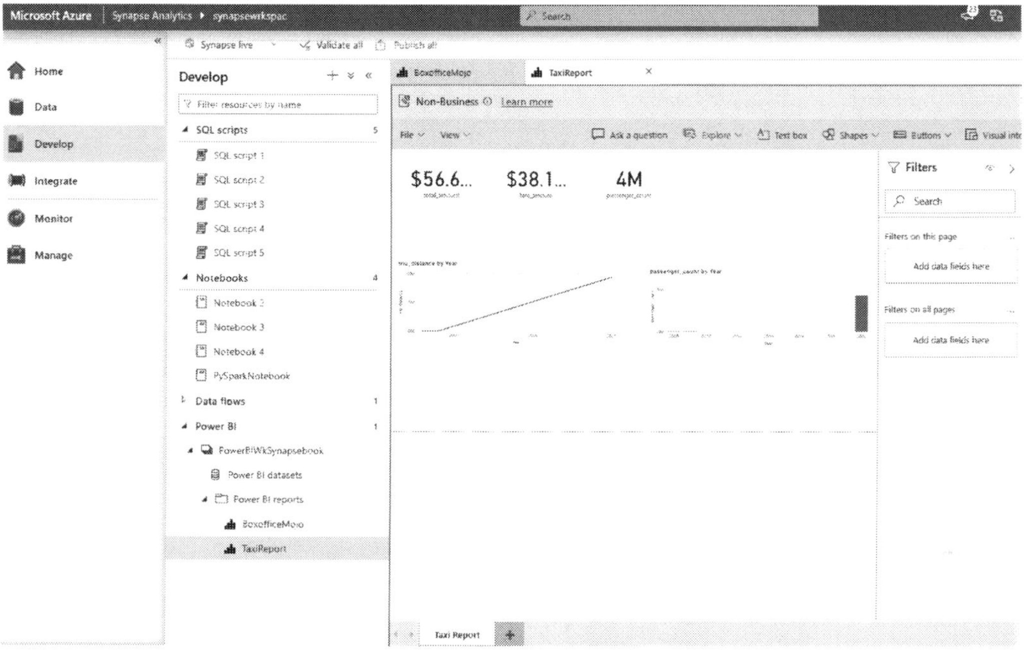

Figure 7.12 – Access the report from Synapse Studio

# Working on a composite model

Let's now learn about the new Power BI **composite model**. With this feature, you can now add data in two different storage modes – either to a direct query or to an import. Previously, using direct query in Power BI did not allow you to add another data source to the model.

In the enterprise scenario, the data comes from multiple sources, and you will be dealing with very large datasets. With the help of composite models, you can combine large datasets and use the direct query method, as well as import data from small data sources. The advantage of this approach is that you can now handle the challenges of dealing with very large data models as well as any performance glitches.

For scenarios when you have very large data in Synapse and you also want to combine data from your local data source, you can connect Synapse data as a direct query and a local data source in import mode and join the datasets. The composite model even gives you the flexibility to do this at an entity level, which provides the most agility.

This is exactly what we will be doing in this recipe, and you will learn how to perform this using a composite model.

# Getting ready

- Make sure you have Power BI Desktop installed.
- Make sure you have access to the Azure Synapse SQL pool to access data.
- Make sure you have the Power BI gateway installed.

# How to do it...

Let's open a new Power BI Desktop and create a new report. We will be using both the DirectQuery method and Import mode for this recipe to build a composite model in Power BI.

Let's begin!

1. Open a new Power BI Desktop, connect to **synapsesqlpool**, and use DirectQuery as the connectivity mode to create the data model, as shown in *Figure 7.13*:

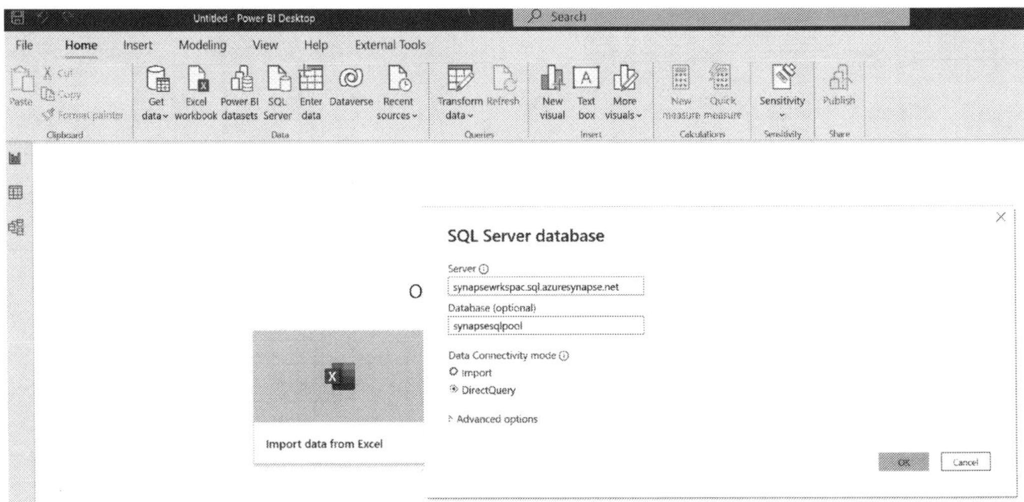


Figure 7.13 – The DirectQuery connectivity mode

2. Let's select one of the fact tables in **DirectQuery** mode so that we are not importing all of the data here:

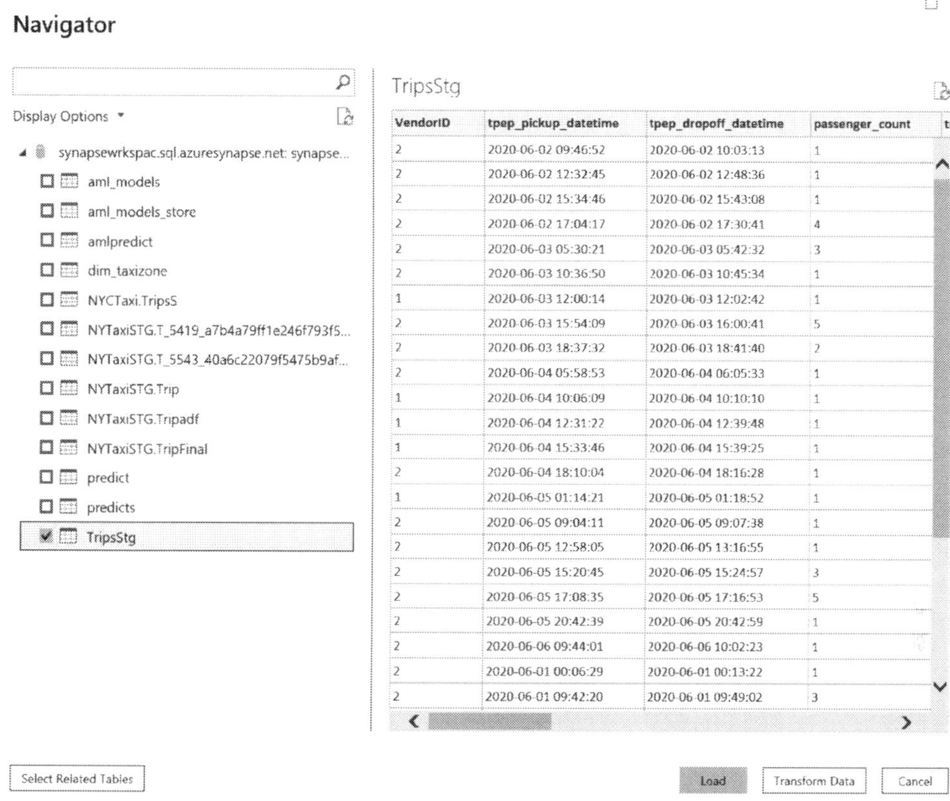


Figure 7.14 – Select the fact table to load as DirectQuery

3. Now, we will use the same **synapsesqlpool** database and connect the data in **Import** query mode, as shown in *Figure 7.15*:

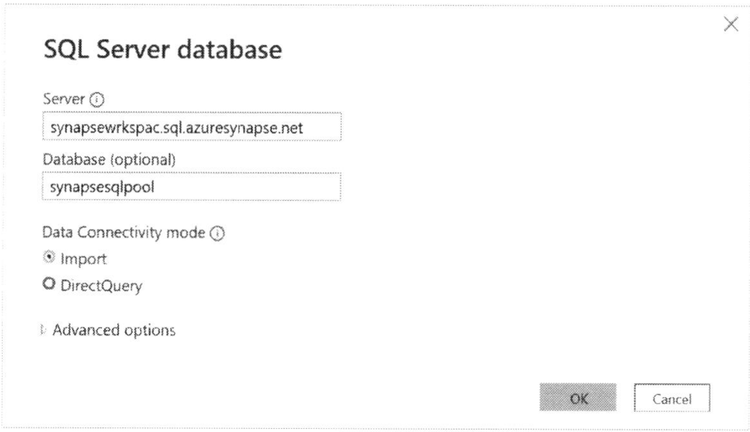


Figure 7.15 – The Import query connectivity mode

4. Now, we are going to import one of the dimension tables, since they don't contain too many records, and make the Power BI composite:

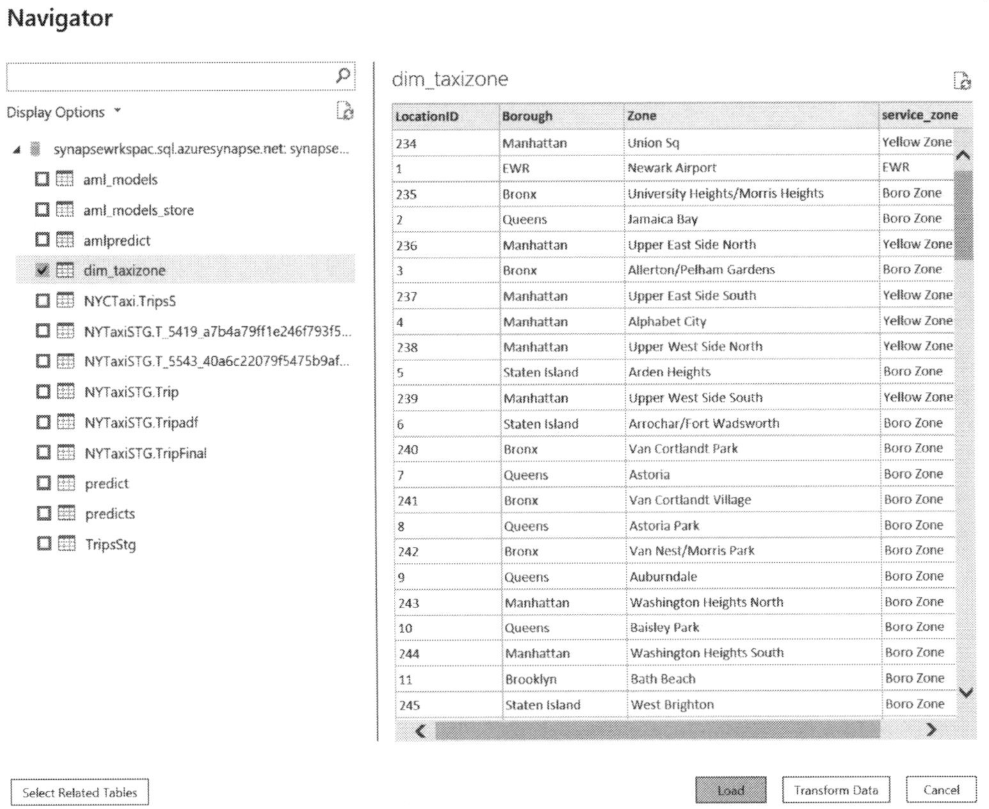


Figure 7.16 – Select a dimension table in Import query mode

5. You can now set the relationship between the two tables using **LocationId**, as shown in *Figure 7.17*:

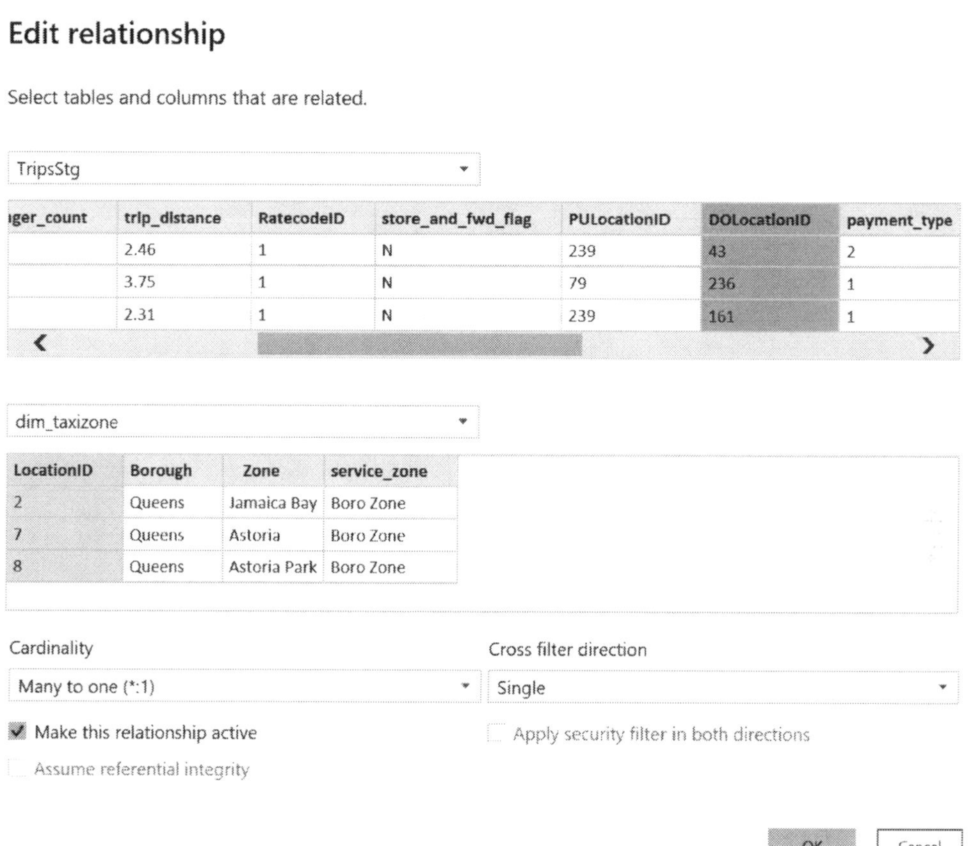


Figure 7.17 – Creating a Many to one relationship

6. This is what the final model will look like after creating a relationship between the two tables that have a composite model of data storage:

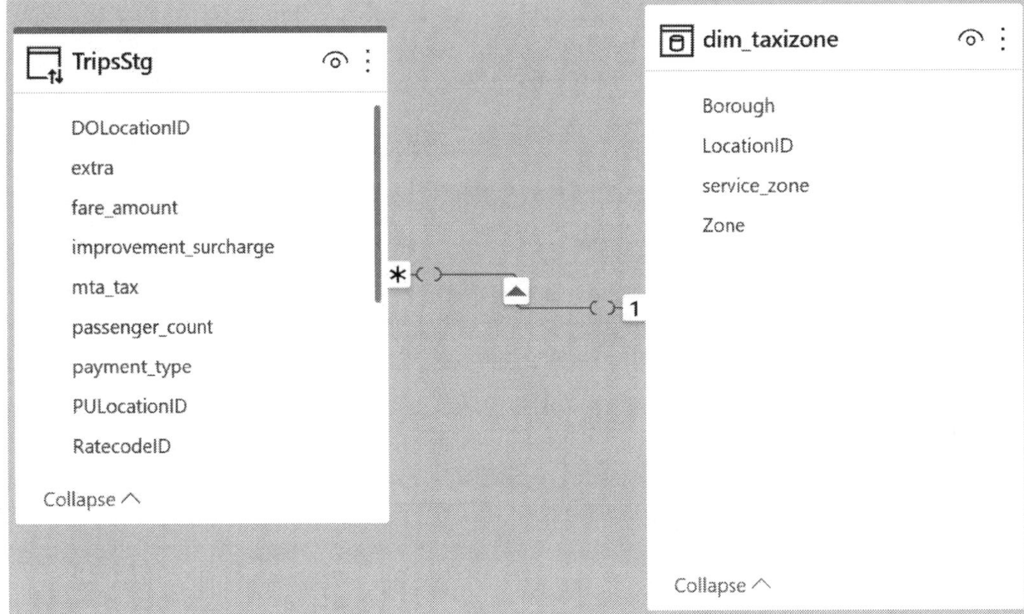


Figure 7.18 – A data model after creating a relationship

## How it works...

This is one of the most interesting features of Power BI when you are dealing with a very large dataset. When you try to visualize data in the Power BI model in the form of a report, as an end user, there won't be any difference in consuming the reports, as you now have the two different storage modes within the same data model, which are Import and DirectQuery.

You can see in *Figure 7.19* how **Storage Mode** is changed to **Mixed**; we can now filter the data based on the `dim_taxizone` dimension and filter records in the reports:

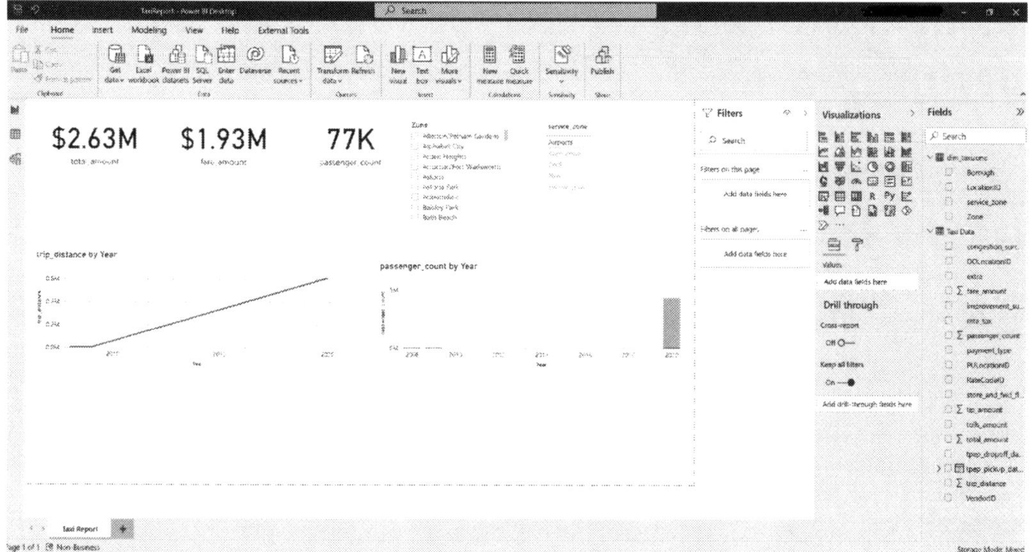


Figure 7.19 – Report creation in Mixed mode

After you deploy this report to the **Synapsebook** Power BI workspace name, you can access the report either from the Power BI service or the Synapse workspace, as shown in *Figure 7.20*:

Figure 7.20 – Accessing the report from the Synapse workspace

The takeaway from this recipe is that you can combine both the DirectQuery and Import storage modes of Power BI and build a single data model. This provides the best flexibility and performance for your Power BI reports.

# Using materialized views to improve performance

In this recipe, you will learn how materialized views can help in solving complex queries that are required for analytical purposes and how you can gain performance. You will learn how to create the materialized view, and when and why to use it in the SQL dedicated pool.

Materialized views are the best option in a large data warehouse, as the data is stored in a pre-processed format, unlike standard views. When you execute a query with a materialized view, it internally keeps processed data within the dedicated SQL pool, just like a physical SQL table.

## Getting ready

Before you begin, make sure you have the following:

- Make sure you have the dedicated SQL pool available in the Synapse workspace.
- You need to ensure that the table in which you are creating a materialized view has a qualifying column that can participate in the columnstore index. You can refer to this document for a list of datatypes that can participate in column store index creation: `https://docs.microsoft.com/en-us/sql/t-sql/statements/create-columnstore-index-transact-sql?view=sql-server-2017#LimitRest`.
- Ensure you have the right permissions to create the views in the SQL pool.

## How to do it...

Let's get back to the same Synapse workspace, and under the **Data** tab, expand the SQL pool database and let the work start on a new SQL query:

1. We will find the total gross amount by joining two tables, `dim_taxizone` and `TripsStg`, within the SQL pool, as shown in *Figure 7.21*.

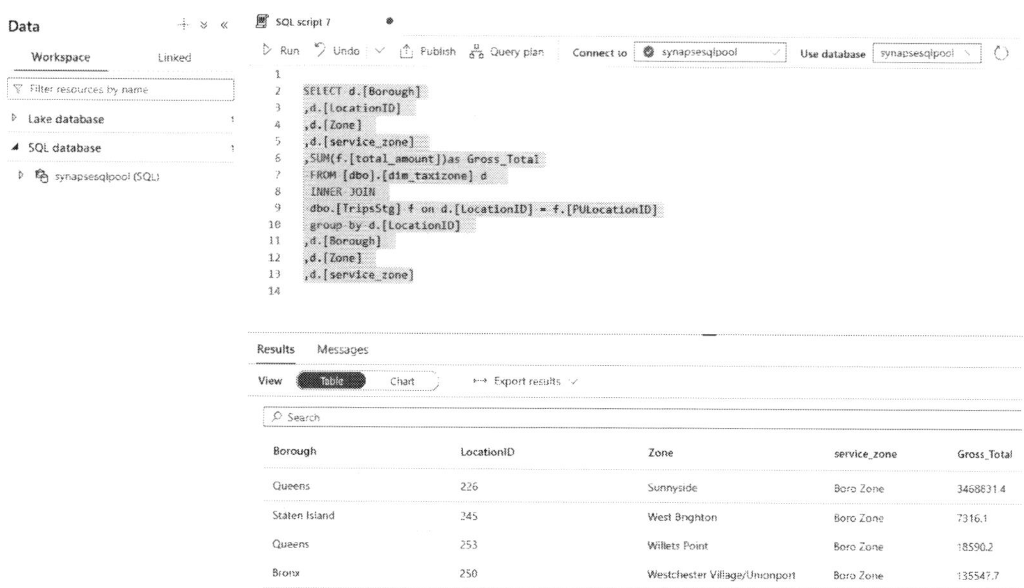

Figure 7.21 – A script to get a gross sum after joining the two tables

The SQL script can be written as follows:

```
SELECT d.[Borough]
,d.[LocationID]
,d.[Zone]
,d.[service_zone]
,SUM(f.[total_amount])as Gross_Total
 FROM [dbo].[dim_taxizone] d
 INNER JOIN
 dbo.[TripsStg] f on d.[LocationID] = f.[PULocationID]
 group by d.[LocationID]
,d.[Borough]
,d.[Zone]
,d.[service_zone]
```

2. You now need to convert the SQL query and create a materialized view to boost the performance and get the data in a pre-compute store within the dedicated SQL pool. Refer to the following script and *Figure 7.22*:

```
CREATE materialized view matViewGrossAmount WITH
(DISTRIBUTION=HASH([LocationID])) AS
SELECT d.[Borough]
,d.[LocationID]
,d.[Zone]
,d.[service_zone]
,SUM(f.[total_amount])as Gross_Total
 FROM [dbo].[dim_taxizone] d
 INNER JOIN
 dbo.[TripsStg] f on d.[LocationID] = f.[PULocationID]
 group by d.[LocationID]
,d.[Borough]
,d.[Zone]
,d.[service_zone]
```

This is shown in the following screenshot:

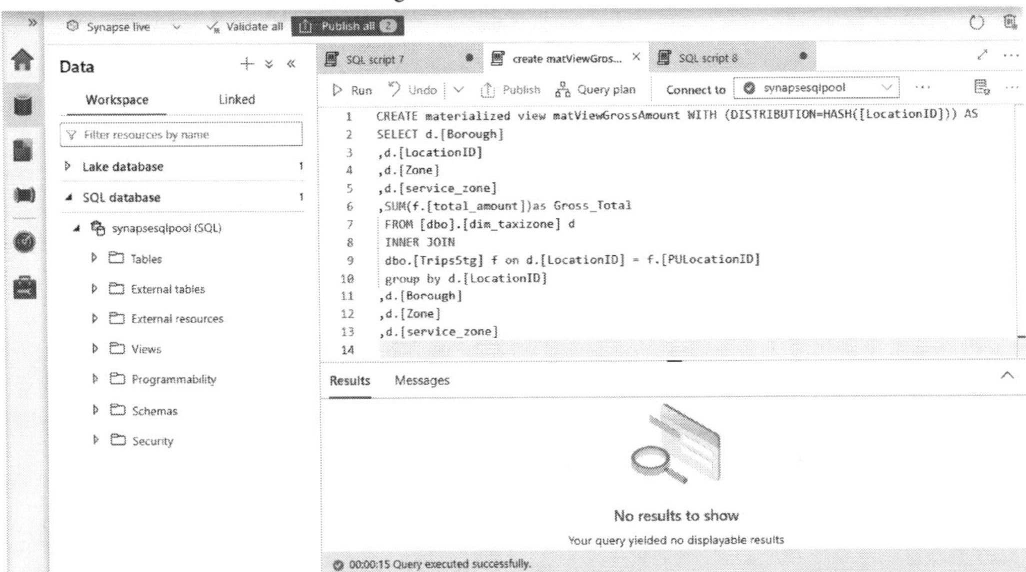


Figure 7.22 – Create a materialized view

3. You can now verify whether the view has been created successfully, as shown in *Figure 7.23*:

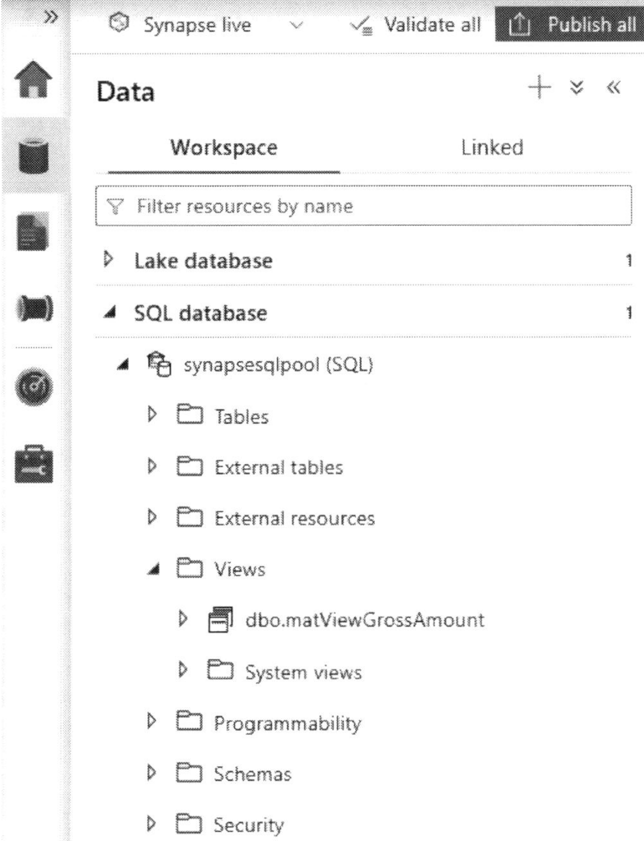


Figure 7.23 – The created materialized view

## How it works...

Let's understand what we have done so far and how this works. The materialized view will act as the physical table and reduce the execution time for complex queries where we have `JOINS` and are using aggregated functions.

The execution plan for the query will get optimized in the dedicated SQL pool and automatically use the best-optimized execution plan.

You can get the best out of the materialized view, as the data in the view is scalable and always available compared to a regular query, where you need to depend on the individual query execution plan.

You can create the Power BI report connecting to the materialized view and get rid of the complex query in the report, which will eventually improve the overall performance of the report.

If you refer to *Figure 7.24*, you can see the `matViewGrossAmount` materialized view as the physical object, which can be loaded to Power BI for further analysis:

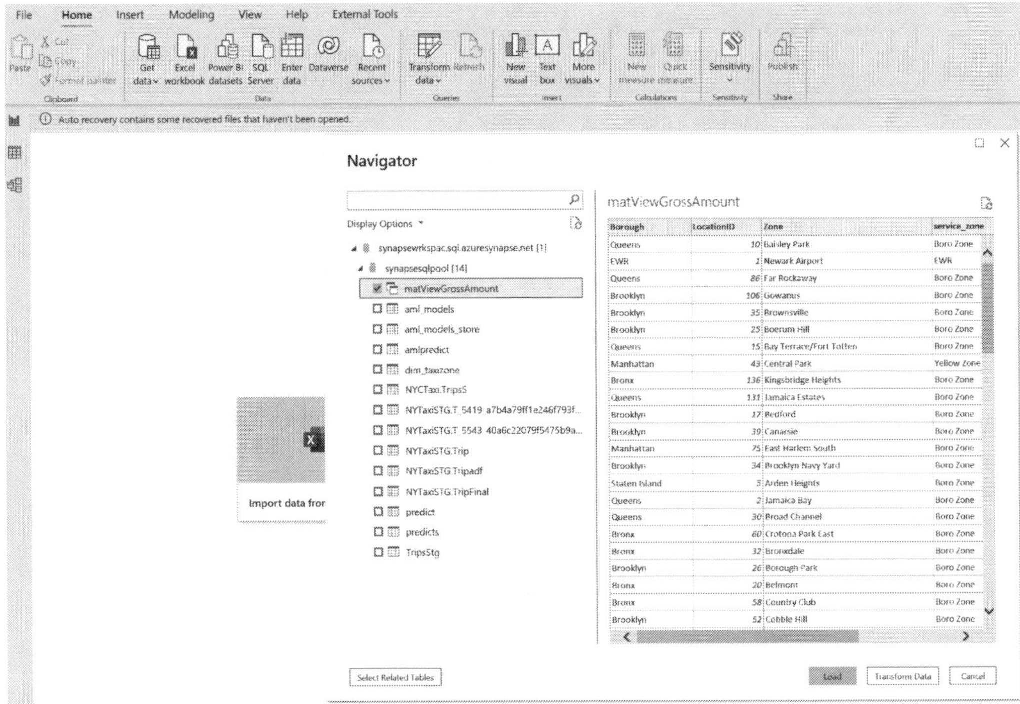


Figure 7.24 – Connected to the view in Power BI

You can create the visuals as required and get an insight within Power BI Desktop, as shown in *Figure 7.25*:

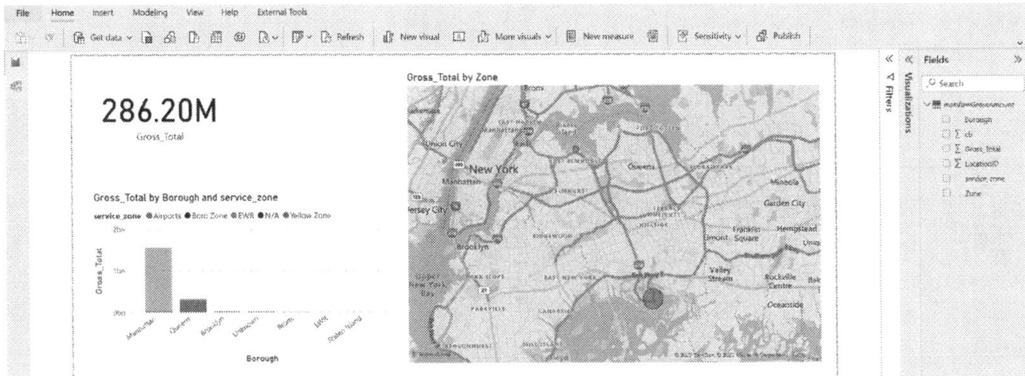


Figure 7.25 – Create a Power BI report

Finally, you can see this report in the Power BI workspace named **Synapsebook**; you can access the report either from the Power BI service or the Synapse workspace, as shown in *Figure 7.26*:

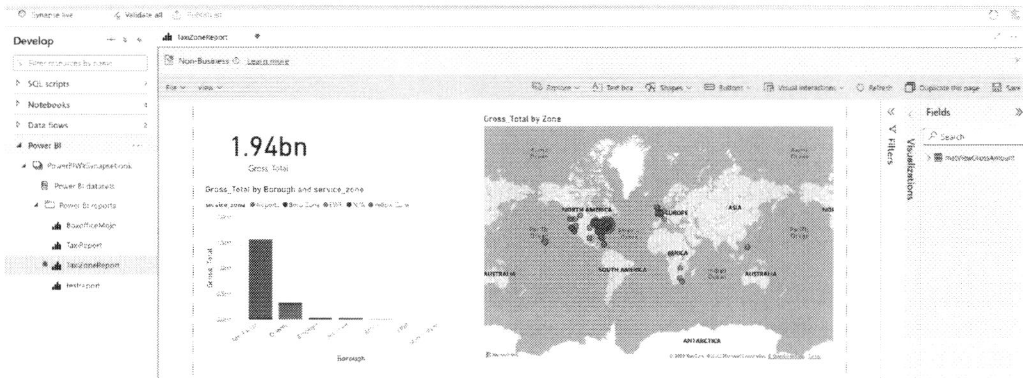


Figure 7.26 – Access the Power BI report from the Synapse workspace

The takeaway from this recipe is that the Synapse is a strong proposition for data storage, data processing, and data transformations. Power BI infuses data visualizations to Synapse for better insights and reporting.

# 8

# Data Cataloging and Governance

In this chapter, we will learn how to integrate **Azure Purview** and **Synapse**. We will be learning how to generate value out of data using metadata and cataloging. This is key to implementing data governance and security. As there are many elements associated with an **enterprise data warehouse** (**EDW**), it is important to understand how the two capabilities, accessing a data catalog and data classification, work when dealing with a very large data warehouse.

We will also learn how to configure and perform data discovery within Synapse Studio with the help of Azure Purview integration. With more than 200+ prebuilt classification, Azure Purview allows you to perform automated data classification. This will help you to integrate and perform data classification for a Synapse Analytics workspace.

> **Azure Purview**
>
> To learn more about Azure Purview, you can refer to the official documentation: `https://docs.microsoft.com/en-in/azure/purview/`.

We will cover the following recipes in this chapter:

- Configuring your Azure Purview account for Synapse SQL pool
- Scanning data using the Purview data catalog
- Enumerating resources within Synapse Studio

# Configuring your Azure Purview account for Synapse SQL pool

The Azure Purview Studio gives you the capability to register multiple data sources so that you can scan the data in the Purview Studio. We will learn how we can register an Azure Synapse workspace and connect to dedicated SQL pool. There are some key steps and configuration that you need to consider in order to register Azure Synapse as the data source within an Azure Purview account.

## Getting ready

We will be working in the Azure Purview Studio for this recipe to create the access and integration.

The prerequisites for this recipe are as follows:

- Make sure you have created an Azure Purview resource and account. Please refer to this link for detailed instructions: `https://docs.microsoft.com/en-us/azure/purview/create-catalog-portal`.
- Data source admin and data reader access are required in order to register a source and manage it in the Azure Purview Studio.
- You need to have an Azure Key Vault connection.
- Make sure you have granted the Azure Purview account access to Key Vault.

## How to do it...

Let's begin this recipe and see how to integrate an Azure Synapse workspace with the Azure Purview Studio:

1. Go to the Azure Purview Studio and under the **Management** tab, click on **Credentials** and then **Manage Key Vault connections**, as shown in *Figure 8.1*:

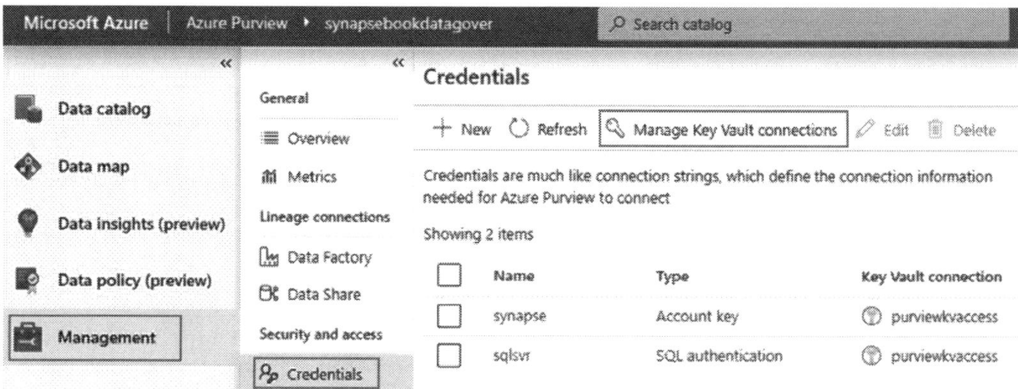


Figure 8.1 – Manage Key Vault connections under Azure Purview

2. You can now create a new Key Vault connection and name it `purviewkvaccess` to bring your existing key vault to Azure Purview in order to create credentials. Grant Purview managed identity access and copy the managed identity name (Azure Purview account), `synapsebookdatagover`, as shown in *Figure 8.2*:

New Key Vault

Name *

purviewkvaccess

Description

Enter description

Azure subscription

Key Vault name *

azurepuvkv

You must grant the Azure Purview managed identity access to your Azure Key Vault.
See less

See more details here
Managed identity name: **synapsebookdatagover**
Managed identity object ID:
Managed identity application ID:

Create Back Cancel

Figure 8.2 – Creating new Key Vault credentials

3. Go to Azure Key Vault and select the **azurepuvkv** key vault, which you associated while creating credentials in Azure Purview under **Access policies** | **+ Add Access Policy**, as shown in *Figure 8.3*:

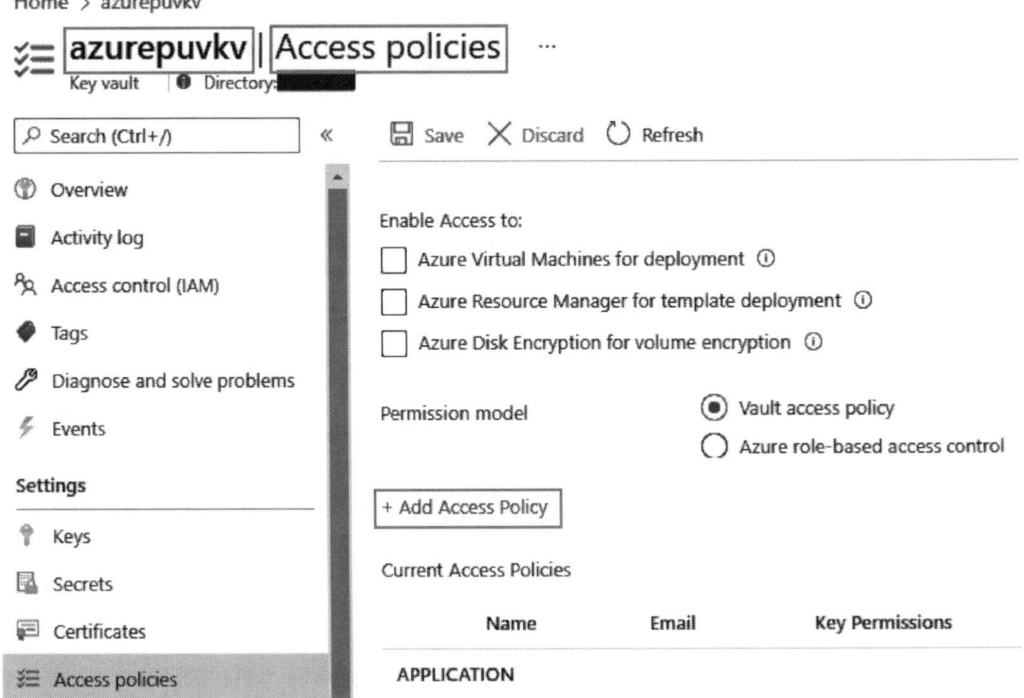


Figure 8.3 – Add Access Policy

4. Under **Add access policy**, select **Secret Management** for the **Configure from template** field and click **None selected** under **Select principal**. Search for the Azure Purview account named `synapsebookdatagover`, as shown in *Figure 8.4*:

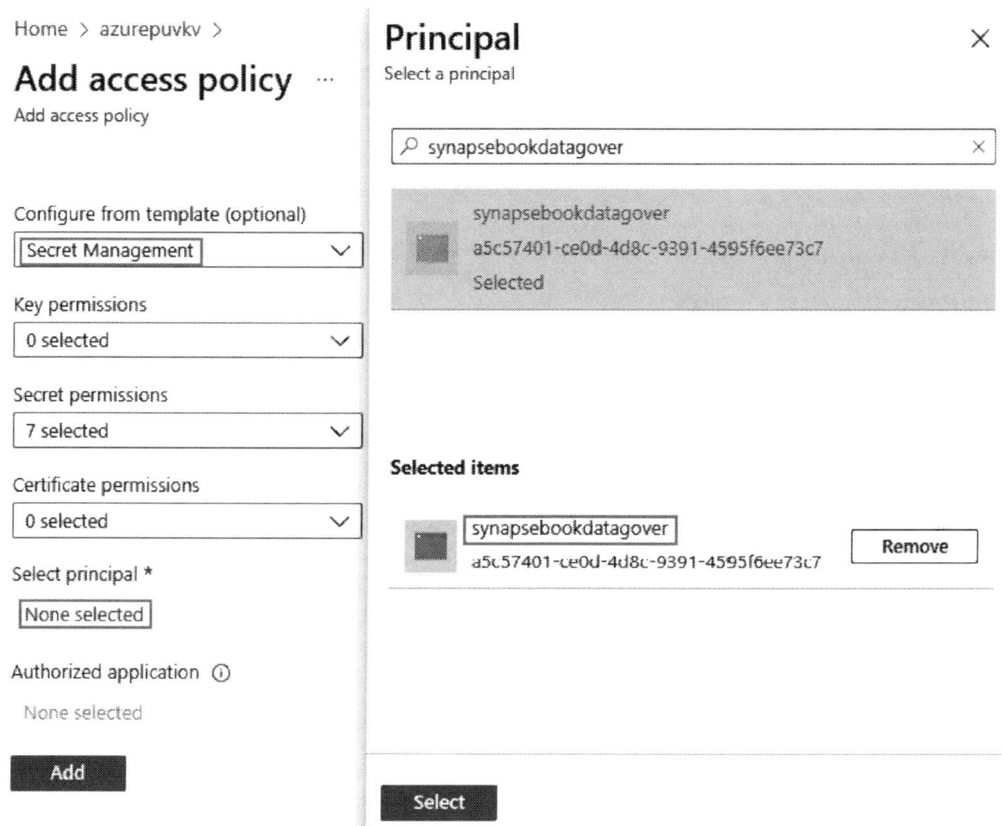


Figure 8.4 – Configuring an access policy service principal

5. Finally, create the new credentials using the existing Key Vault connection that we created in *step 2* with the name **purviewkvaccess**. Set **Authentication method** to **Account key**, and set the Key Vault name as **purviewkvaccess**, as shown in *Figure 8.5*:

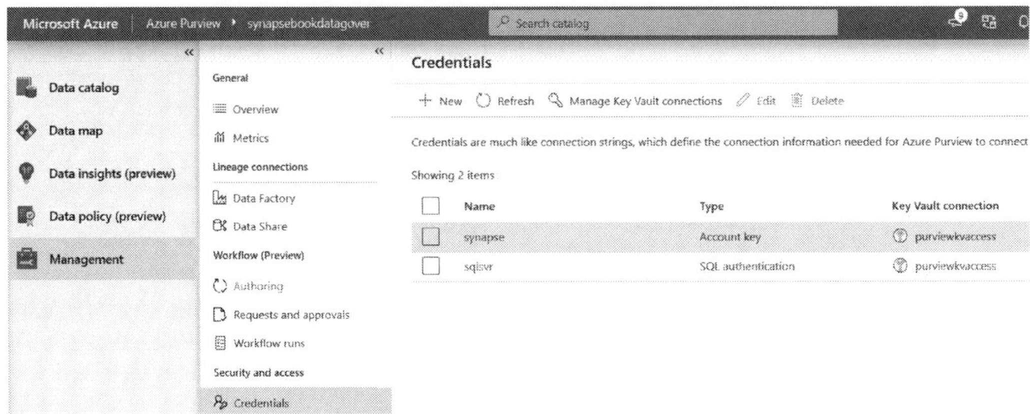


Figure 8.5 – Creating new credentials

## How it works...

Azure Purview allows you to register and access multiple data sources for data cataloging and governance. There are two different methods to set up authentication for multiple sources:

- With a service principal
- With a managed identity

Before you go ahead with creating any credentials, make sure you understand the data source and its type. Every data source will have its own networking and authentication method, which may differ for data sources such as Azure Synapse and Azure SQL Database.

If you check the **Credentials** tab under **Management**, you should be able to see the credentials `Type` and `Key Vault connection` for different types of data sources. You can see this in *Figure 8.6*:

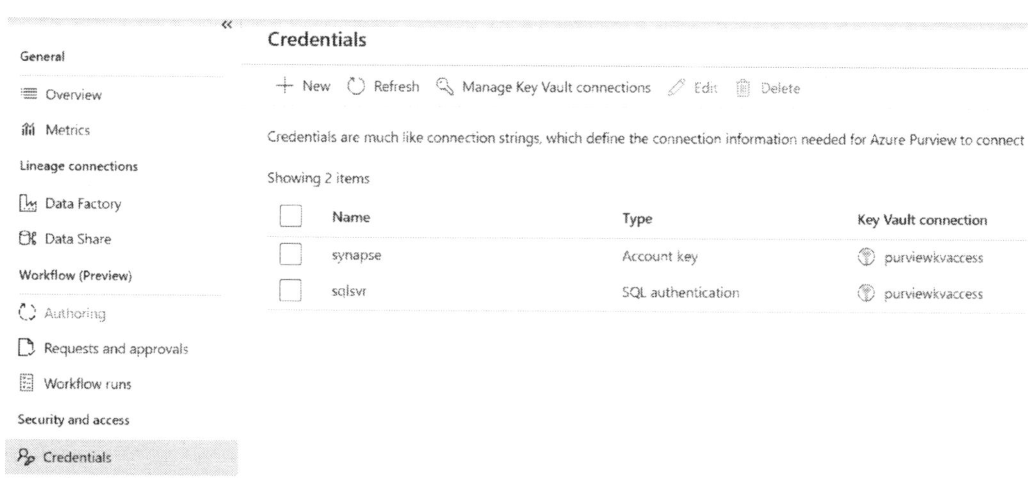


Figure 8.6 – Azure Purview credentials type

You can see there are two types of data sources, Azure Synapse and Azure SQL, and both have the **purviewkvaccess** Key Vault connection. However, the authentication type for Azure Synapse is **Account key**, and **SQL authentication** is the type for Azure SQL.

# Scanning data using the Purview data catalog

Let's now learn how to scan data inside Azure Purview and how to create an Azure Purview data map and a data catalog with data insights. This will give you a unified experience for data cataloging and governance.

To extract the metadata, classification, and lineage from your existing data sources, we will be creating a data map for Azure Synapse SQL dedicated pool.

Azure Purview provides you with an intuitive UI that is very user-friendly to create your data map. A data map keeps your metadata up to date and with the help of the on-demand and schedule scan, you can identify and classify the type of data, including tagging data sensitivity.

## Getting ready

Make sure you meet the following requirements before we begin:

- You have created and followed the steps mentioned in the previous recipe, *Configuring your Azure Purview account for Synapse SQL pool*.
- You must have data administrator and data reader access to register and manage a data source within the Azure Purview Studio.

## How to do it...

Let's understand how it works and how we create a Data map and register different data sources.

1. Open Azure Purview Studio. Under **Data map**, register the data source as **Azure Synapse Analytics**, as shown in *Figure 8.7*:

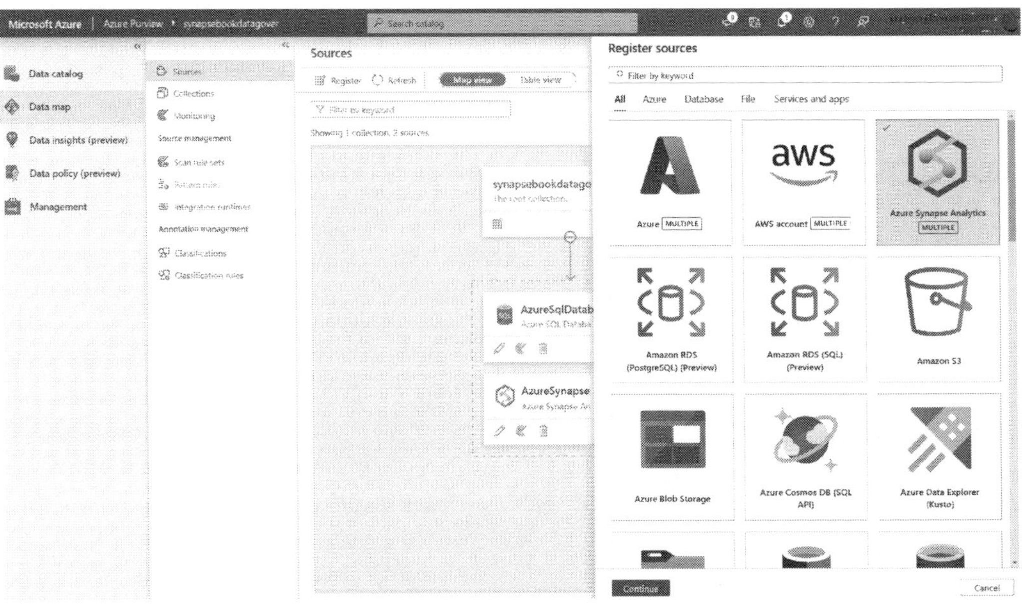


Figure 8.7 – Registering a data source under Data map

2. Let's fill in the required fields to complete the data source registration, as shown in *Figure 8.8*, and click **Register**:

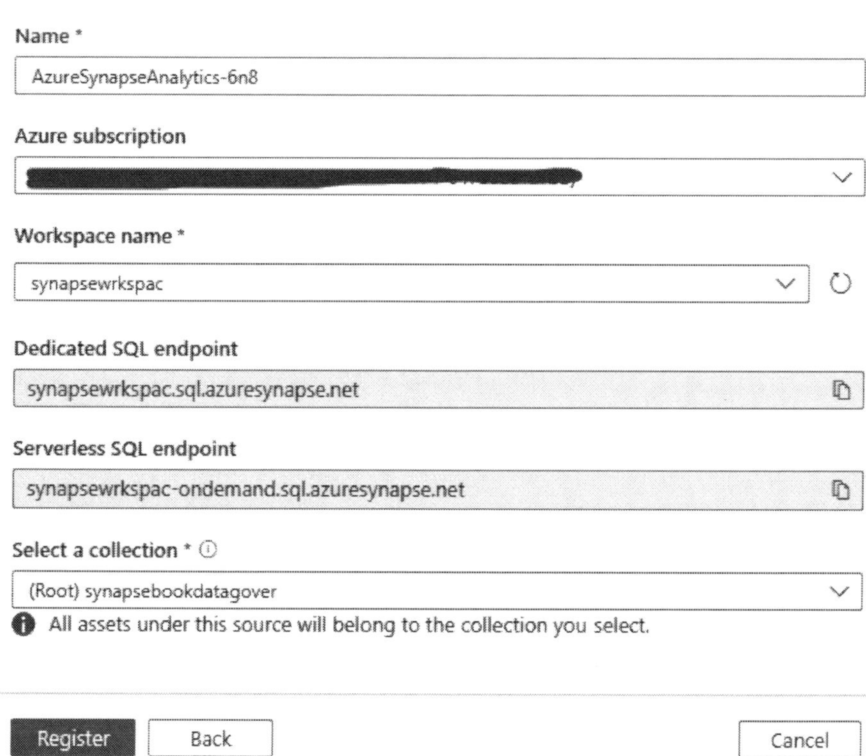


Figure 8.8 – Data source registration resources

3. Now, create a new scan to scan Azure Synapse dedicated SQL pool and its data, as shown in *Figure 8.9*. The scan can run once or can be scheduled to run regularly:

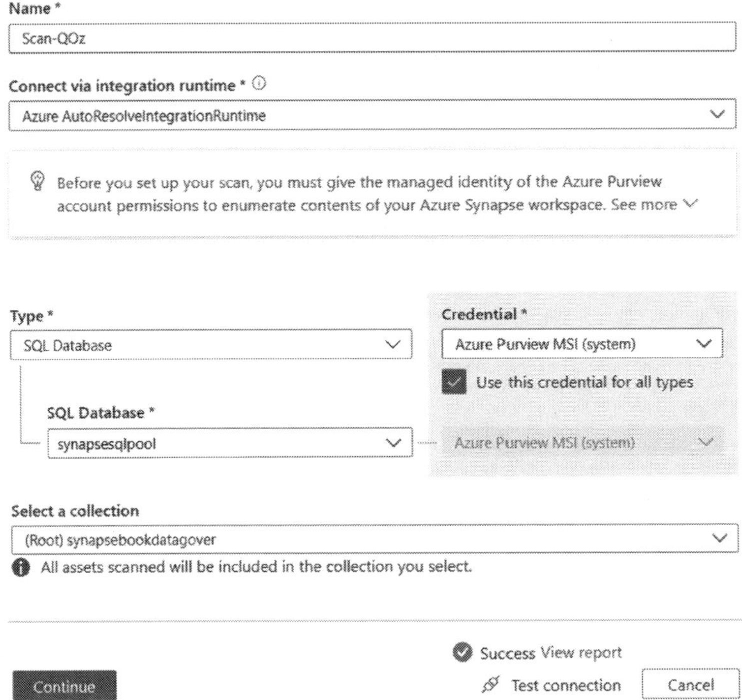


Figure 8.9 – Creating a new scan

4. Once the scan is created, you can start scanning SQL dedicated pool artifacts, as shown in *Figure 8.10*:

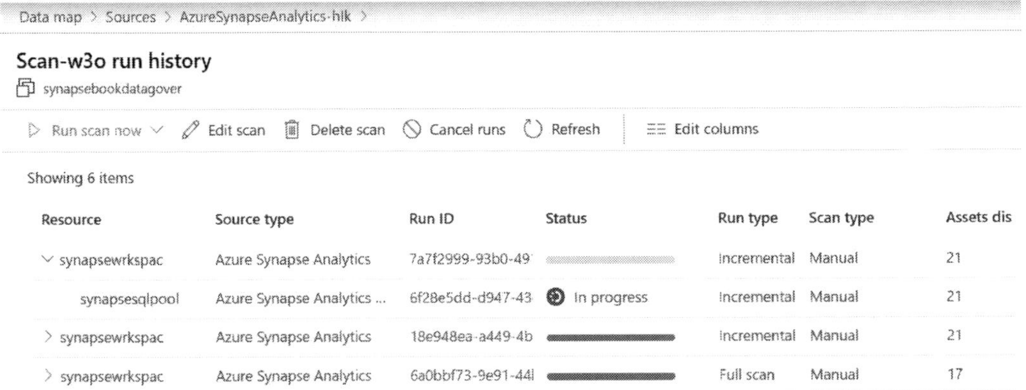


Figure 8.10 – Running the scan

## How it works...

This is a very interesting feature of Azure Purview. Once you have completed the data source scanning, it's time to look into the data catalog, which was built after the data scan. The data catalog stores the data about your data source in a searchable format. End users can enumerate various data artifacts and see data classifications, data sensitivity, the business glossary, data lineage, and catalog insights.

Just navigate to the **Data catalog** tab. You can see the collection where you can browse the assets by collection, source type, classification, label, and glossary term. You can refer to *Figure 8.11* for an idea of what it looks like:

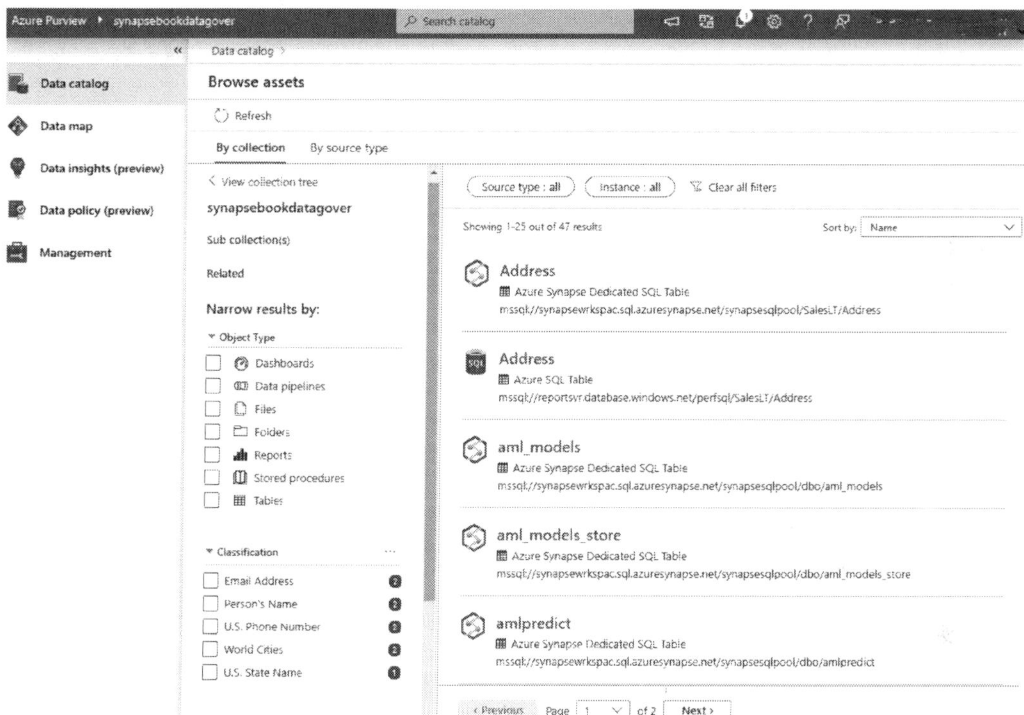


Figure 8.11 – Browsing data catalog assets

You can see there are data classifications that Azure Purview has identified, based on the data map that we have created. You can browse the customer table and see these schema classifications within the data catalogs, as shown in *Figure 8.12*:

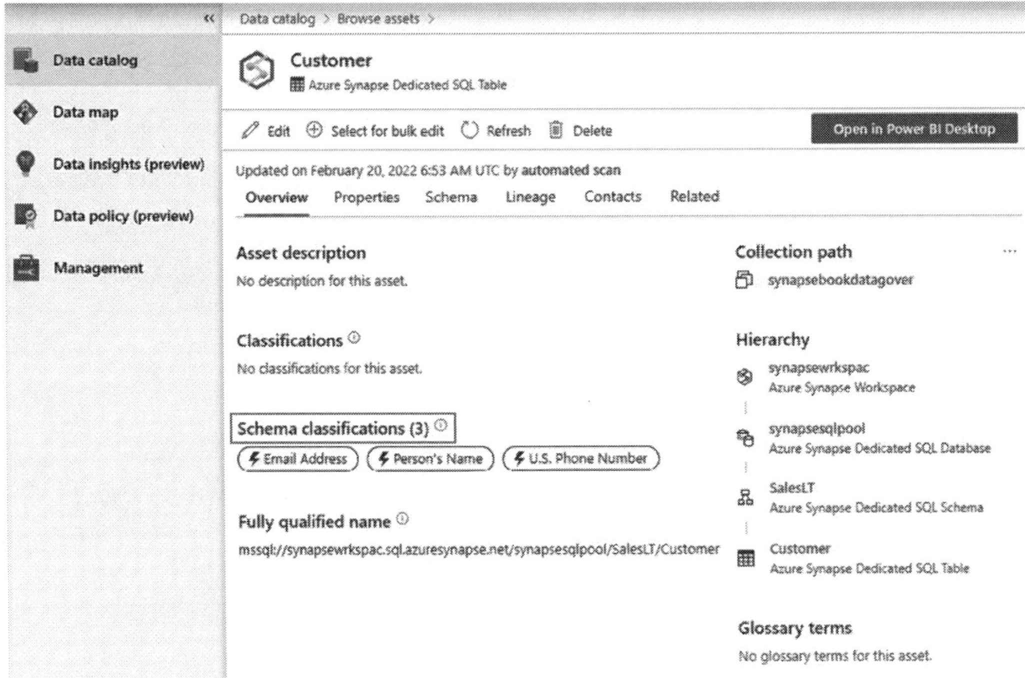


Figure 8.12 – Schema classification

# Enumerating resources within Synapse Studio

In this recipe, you will learn how to integrate Azure Purview with an Azure Synapse workspace for data discovery and exploration. You will understand how you can browse the Azure Purview data catalog within Azure Synapse Studio. You will also learn how data lineage is tracked and understand the detailed coverage at different levels of data preparation, such as data transformation, data extraction, and data loading from source to destination.

The integration between Azure Synapse and Azure Purview will give you a seamless experience for data governance and data exploration.

## Getting ready

Before we begin, ensure you have met the following prerequisites:

- You have dedicated SQL pool available in the Synapse workspace.
- You have the right permission to link an Azure Purview account to the Synapse workspace.

## How to do it...

Let's go back to the same Synapse workspace as we will be working on Synapse Studio to link the Azure Purview account. This will integrate Azure Purview within Synapse Studio so that you will be able to browse the Purview assets within the Synapse workspace:

1. Go to the Synapse workspace and under the **Manage** tab, click on **Azure Purview** and then **Connect to a Purview account**. Choose **synapsebookdatagover** as the account, as shown in *Figure 8.13*:

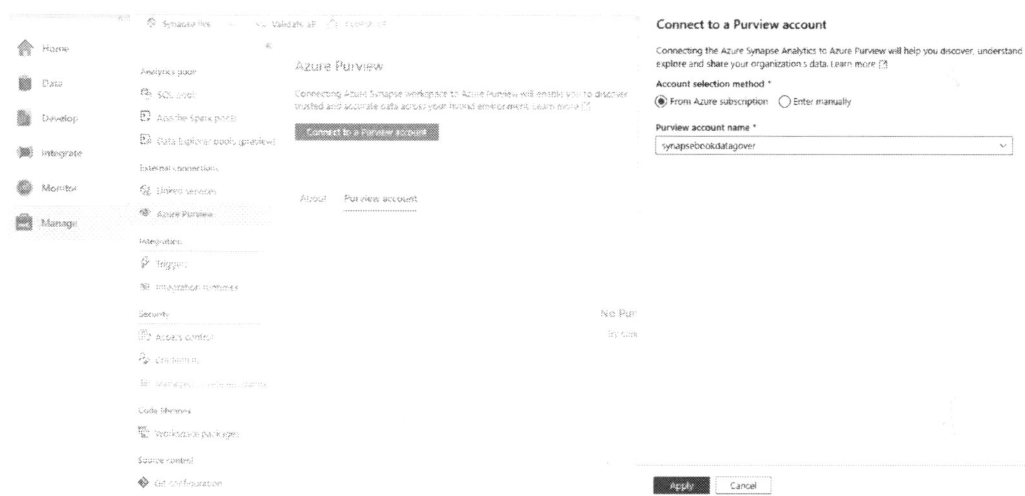

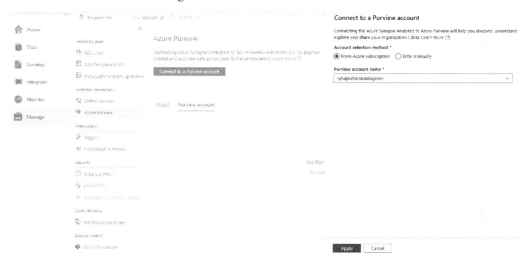

Figure 8.13 – Connecting to a Purview account in a Synapse workspace

2. You should be able to see the **Data Lineage - Synapse Pipeline** integration status as **Connected**, as shown in *Figure 8.14*:

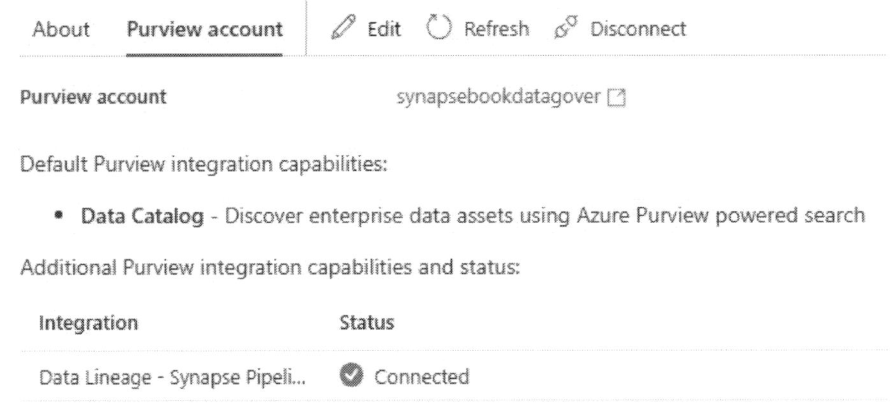


Figure 8.14 – Azure Purview connected account

3. Go to the **synapsebookdatagover** Purview workspace and under the **Management** tab, click on **Data Factory** and connect to an existing data factory from your **synapseadfintegration** subscription, as shown in *Figure 8.15*:

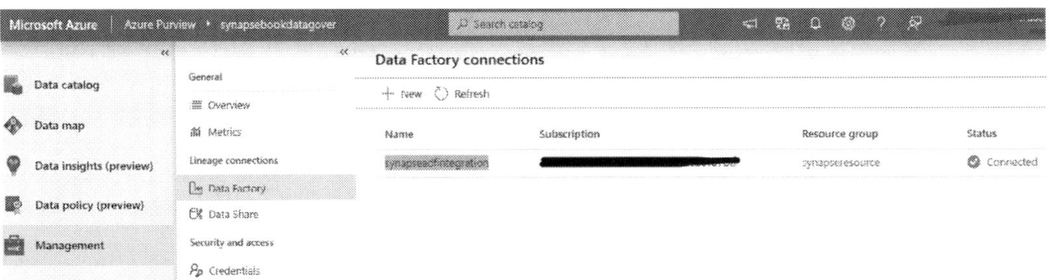


Figure 8.15 – Connecting to Data Factory in Azure Purview

4. You can now go to the search box in the Azure Synapse workspace, and you will see that it is now driven by Azure Purview to access the data. You can now start searching to get the intuitive search within the Synapse workspace.

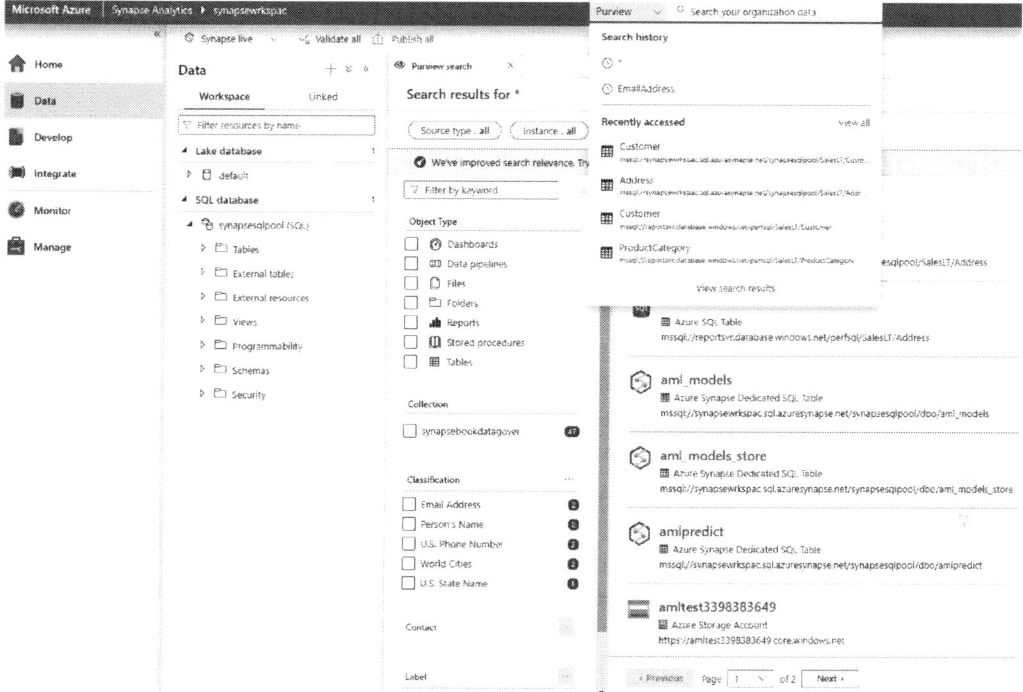


Figure 8.16 – Purview tab on the search bar

## How it works...

Let's understand what we have done so far and how this works. We have just linked Azure Purview to the Azure Synapse workspace. However, linking these two doesn't build the data catalog and it will not automatically apply data governance or classification. To perform data classification and data cataloging, you must first build the Azure Purview data catalog, which we did in the *Scanning data using the Purview data catalog* recipe.

So, regardless of whether you have linked the Azure Purview account to the Synapse workspace or not, you will still not be able to browse the data catalog until you first build the data map within Azure Purview for the Synapse data resources.

You can search for any assets in the Synapse workspace search bar, which will show you the entire overview of it, including asset classification, schema classification, and lineage, as shown in *Figure 8.17*:

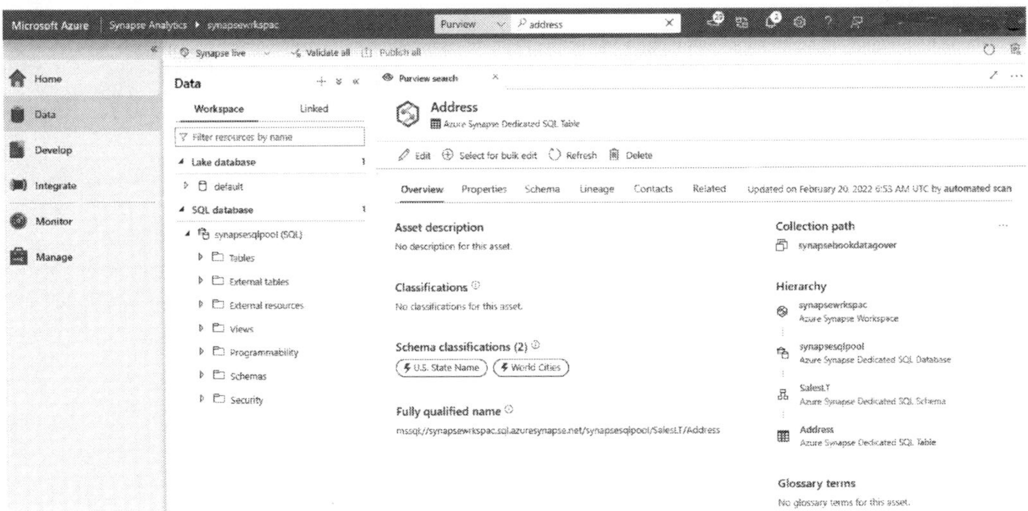


Figure 8.17 – Searching for assets in Synapse Studio

Here is what you see under the data pipelines: there is a **Copy** activity, using Azure Data Factory, which copies the data from Azure Storage to Azure Synapse. You can see the data lineage in *Figure 8.18*:

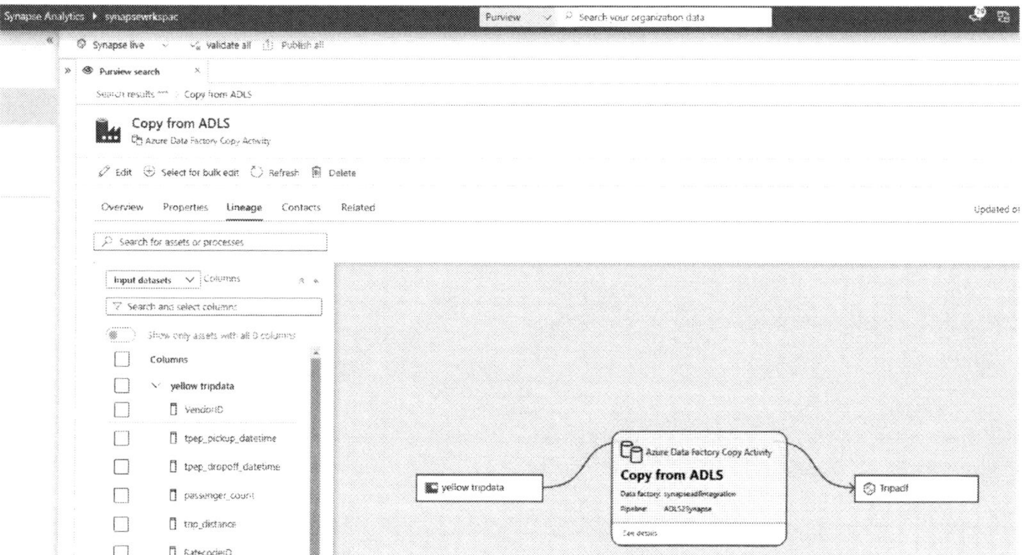


Figure 8.18 – Azure Data Factory data lineage

Azure Purview keeps the lineage metadata updated in real time after the end of each pipeline run. This keeps the details up to date, such as the pipeline run status, column lineage, row count, and other metadata details.

# 9
# MPP Platform Migration to Synapse

In this chapter, we will learn how to get started with the process of migrating a legacy data warehouse to a Synapse SQL pool using Azure Synapse Pathway. Customers are adopting modernized cloud data warehouses to leverage the advantages in terms of costs, agility, and managed services that are associated with the cloud. Migration to the cloud involves many challenges and requires careful assessment planning prior to migration. To guide us through this overwhelming migration process, it is essential to learn the following recipes for efficient migration:

- Understanding data migration challenges
- Configuring Azure Synapse Pathway
- Evaluating a data source to be migrated
- Generating a data migration assessment
- Supported data sources for migration

# Understanding data migration challenges

In this section, we will cover the data migration challenges that we face while migrating an on-premises data warehouse to the cloud, the ways of mitigating these challenges, and the successful migration journey to Synapse using Azure Synapse Pathway.

Data warehouses are usually used to store large amounts of data for analytical purposes. The data is ingested from a variety of sources and transactional systems into this data warehouse store, where raw data is transformed based on the schema and stored for future analytical purposes to derive business insights. Over a period of time, the data becomes overwhelming, such that the scalability becomes bottlenecked in an on-premises store, which is one of the compelling reasons for most organizations to adopt cloud data warehouses.

Let's take an example of an on-premises Teradata Data Warehouse where the customer intends to move it to Azure Synapse. There are significant design differences between the two platforms and it is essential to understand the differences and challenges as well as the ways to mitigate or compensate for the destination Synapse.

## Tables and databases

Teradata typically has multiple databases for ingestion and staging. The design will have a database for core tables and a database for the semantic layer that act like data marts. If we translate the same pattern to Synapse, then we may need to use cross-database joins and data movement between these databases, which is inefficient. Azure Synapse environments usually have a single database, and schemas are used to logically separate groups and tables. This is one of the design changes that is considered challenging due to data warehouse migration.

## Data modeling

There are differences in data type mapping between Teradata and Synapse for a few data types that require changes in consumption by downstream applications following migration. Some of the data types require data transformation during migration to Synapse. The majority of data types, including `int`, `bigint`, `char`, `decimal`, `float`, `timestamp`, and `varchar`, remain the same on both platforms. The following table shows a few of the data types that will require data transformation logic before we migrate to Synapse:

| Teradata data type | Synapse data type |
|---|---|
| Bool or Boolean | bit |
| Char varying | varchar |
| Interval | Not supported |
| Timespan | Not supported |
| Time with time zone | Datetimeoffset |
| National character varying | nvarchar |
| Double | float |

Figure 9.1 – Teradata data type versus the Synapse data type

Teradata supports time series and temporal data, whereas Azure Synapse does not. We will need to migrate the data from the time series table in Teradata to a standard table in Azure Synapse.

## Data Manipulation Language statements

There are a few differences in terms of using **Data Manipulation Language** (**DML**) statements between the two platforms. Teradata uses the qualify operator, whereas the equivalent is not available in Synapse. We should use subqueries and mitigate the challenges during migration. Likewise, Teradata supports direct addition or subtraction of dates, whereas in Synapse, we should change these statements by using `Dateadd` and `Datediff` statements.

## Functions, stored procedures, sequences, and triggers

Most of the migration involves planning for the migration of functions, stored procedures, triggers, and sequences. There are cases where we can find the equivalent in Synapse, but in a few instances, we might need to re-code to replicate the functionality of Teradata in Synapse.

### Functions

**Functions** involves both system- and user-defined functions. There are equivalents for system functions in Synapse. The syntax is different, however, so we may need to change it when migrating to Synapse, but we may also need to re-code all user-defined functions in Synapse using T-SQL since there will be multiple differences between Teradata syntax and Synapse.

## Stored procedures

We have to re-code all stored procedures in T-SQL syntax when we intend to migrate all stored procedures from Teradata to Synapse.

## Sequences

Teradata and Synapse handle sequences similarly, hence they can be migrated directly.

## Triggers

Triggers are not supported in Azure Synapse as they are in Teradata, and we should find ways of triggering along with Azure Data Factory.

## Data partitioning

Data partitioning should be considered after initial loading, using various partitioning techniques provided by Azure Synapse.

## Data indexing

Indexing options and usage are wholly different between Teradata and Synapse. However, we can use the existing data indexing design of Teradata and re-design it in Synapse with the syntax and options provided by Synapse.

## Other data migration challenges

The following questions articulate the other data migration challenges and complexity involved in the migration of an on-premises data warehouse to Azure Synapse:

- *When the data was housed on-premises, it was protected by our security measures. Now that it's in the cloud, how do we minimize the risks associated with cloud security?*

  Additional security features, such as transparent data encryption or moving the data by means of a secure VPN or express route, have to be considered in order to mitigate the challenges. Encrypt the data during migration for additional security.

- *How quickly can we realize improved performance?*

  Design decisions on partitions and indexing will improve query performance and yield improved cost savings.

All the data migration challenges should be considered in the assessment plan prior to migration. A tool that addresses all the challenges and automates the migration process with a proper assessment will be helpful.

# Configuring Azure Synapse Pathway

Azure Synapse Pathway is a code translation tool that helps with the migration of legacy on-premises data warehouses to Synapse. It helps with automating the code translation of on-premises data warehouses to Azure Synapse and aids quicker migration. Azure Synapse Pathway understands the data migration challenges between Synapse and on-premises data warehouses and assists in the translation of **data definition language** (**DDL**) and **data manipulation language** (**DML**) into T-SQL. It supports the code translation of databases, tables, schemas, and views.

**Azure Synapse Pathway** is a free tool that is used for automated data warehouse migration. Azure Synapse Pathway supports the automatic translation of schemas, tables, views, and functions from Amazon RedShift, Google BigQuery, IBM Netezza, SQL Server, Snowflake, and Teradata Data warehouses into T-SQL-compliant SQL code to Azure Synapse.

It is a proven tool for significantly reducing migration costs by converting 100 K lines of SQL code in minutes, thereby accelerating the migration time from months to minutes.

It will not scan the environment, and the link for DDL/DML scripts must be provided for translation. Some pre-defined errors and warnings are provided for troubleshooting automation and migration.

In this recipe, we will cover the prerequisites, installation, and minimum requirements for Azure Synapse Pathway.

## Getting ready

Download the prerequisites and installation from the following Microsoft installation path:

- **.NET 5.0**: `https://dotnet.microsoft.com/download/dotnet/5.0`
- **Azure Synapse Pathway 0.5**: `https://www.microsoft.com/en-us/download/confirmation.aspx?id=103597`

## How to do it…

Let's get started.

1. Install .NET Core Desktop Runtime 5.0.8 or later from the path mentioned in the *Getting ready* section.
2. Then, download the latest version of Azure Synapse Pathway and install the `.msi` file. The supported operating system is Windows, with .NET Framework pre-installed.

3. Open the Azure Synapse Pathway setup wizard to begin the installation process.
4. Click **Next** on the end user license agreement.
5. Once the agreement is accepted, click **Next**, followed by **Install**, to begin the installation process.
6. Click **Finish** to complete the installation and you will be redirected to the Azure Synapse Pathway home screen.

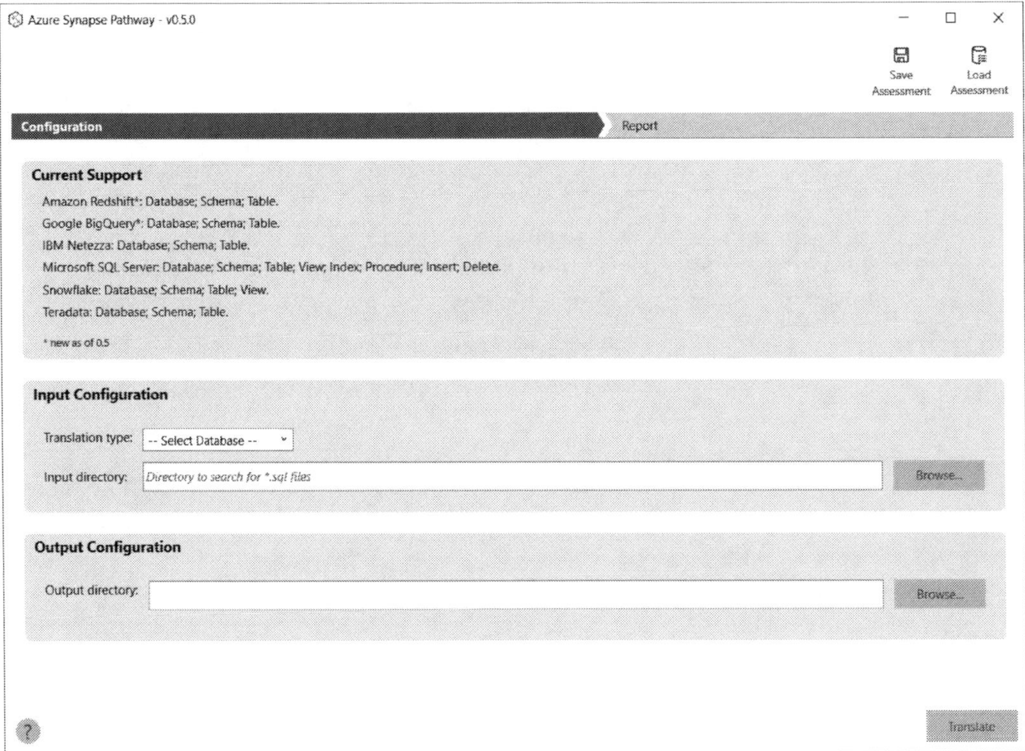


Figure 9.2 – Azure Synapse Pathway wizard

This screen helps us to configure the input database and output directory so that the scripts can be generated.

## How it works...

We will learn the internal three-step process of Azure Synapse Pathway in terms of translation to T-SQL code from an on-premises data warehouse to Azure Synapse. Let's learn about each process step by step.

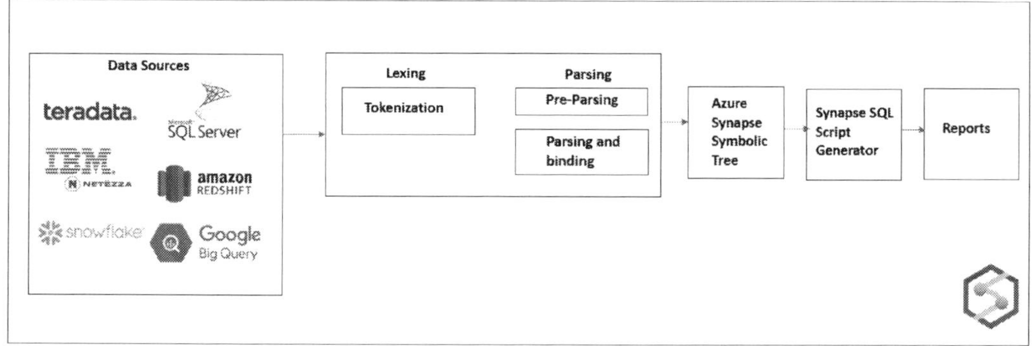


Figure 9.3 – Azure Synapse Pathway internal functionality

### Step 1 – Lexing and parsing

A source statement from SQL is broken down into a series of logical tokens. Each token is then executed against a set of parser rules. It is then bound to those rules, which generate the output. Azure Synapse Pathway defines parser rules or grammar and allows the tool to identify and process the SQL input into a tree called an **Abstract Syntax Tree** (**AST**), which is used in the next processing step.

### Step 2 – Abstract Syntax Tree (AST)

Azure Synapse Pathway defines all objects in the AST. This AST includes metadata, which assists in the proper conversion of a statement. The source system function is broken down into a series of steps and assigned a token that is used to track the script generation and can make smarter decisions in translating to Synapse SQL.

The tool understands the implicit conversion required by default and no type casting functions are required. For example, if the source system has a function with a numeric data type and Synapse SQL requires that function to have a float as a parameter, it implicitly converts the numeric parameter to a float without the expectation of having a type cast function used to convert the parameters from a numeric parameter to a float.

### Step 3 – Syntax generation

The final step in the process is to generate SQL syntax for Synapse. Using an AST structure, Azure Synapse Pathway writes each object to an individual file. Then it optimizes statements accordingly and generates an assessment report.

Now that we have seen the different steps in terms of the internal functionality of Azure Synapse Pathway, let's look at the different data sources that it is compatible with.

# Evaluating a data source to be migrated

In this recipe, we will learn how to work with Azure Synapse Pathway and get started with using it for data source migration.

## Getting ready

Before we begin, you'll need to do the following preparation:

1. Extract `.SQL` files from your legacy data warehouse and download them to your system's folder. If you are in experimentation mode to learn how Azure Synapse Pathway works, you can download Microsoft SQL Server's sample data warehouse from the following link and keep the .SQL DDL/DML files ready in your system folder: `https://github.com/microsoft/sql-server-samples/tree/master/samples/databases/contoso-data-warehouse`.
2. Copy the contents of `load-contoso-data-warehouse-to-sql-data-warehouse.sql` into a notepad and save it as `contoso.sql` in your system folder.

Let's now start to use the Azure Synapse Pathway tool.

# How to do it...

Let's open the Azure Synapse Pathway tool and keep the .SQL files ready from one of the data sources:

1. Set the translation type as **IBM Netezza or Microsoft SQL Server** or whichever data source you intend to migrate.

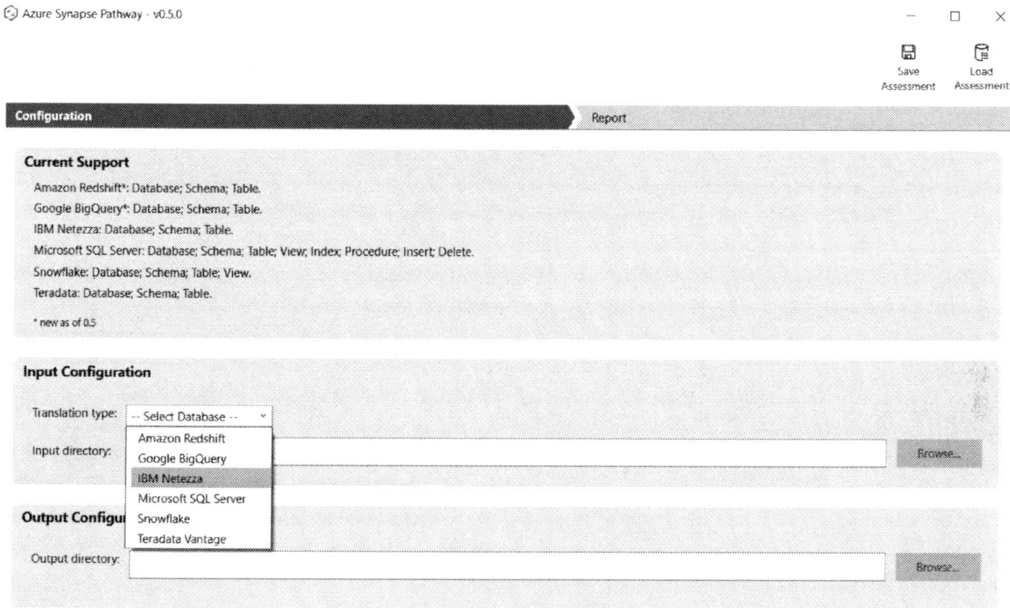


Figure 9.4 – Selecting the translation type – Azure Synapse Pathway wizard

2. Select **Input directory** and browse to the folder where the input data source `.SQL` files are stored. Also, browse to the output directory folder where the results have to be stored.

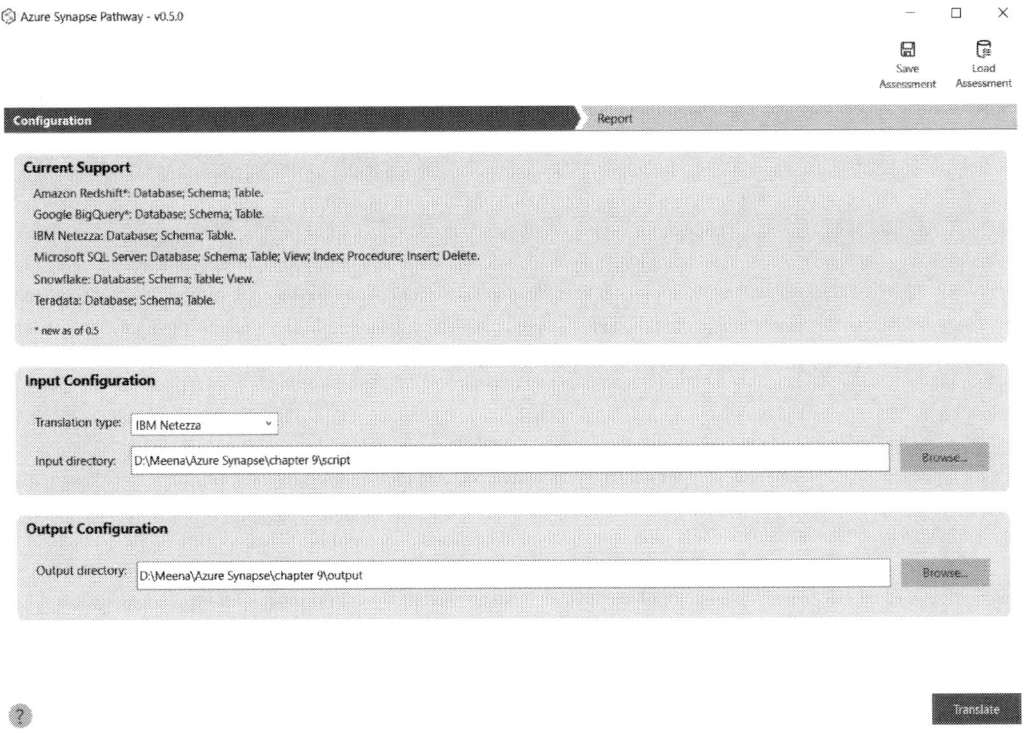


Figure 9.5 – Selecting the Input and Output configurations of Azure Synapse Pathway

3. Click **Translate** and view the results.

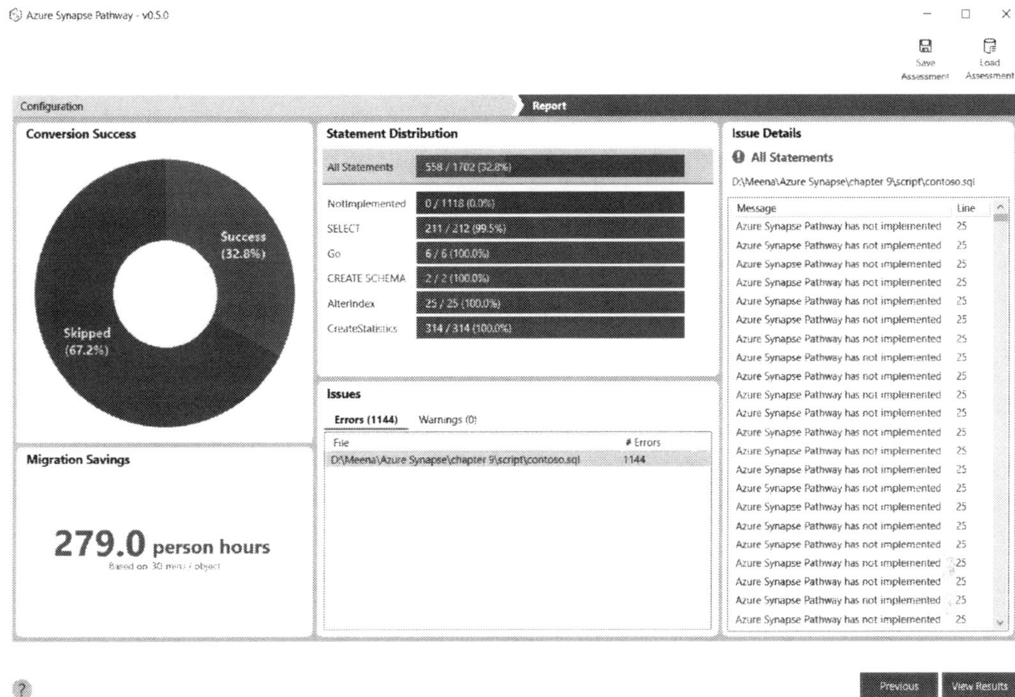


Figure 9.6 – Azure Synapse Pathway report summary

4. Generate results for the DDL statements. The sample is as follows:

Figure 9.7 – Azure Synapse Pathway DDL report summary

All done!

# Generating a data migration assessment

In this recipe, we will learn how to save and load assessments and how to read the report summary generated by Azure Synapse Pathway.

## Getting ready

Keep the Azure Synapse Pathway wizard open with the results generated in the previous recipe.

Let's get started by saving this assessment and loading it back up.

## How to do it...

We're starting from the final step of the previous recipe:

1. Go to the results window and click **Save Assessment**.

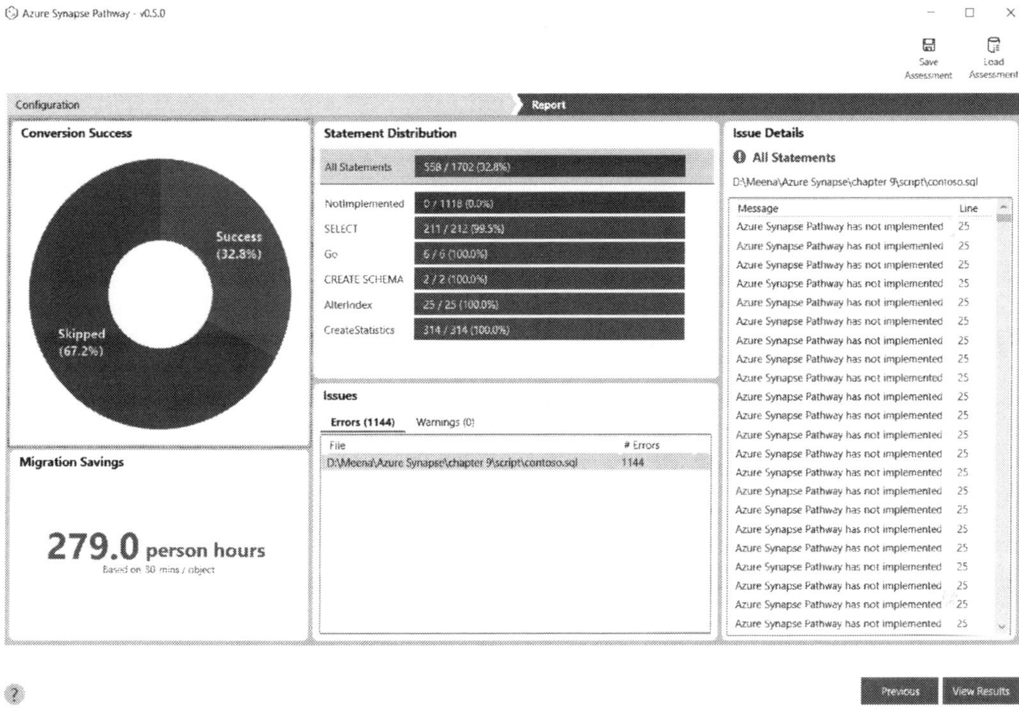


Figure 9.8 – Report summary deep dive

2. Save it in the output folder as a `Netezzaconfig.aspproj` file.

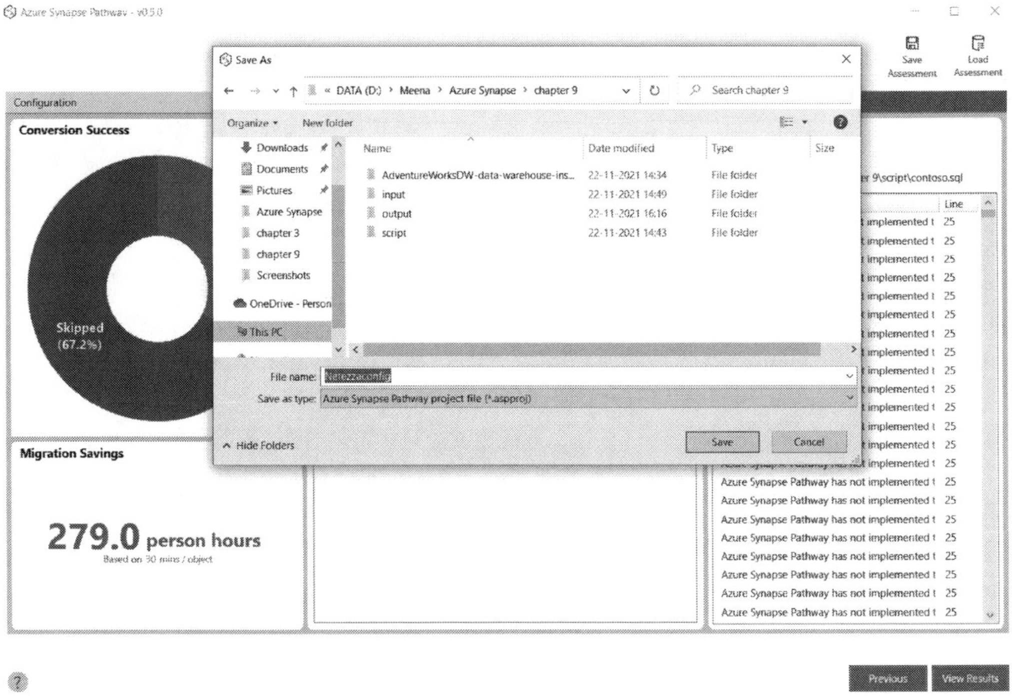

Figure 9.9 – Report summary save assessment

3. Click **Load Assessment** to re-load the assessment results.
4. Now, let's understand the report summary sections. Look at the conversion success and it provides the success ratio of DDL and DML files translated for the IBM Netezza data source.

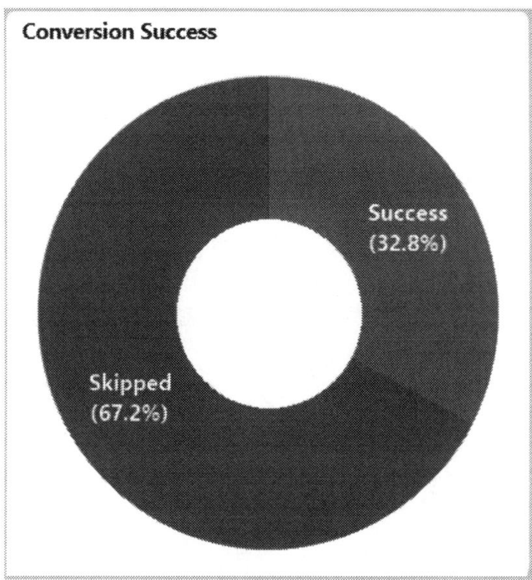


Figure 9.10 – Report summary conversion success

5. **Migration Savings** in the report summary is the auto-calculated number of hours by Azure Synapse Pathway per object. In total, there are 1700+ objects, while 279 person-hours can be saved by using Azure Synapse Pathway.

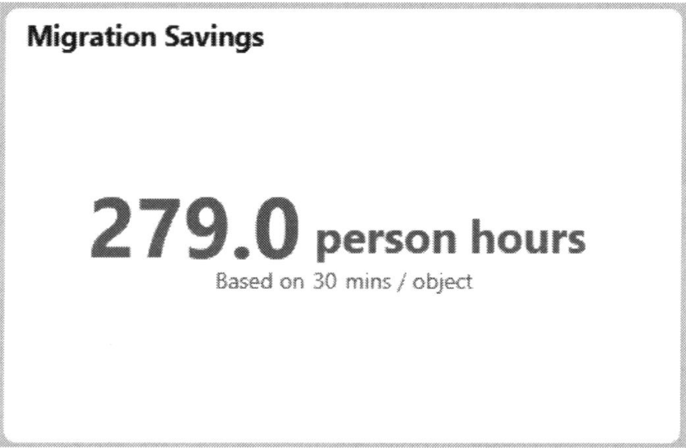


Figure 9.11 – Report summary migration savings

6. The **Statement Distribution** section details the number of DDL and DML statements translated, including the **SELECT**, **CREATE SCHEMA**, **AlterIndex**, and **CreateStatistics** statements. Ideally, it includes tables, schemas, and databases created.

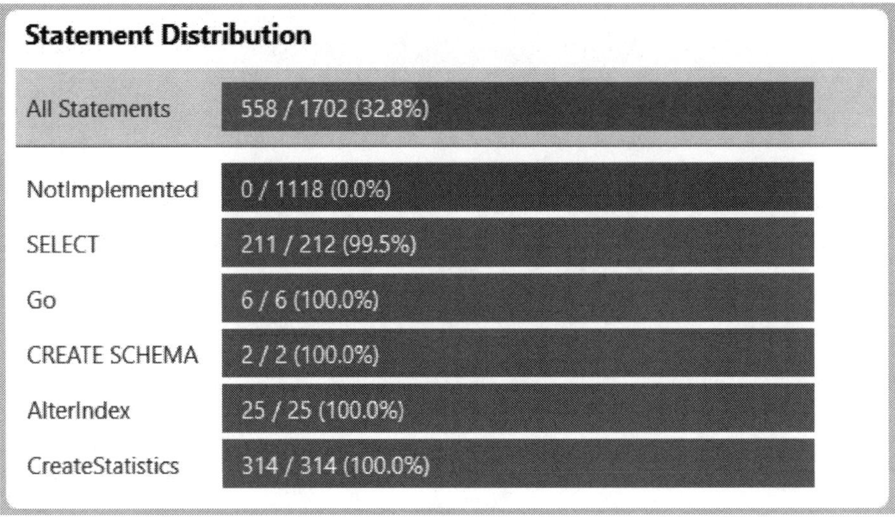


Figure 9.12 – Report summary statement distribution

This screen also has a **NotImplemented** field, which tells us the number of statements and the percentage of the same that cannot be assessed.

# Supported data sources for migration

In this recipe, we will learn the different data sources supported for migration to Azure Synapse.

Following are the data warehouses that are supported as data sources by Synapse Pathway for the translation of T-SQL code to Azure Synapse:

| Data warehouse | Supported objects |
|---|---|
| Amazon Redshift | Database, Schema, Table |
| Google BigQuery | Database, Schema, Table |
| IBM Netezza | Database, Schema, Table |
| Microsoft SQL Server | Database, Schema, Table, View, Index, Procedure, Insert, Delete |
| Snowflake | Database, Schema, Table, View |
| Teradata | Database, Schema, Table |

Figure 9.13 – Supported data sources

We went through the data migration challenges in our first recipe with Teradata as an example. There are many data types, functions, stored procedures, and sequences that support the differences between the source data warehouses and Azure Synapse.

Let's now learn the differences between IBM Netezza, Oracle Exadata, Snowflake, Microsoft SQL Server, and Azure Synapse.

# IBM Netezza and Azure Synapse platform differences

We will compare these platforms using several different criteria.

## Data modeling

There are differences in data type mapping between Netezza and Synapse as regards a few data types and this requires changes in the consumption of downstream applications following migration. Some of the data types require data transformation during migration to Synapse. However, the majority of data types, such as int, bigint, char, decimal, float, and timestamp, remain the same on both platforms. The following tables show a few of the data types that will require data transformation logic prior to migration to Synapse:

| Netezza data type | Synapse data type |
|---|---|
| boolean | bit |
| bpchar | varchar |
| dataslice | Not supported |
| Interval (a)Timespan | Not supported |
| Time with time zone | Datetimeoffset |
| rowid | Not supported |
| st_geometry | Not supported |
| transactionid | Not supported |

Figure 9.14 – Netezza data type versus the Synapse data type

## DML statements

There are a few differences in terms of using DML statements between the two platforms. Netezza supports the AGE operator, whereas the equivalent is not available in Synapse. We should use `DateDiff` and mitigate the challenges during migration.

## Functions, stored procedures, and sequences

We might need to re-code to replicate the functionality of Netezza in Synapse.

### Functions

Functions involve both system- and user-defined functions. There are equivalents for system functions in Synapse. The syntax is different and we may need to change it while migrating to Synapse. However, we may also need to re-code all user-defined functions in Synapse using T-SQL since there will be multiple differences between Netezza syntax and Synapse.

### Stored procedures

We have to re-code all stored procedures in T-SQL syntax from PL/pgSQL when intending to migrate all stored procedures from Netezza to Synapse.

### Sequences

A unique value is handled via the `NEXT()` method, whereas in Azure Synapse, we should use the identity column, while complete re-coding is required during the migration sequences.

## Data partitioning

Data partitioning should be considered after initial loading using various partitioning techniques provided by Azure Synapse.

## Data indexing

Indexing options and use are entirely different between Netezza and Synapse. We can use the existing data indexing design of Netezza and re-design it in Synapse with the syntax and options provided by Synapse.

# Oracle Exadata and Azure Synapse platform differences

The Oracle data warehouse is wholly different from Azure Synapse. Oracle bit map indexes, function-based indexes, domain indexes, clustered tables, row-level triggers, user-defined data types, and PL/SQL stored procedures are not supported by Azure Synapse, which requires all the database objects to be re-designed and re-coded. Materialized views can be used instead of clustered tables.

Oracle typically has multiple databases for ingestion and staging. If we translate the same pattern to Synapse, then we may need to use cross-database joins and data movement between these databases, which is inefficient. The Azure Synapse environment usually has a single database and schemas are used to logically separate groups and tables. This is one design change that needs to be considered during data warehouse migration.

## Snowflake and Azure Synapse platform differences

The following table shows a few of the data types that will require data transformation logic prior to migration to Synapse:

| Snowflake data type | Synapse data type |
|---|---|
| Array | Not supported |
| boolean | bit |
| double | float |
| geography | Not supported |
| object | Not supported |
| String, text | varchar |
| timestamp | datetime |
| variant | Not supported |

Figure 9.15 – Snowflake data type versus the Synapse data type

## Microsoft SQL Server and Azure Synapse platform differences

The following table shows a few of the data types that will require data transformation logic prior to migration to Synapse:

| SQL Server data type | Synapse data type |
|---|---|
| cursor | Not supported |
| geometry | Not supported |
| hierarchyid | Not supported |
| geography | Not supported |
| image | Varbinary(max) |
| String, text | varchar |
| timestamp | datetime |
| ntext | Nvarchar(max) |
| rowversion | Not supported |
| Sql_variant | Not supported |
| table | Not supported |
| Text | Varchar(max) |
| xml | Nvarchar(max) |

Figure 9.16 – SQL Server data type versus the Synapse data type

In this recipe, we learned about different data warehouses and their differences with respect to Synapse. It is essential that we consider the differences in our design and mitigate the data migration challenges so that we can leverage the features of Azure Synapse effectively.

# Index

## Symbols



## A

## B



## C



## D

## F



## H



## I



## L



## M

## N



## O



## P



## R

## S



## T

# W

# Other Books You May Enjoy

If you enjoyed this book, you may be interested in these other books by Packt:

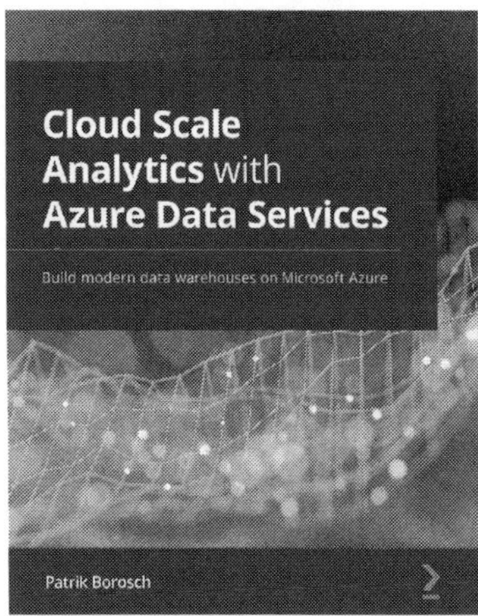


**Cloud Scale Analytics with Azure Data Services**

Patrik Borosch

ISBN: 978-1-80056-293-6

- Implement data governance with Azure services
- Use integrated monitoring in the Azure Portal and integrate Azure Data Lake Storage into the Azure Monitor
- Explore the serverless feature for ad-hoc data discovery, logical data warehousing, and data wrangling
- Implement networking with Synapse Analytics and Spark pools

- Create and run Spark jobs with Databricks clusters
- Implement streaming using Azure Functions, a serverless runtime environment on Azure
- Explore the predefined ML services in Azure and use them in your app

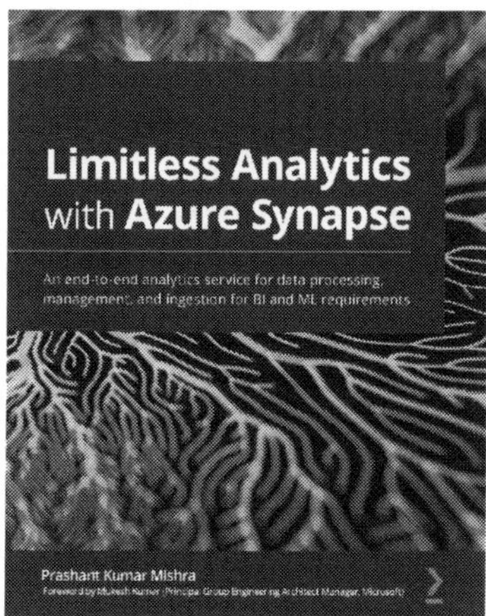


**Limitless Analytics with Azure Synapse**

Prashant Kumar Mishra

ISBN: 978-1-80020-565-9

- Explore the necessary considerations for data ingestion and orchestration while building analytical pipelines
- Understand pipelines and activities in Synapse pipelines and use them to construct end-to-end data-driven workflows
- Query data using various coding languages on Azure Synapse
- Focus on Synapse SQL and Synapse Spark
- Manage and monitor resource utilization and query activity in Azure Synapse
- Connect Power BI workspaces with Azure Synapse and create or modify reports directly from Synapse Studio
- Create and manage IP firewall rules in Azure Synapse

## Packt is searching for authors like you

If you're interested in becoming an author for Packt, please visit `authors.packtpub.com` and apply today. We have worked with thousands of developers and tech professionals, just like you, to help them share their insight with the global tech community. You can make a general application, apply for a specific hot topic that we are recruiting an author for, or submit your own idea.

## Share Your Thoughts

Now you've finished *Azure Synapse Analytics Cookbook*, we'd love to hear your thoughts! Scan the QR code below to go straight to the Amazon review page for this book and share your feedback or leave a review on the site that you purchased it from.

`https://packt.link/r/1-803-23150-5`

Your review is important to us and the tech community and will help us make sure we're delivering excellent quality content.